ECONOMIC DEVELOPMENT
FOR EASTERN EUROPE

Other International Economic Association symposia

*

THE ECONOMICS OF INTERNATIONAL MIGRATION
Edited by Brinley Thomas

THE BUSINESS CYCLE IN THE POST-WAR WORLD
Edited by Erik Lundberg

INFLATION
Edited by D. C. Hague

STABILITY AND PROGRESS IN THE WORLD ECONOMY
Edited by D. C. Hague

THE THEORY OF CAPITAL
Edited by F. A. Lutz and D. C. Hague

THE THEORY OF WAGE DETERMINATION
Edited by J. T. Dunlop

CLASSICS IN THE THEORY OF PUBLIC FINANCE
Edited by R. A. Musgrave and A. T. Peacock

THE ECONOMIC CONSEQUENCES OF THE SIZE OF NATIONS
Edited by E. A. G. Robinson

ECONOMIC DEVELOPMENT FOR LATIN AMERICA
Edited by Howard S. Ellis assisted by Henry C. Wallich

THE ECONOMICS OF TAKE-OFF INTO SUSTAINED GROWTH
Edited by W. W. Rostow

ECONOMIC DEVELOPMENT WITH SPECIAL REFERENCE TO EAST ASIA
Edited by Kenneth Berrill

INTERNATIONAL TRADE THEORY IN A DEVELOPING WORLD
Edited by R. F. Harrod and D. C. Hague

ECONOMIC DEVELOPMENT FOR AFRICA SOUTH OF THE SAHARA
Edited by E. A. G. Robinson

THE THEORY OF INTEREST RATES
Edited by F. H. Hahn and F. P. R. Brechling

THE ECONOMICS OF EDUCATION
Edited by E. A. G. Robinson and J. E. Vaizey

PROBLEMS IN ECONOMIC DEVELOPMENT
Edited by E. A. G. Robinson

THE DISTRIBUTION OF NATIONAL INCOME
Edited by Jean Marchal and Bernard Ducros

ECONOMIC DEVELOPMENT
FOR
EASTERN EUROPE

Proceedings of a Conference
held by
the International Economic Association

EDITED BY

M. C. KASER

MACMILLAN
London · Melbourne · Toronto
ST MARTIN'S PRESS
New York
1968

© The International Economic Association 1968

Published by
MACMILLAN & CO LTD
Little Essex Street London W C 2
and also at Bombay Calcutta and Madras
Macmillan South Africa (Publishers) Pty Ltd Johannesburg
The Macmillan Company of Australia Pty Ltd Melbourne
The Macmillan Company of Canada Ltd Toronto
St Martin's Press Inc New York

Library of Congress catalog card no. 68-15301

Printed in Great Britain by
R. & R. CLARK LTD
Edinburgh

CONTENTS

Contents

SESSION IV

ECONOMIC RELATIONS BETWEEN CAPITALIST AND SOCIALIST COUNTRIES

SESSION V

PRICE SYSTEMS

SESSION VI

MATERIAL INCENTIVES AND COST ACCOUNTING

SESSION VII

AGRICULTURAL PRICES

Contents

ACKNOWLEDGEMENTS

The International Economic Association is grateful to the organizations and persons who helped to make practicable the Conference reported in this volume. It was financed under a general subsidy from UNESCO and by a subsidy from the Ford Foundation to the Association, supplemented by various contributions from the host country.

The Meeting was held at the Hotel Trimontium, Plovdiv (Bulgaria), in December 1964, and the Association desires to record its appreciation to the organizing committees. The Programme Committee was composed of Professor E. Kamenov (Chairman), Professor E. A. G. Robinson (Vice-Chairman), Professor E. Lundberg, Professor E. Lipiński, Professor G. M. Sorokin, Professor O. Šik, and Professor J. Sirotković. Of these, Professor Lundberg, Vice-President of the Association, and Professor Šik, President of the Czechoslovak Economic Association and Director of the Institute of Economics of the Czechoslovak Academy of Sciences, were unable to attend the Conference. The Committee of Organization in Bulgaria comprised Professor Kamenov (Chairman), Professor K. Dobrev, Professor I. Stefanov, Dr. L. Chaushev, and Professor D. Bradistilov ; of these, Dr. Chaushev, Rector of the Karl Marx Higher School of Economics, Sofia, was unable to attend. The Institute of Economics of the Bulgarian Academy of Sciences seconded a number of its staff, led by Mme. Gocheva and Mr. D. Kinov, to form the Secretariat.

The participants were the guests of the Plovdiv Municipality at a reception opening the Conference, and Mr. Kirev, Deputy President of the Plovdiv Town Council, welcomed members at the first session. Mr. V. Gavriliouk, a member of the Division of Applied Social Sciences, UNESCO, expressed the interest of his Organization in the Conference. The United Nations Economic Commission for Europe, which was particularly involved in East-West economic relations, was represented by Mr. R. Jauković, a member of its Research and Planning Division.

The Conference was the fourth in a series of regional meetings on economic development organized by the Association following an initiative of the Social Sciences Department of UNESCO ; the previous meetings had concerned Latin America, East Asia, and Africa. The Programme Committee invited economists from Eastern Europe to present papers and their colleagues from other countries to initiate the discussion at each session. The Conference was opened by Professor Kamenov, who welcomed the analysis of development as an essential for continued economic growth, in Bulgaria as elsewhere, and by Professor L. Fauvel (Secretary-General of the Association), who emphasized that there were no national delegations but individual participants speaking in their own professional capacities. The closing speeches of the Meeting were made by Academician K. Ostrovityanov, who believed that the economists from socialist states had found exchanges with Western colleagues extremely fruitful and that acute discussion had not disturbed the amicable atmosphere of the sessions, and by Professor Robinson, who declared himself impressed by the transcendence of political systems by the problems of economics. The Conference expressed its appreciation to the management and staff of the Hotel Trimontium, to the staff of the Bulgarian Academy of Sciences who serviced the Meeting, and to the translators and interpreters : the working languages were English, French, and Russian, and interpretation was available into Bulgarian.

The record of the proceedings was made by the Editor, Mr. M. C. Kaser, who was greatly aided by the notes of their contributions which participants subsequently sent him ; Professor M. Flamant made an independent record of statements in French, which was of great value in editing the final text. Mr. Richard Portes, Fellow of Balliol College, Oxford, kindly verified the editing of the mathematical notation. The preliminary work of collating the discussion record from these three sources was performed by Mr. Richard Batsavage, a graduate student in the Department of Economics, University of Michigan (under a grant from the Department's Project in Comparative Economics : Director, Professor A. Eckstein) while the Editor was Visiting Professor of Economics.

LIST OF PARTICIPANTS

Dr. Jiří Bouška, Econometric Laboratory, Institute of Economics, Czechoslovak Academy of Sciences, Prague, Czechoslovakia.

Professor Dobri Bradistilov, Institute of Economics, Bulgarian Academy of Sciences, Sofia, Bulgaria.

Dr. Slobodan Branković, Institute of International Politics and Economics, Belgrade, Yugoslavia.

Professor Nikola Čobeljić, University of Belgrade, Yugoslavia.

Dr. J. Desmireanu, Institute of Economics, Rumanian Academy of Sciences, Bucharest, Rumania.

Professor Kristyu Dobrev, Institute of Economics, Bulgarian Academy of Sciences, Sofia, Bulgaria.

Professor Evsey D. Domar, Massachusetts Institute of Technology, Cambridge, Mass., U.S.A.

Professor Léon H. Dupriez, Institut de Recherches Économiques, Sociales et Politiques, Louvain, Belgium.

Professor Luc Fauvel, University of Paris, France, Secretary-General, International Economic Association.

Professor Maurice Flamant, University of Dijon, France.

Mr. Vassili Gavriliouk, Division of Applied Social Sciences, UNESCO, Paris, France (Observer).

Professor Gregory Grossman, University of California, Berkeley, Calif., U.S.A.

Professor Hasan Hadziomerović, University of Sarajevo, Yugoslavia.

Sir Roy Harrod, University of Oxford, U.K.

Dr. András Hegedüs, Sociology Unit, Hungarian Academy of Sciences, Budapest, Hungary.

Professor Erwin Hutira, Institute of Economics, Rumanian Academy of Sciences, Bucharest, Rumania.

Mr. Raško Jauković, Research and Planning Division, United Nations Economic Commission for Europe, Geneva, Switzerland (Observer).

Professor J. M. Jeanneney, University of Paris, France.

Professor Evgeni Kamenov, Bulgarian Academy of Sciences, Sofia, Bulgaria.

Mr. Michael Kaser, University of Oxford, U.K.

Dr. Zygmunt Knyziak, Higher School of Planning and Statistics, Warsaw, Poland.

Dr. W. Krencik, Economics Department, Polish Academy of Sciences, Warsaw, Poland.

Dr. Oldřich Kýn, Charles University, Prague, Czechoslovakia.

Dr. Věra Kyprová, Higher School of Economics, Prague, Czechoslovakia.

List of Participants

Dr. János László, Institute of Economics, Hungarian Academy of Sciences, Budapest, Hungary.

Professor Eduard Lipiński, Polish Academy of Sciences, Warsaw, Poland.

Mr. L. Machoň, Scientific-Research Institute on Finance, Prague, Czechoslovakia.

Professor Ivan Maksimović, University of Belgrade, Yugoslavia.

Miss Era I. Matvievskaya, Institute of the Economics of the World Socialist System, U.S.S.R. Academy of Sciences, Moscow, U.S.S.R.

Professor Kiril Miljovski, University of Skopje, Yugoslavia.

Mr. Veselin Nikiforov, Institute of Economics, Bulgarian Academy of Sciences, Sofia, Bulgaria.

Professor Aleksandr Ilich Notkin, Institute of Economics, U.S.S.R. Academy of Sciences, Moscow, U.S.S.R.

Dr. Jiří Novozámský, Research Institute of National Economic Planning, Prague, Czechoslovakia.

Professor Fred Oelssner, Institut für Wirtschaftswissenschaften bei der DAdW zu Berlin, Berlin, German Democratic Republic.

Dr. Tsvi Ophir, The Hebrew University, Jerusalem, Israel.

Academician Konstantin Vasilievich Ostrovityanov, U.S.S.R. Academy of Sciences, Moscow, U.S.S.R.

Professor Zoran Pjanić, University of Belgrade, Yugoslavia.

Professor I. Rachmuth, Institute of Economics, Rumanian Academy of Sciences, Bucharest, Rumania.

Professor E. A. G. Robinson, University of Cambridge, U.K.

Professor Gennady Sorokin, Institute of the Economics of the World Socialist System, U.S.S.R. Academy of Sciences, Moscow, U.S.S.R.

Professor Ivan Stefanov, Institute of Economics, Bulgarian Academy of Sciences, Sofia, Bulgaria.

Professor Radmila Stojanović, University of Belgrade, Yugoslavia.

Professor I. A. Zakhariev, Bulgarian Academy of Sciences, Sofia, Bulgaria.

Diacritic marks are shown on eastern European names in the above list and in bibliographical footnotes, but, for typographical simplicity, have been omitted from the text.

SESSION I

THEORETICAL PROBLEMS OF A
SOCIALIST ECONOMY

Chapter 1

BASIC TRENDS OF ECONOMIC DEVELOPMENT IN THE SOCIALIST COUNTRIES OF EUROPE

BY

G. M. SOROKIN

Institute of Economics of the World Socialist System, Moscow

ONE of the outstanding events of recent times is the establishment of more than a dozen new socialist states, which emerged, after the collapse of fascism in the Second World War, as the echo in eastern Europe and Asia of the October Socialist Revolution in Russia. Together with the Soviet Union, they form a world socialist system, the characteristics of which must be considered in any attempt at solving the political, sociological, or economic problems of today.

The approach to the analysis of the economic and social institutions of these states — which, while still in their infancy, are already extremely complex — should be illuminated by an understanding not only of their historical evolution, but, above all, of their potential for the future. A dispassionate examination of those features which are fundamental to economic development in the socialist countries involves the sifting of factors due to prejudice and accident from an objective review of the errors in practical policy.

The historical perspective necessary for such a study conduces to a distinction between characteristics exhibited during the transition period from capitalism to socialism, and those when socialism has been achieved (as in the Soviet Union) and when the wide-scale building of communism is in progress. The disturbing transitional years were characterized by an acute class struggle, as for example in Hungary in 1956. The socialist reorganization of each country's economic life was inevitably accompanied by some retardation and instability in economic development, which are disappearing with better balance within each economy, accompanied by rapid technical advance, higher productivity, and the improvement of living standards.

The study of society rightly leads one to believe that the main

3

criterion of social progress is the degree of development of productive forces.[1] Since their rejection of capitalism, the majority of the socialist countries have had — if the period covering post-war rehabilitation is discounted — little more than a decade to construct their economies on the new principles.

THE CRUCIAL DEVELOPMENT OF PRODUCTIVE FORCES AND PRODUCTIVE RELATIONS

The rate of growth of material product is a generally accepted indicator of the development of productive forces, and it is clear that since their revolutions the material product of socialist countries has risen faster than in the capitalist states. Statistics for the years following the rehabilitation period (1950–62) show that the European socialist countries not only made great advances over their pre-war levels, but developed twice as fast as the average for capitalist states.

In 1962, industrial output in Albania and Bulgaria was 15–18 times that of the pre-war level; in the U.S.S.R., Poland, and Rumania 6·3–8 times; and in Hungary, Czechoslovakia, the German Democratic Republic (G.D.R.), and Yugoslavia, 3·6–5·5 times. In aggregate the European socialist countries increased their industrial output 3·6 times during 1950–62, while in capitalist countries the mean growth was no more than 1·8 times. In the same period their share in world production greatly increased : that of electric power, of cement, of cotton fabrics, and of sugar rose from one-seventh to one-fifth, that of coal from 25 to 36 per cent, of sawn timber from 28 to 40 per cent, and of synthetic fibre from 10 to 15 per cent.

According to United Nations estimates, agricultural output *per capita* in eastern Europe and the U.S.S.R. in 1962–63 was 50 per cent above pre-war, whereas the mean increment for the world was 13 per cent. The share of the European socialist countries in grain production rose from 17 to 20 per cent between 1950 and 1962.

National income in those 12 years more than doubled in Poland, Hungary, Czechoslovakia, and Yugoslavia, and increased between 2·5 and 3·1 times in the U.S.S.R., Albania, Bulgaria, the G.D.R., and Rumania. In the U.S.S.R., the rate of growth of the national income for the years concerned was 2·1 to 2·3 times higher than that in the U.S.A. and England, while, compared with the G.F.R. and France, it was 1·3 to 1·8 times higher.

[1] See V. I. Lenin, *Sochineniya*, vol. 13, Fourth edn., Moscow, 1947, p. 219 ; *Works*, English trans., vol. 13, Fourth edn., Moscow, 1962, p. 276.

It should be noted that 1963 proved unfavourable for some socialist countries : notably, the Soviet crop was smaller than in 1962, and industrial production in Czechoslovakia failed to expand. The reduction of the crops in the U.S.S.R. was purely attributable to bad weather, and measures were taken to compensate for the immediate shortfall and to support an expansion during 1964–65. In Czechoslovakia significant difficulties have been encountered, connected with the reorganization of industrial production and the introduction of technological changes ; these were intensified by faults in planning and neglect of incentives. A broad programme to reassert the expansion of industry and agriculture is now being put into practice in that country.

These examples show some of the serious problems to be overcome if a world socialist economy is to be achieved. Many socialist countries inherited poorly-developed productive forces, and politico-economic hindrances to progress have been attempted from outside. The disruption of economic relationships with the Chinese People's Republic had a negative effect on the economy of some, in particular Czechoslovakia.

The steady rapid growth of productive forces which is nevertheless being maintained in the European socialist countries may be ascribed to their economic system based on social ownership, that is on socialist productive relations : indeed, the countries of eastern Europe are on the point of achieving all the material and technical foundations of socialism. Their features include the socialist organization of labour on the basis of the obligation of all members of society to work and to be remunerated according to the quantity and quality of work ; the balanced subordination of production to gradual growth of popular welfare, notably by increasingly accurate assessment of the volume and pattern of production to provide for the growing needs of the people ; the organization of the economy along the lines of democratic centralism, economic accounting, and a combination of state and co-operative enterprise ; and the active participation of the entire working community in establishing policies and incentives. All these radical constituents of socialism are pertinent, but not every country concerned displays them equally : thus the fulfilment of collectivization of peasant households in Rumania and Hungary in 1961–62 can be considered one of the major victories of socialism. New forms of economic organization are being set up in the young socialist countries, and with maturity their great potential will be fully revealed. This is the historical perspective which cannot be ignored : however outstanding the achievements of socialist construction in the transition period, they will be far weightier when socialism is fully attained. The more favourable the international situation, the sooner those advantages will appear.

Some of the problems of this forthcoming development may now be considered, with particular reference to the distinct characteristics of industry and agriculture. The former must be expected to develop faster than the latter, for a socialized industry has many valuable features enabling it to undergo rapid development : an unlimited market ; expanding sources of accumulation ; the state-wide exploitation of technical achievements and scientific research ; and controlled access to a skilled labour force and professional and technical manpower.

The main practical conditions for the present industrial growth in the European socialist countries are intensive investment and a shift in the production pattern to accommodate industrialized construction methods and technically novel processes. The share of investment in the national income of the socialist countries has greatly increased since the inception of industrialization, and thus increased financing of industry has been possible. In 1962, as compared with 1958, investment in industry has increased in the U.S.S.R. and G.D.R. 1·4 times, in Czechoslovakia and Poland 1·5 times, and has more than doubled in Rumania, Bulgaria, and Hungary. An impression of these changes may be obtained from Table 1.

TABLE 1

INDEX NUMBERS OF GLOBAL INDUSTRIAL OUTPUT IN 1962

1950 = 1

	All Industry	Group A	Fuel and Power	Engineering and Metal-working	Chemicals	Construction Materials
Albania	6·9	..	14·8	6·7	..	..
Bulgaria	4·9	6·6	8·6	10·0	11·0	11·4
Czechoslovakia	3·3	3·7	3·4	5·5	5·5	5·1
G.D.R.	3·3	..	2·4	4·5	3·4	2·9
Hungary	3·2	..	3·4	4·2	6·1	3·2
Poland	4·0	4·7	4·6	10·8	6·8	4·3
Rumania	4·5	5·4	6·0	8·3	10·4	5·6
U.S.S.R.	3·6	4·0	4·6	5·6	5·2	6·8
Yugoslavia	3·0	..	4·7	..	5·6	..

Output of the means of production (Group A), and in particular that of engineering, electric power, chemicals, and building materials, grows almost invariably faster than that of industry as a whole : this derives from the preferential growth accorded the most important material components for further investment and hence for the expansion of industry.

For the future, all the socialist countries face the urgent problems of consolidating their high rates of accumulation and intensive investment in industry, together with those of further change in the industrial pattern, of the establishment of the most effective types of enterprises, and of the rapid advance of technology. The new long-term plans (or 'general plans' as they are sometimes known) envisage the task of creating the most advanced pattern of industry with all possible speed. According to the general plan of economic development in the U.S.S.R., it is proposed to increase considerably the share in output of the following branches : electric power, chemicals (especially the production of polymers), the production of facilities for complete mechanization and automation (*i.e.*, instruments, electrotechnical and radiotechnical appliances, semi-conductors, and precision engineering), oil, gas, and ferrous metals. The growth of power and machinery will be 50 per cent faster than the mean for industry, and that of synthetic resins and plastics will be 9 times greater.

In Poland electric power is planned to be developed 20 per cent faster than industry as a whole, engineering 50 per cent, and the chemical industry 2·2 times faster. Roughly the same priority for these branches of industry has been planned in Hungary. Nowhere is growth simply a repetition of existing production patterns.

The significant efforts directed to the enlargement of fuel and power resources and to the creation of chemical and metallurgical industries, and the measures taken to rationalize the use of raw materials and their substitutes, testify to the fact that the foundation is being laid for further industrial advance in the European socialist countries.

As Table 2 shows, the use of raw materials has been greatly expanded : during 1950–62 the European socialist countries have been able to increase the output of power 3·7 times, the mining of hard coal 1·9 times, oil extraction 4·6 times, and steel and sulphuric acid output 2·8 times. The problem of raw materials remains, however, considerable, and chemicals are being increasingly used to supplement natural and agricultural resources. Chemicals now have

TABLE 2

OUTPUT OF POWER AND VARIOUS RAW MATERIALS
IN THE EUROPEAN SOCIALIST COUNTRIES

	Electric Power (billion kWh)		Hard Coal (million tons)		Oil (million tons)		Steel (million tons)		Sulphuric Acid (thousand tons)	
	1950	1962	1950	1962	1950	1962	1950	1962	1950	1962
Albania	0·02	0·24	0·02	0·15	0·1	0·8	—	—	—	
Bulgaria	0·8	6·0	3·0	10·7	—	0·2	0·0	0·4	—	247
Czecho-slovakia	9·3	28·7	33·9	68·5	0·06	0·18	3·1	7·6	252	649
G.D.R.	19·5	45·1	48·5	84·2	—	—	1·0	3·6	245	703
Hungary	3·0	9·1	8·5	18·5	0·5	1·6	1·0	2·3	62	219
Poland	9·4	35·4	80·4	115·0	0·16	0·20	2·5	7·7	285	852
Rumania	2·1	10·1	3·1	4·4	5·0	11·9	0·6	2·5	52	326
U.S.S.R.	91·2	369·0	224·5	453·0	37·9	186·2	27·3	76·3	2,125	6,132
Yugoslavia	2·4	11·3	7·0	12·9	0·1	1·5	0·4	1·6	83	287
Total	137·7	514·9	408·2	767·4	43·8	202·6	35·9	102·0	3,058	9,408

as much significance in development as electric power — a situation which the Soviet Communist Party has characterized by adapting Lenin's definition to 'Communism is Soviet power plus the electrification of the whole country, plus the intensive use of chemicals'.

According to the published drafts of the plans for the coming 20 years, production of electricity in the member-countries of Comecon[1] is intended to grow 8·5 times, of fuel — 3·5 times, and of steel — 3·8 times. Particularly advanced growth of the chemical industry is envisaged for the near future. In the Soviet Union it is planned to increase the gross output of the major branches of chemical industry more than thrice the 1963 figure by 1970 ; the production of mineral fertilizers will be increased 3·5 to 4 times, chemical pesticides 7·5 times, plastics and synthetic fibres 6 to 6·8 times, chemical fibres 4·4 times, and tyres doubled. In the G.D.R. chemical production will rise 70 per cent during 1964–70. In Poland, Czechoslovakia, Hungary, and Rumania the growth rate of the chemical industry has been, or is to be, significantly higher than that of industry as a whole.

The special attention paid to the organization of science in the socialist countries must be stressed. The development of science and technology is being increasingly subsidized, and the population at large is becoming increasingly involved in the activities of technical research. State allocations for scientific research, education, and

[1] Council for Mutual Economic Assistance (CMEA).

cultural measures over 1958–62 increased in the U.S.S.R. 1·8 times, in the G.D.R. 1·4 times, and in Poland 1·5 times. The growing creative activities of the population at large in science and technology are evident in the great number of technical innovations : in the U.S.S.R. in 1962 these reached 2·7 millions, representing an increase of 1·6 times over the five years concerned ; the total savings resulting from the introduction of the innovations amounts to 1·7 billion rubles (equivalent to two-fifths of all investment in science). In other socialist countries the figures for 1958–62 were 2·5 times in the G.D.R., 46 per cent in Czechoslovakia and 1·9 times in Bulgaria.

The most acute and vitally important problem in the socialist countries is the growth of agricultural production, the needs for which continue to expand. The European socialist countries could completely satisfy their needs in agricultural products and create the necessary reserves of grain, sugar, livestock products, etc. The prerequisites are already there — large state farms and collective farms are organised and the relevant branches of industry have been developed for providing machinery and chemicals — and it now remains to create the appropriate technical basis, and effectively to organize the labour of collective and state farmers and other agricultural personnel.

The growing mechanization and use of chemicals in agriculture is reflected in Table 3.

TABLE 3

GROWTH OF THE TRACTOR STOCK AND THE PRODUCTION OF
MINERAL FERTILIZERS IN THE SOCIALIST COUNTRIES OF EUROPE

	Tractor Stock (Thousands of Conventional 15-h.p. Units)		Output of Mineral Fertilizers (Millions of Tons)	
	1950	1962	1950	1962
Albania	0·4	5·9	—	—
Bulgaria	8·7	48·0	—	164
Czechoslovakia	26·0	125·8	96	334
G.D.R.	12·7	74·2	256	512
Hungary	12·7	49·4	40	426
Poland	25·6	99·3	160	573
Rumania	16·7	57·5	1	131
U.S.S.R.	93·3	2,293·0	5,497	17,258
Yugoslavia	6·2	37·0	4	83

Over the 12 years, in all the countries enumerated, the number of tractors increased 2·6 times, and the output of mineral fertilizers rose 3·2 times. This and measures now being put into practice promise rapid growth of agricultural production in the long-term plan. Towards 1980 it is planned that agricultural production in the U.S.S.R. be 3·5 times, in Hungary 2 to 2·5 times, and in Bulgaria 2·5 times the 1960 level. There is adequate potential in the socialist countries for enlarging fixed and working capital and general and skilled manpower. The use of this potential by improved organization of labour and production will contribute to the high rates of growth achieved in all the socialist countries.

An economic system can expand only if conditions are created for the training of manpower on a wide scale. Socialism offers the most favourable circumstances for such programmes, and, as time passes, the education and training of the workers, the rise in their living standards, and in those of their children will more and more influence productivity. Among the new conditions arising under socialism for a favourable evolution of the labour force are full employment, a shorter working day, free education and medical care, and security in old age. In all the socialist countries efforts are being made to expand consumption, improve distribution, and raise production, thus paving the way for a new rise in living standards.

THE ESTABLISHMENT AND DEVELOPMENT OF THE NEW TYPE OF INTERNATIONAL ECONOMIC RELATIONS

The economy of individual socialist countries cannot be fully understood without taking into consideration the development of the world socialist economy as a whole. The European socialist countries are members of a system based on co-operation and mutual assistance, and determined by the predominance of socialist ownership of the means of production.

Two types of development are characteristic of the European socialist countries. First, national complexes are formed. Underdeveloped agricultural countries such as Rumania and Bulgaria have now overcome their economic one-sidedness, everywhere modern industry is established and the most appropriate economic pattern is being created. Natural resources such as minerals, arable land, climatic conditions, labour, etc., are more fully exploited. However, such a national economic grouping does not lead to autarky, which is economically absurd in conditions of international co-operation. Specialization in those branches of industry which form a natural part of the national economic complexes is correlated with the needs of the world's socialist system on the whole.

Secondly, co-operative principles are being introduced into the national economies, and international economic relationships are becoming increasingly important. Both these types of economic development supplement each other : the faster effective national complexes are created in each country, the higher is its productivity developed, and the more valuable its integration into the system of international division of labour. International collaboration in turn allows the partners to obtain scarce products at minimum cost. This international co-operation of socialist countries in the economic field has harnessed new productive forces for the benefit of society. The economic sovereignty of the state in the socialist countries is thereby strengthened, and forms the economic foundations of world socialism.

As the statement of a Conference of Representatives of the Communist and Workers' Parties put it: 'Under socialism national economic and cultural progress and the development of the state system are naturally integrated with the strengthening and promotion of the whole world socialist system, and with the closer uniting of nations. The interests of the socialist system as a whole are harmoniously integrated with those of the nation.'

The concept of socialist internationalism which underlies this statement has been less investigated, and may now be examined in some detail.

The steady growth of the division of labour among socialist countries in agriculture and industry, and the expansion of trade with the rest of the world are the goals of economic development in the European socialist countries. The foreign trade of the countries participating in the Council for Mutual Economic Assistance (Comecon) in 1961 was 3·5 times that of 1950. The growth of foreign trade outstrips that of material production, which fact testifies to the enlargement of the international socialist division of labour. Even so, in the light of future tasks, the present procedure for planning foreign trade inadequately promotes the international division of labour. Foreign trade planning should involve the creation of markets for the branches which undertake specialization, and provide for the fulfilment of projects established under schemes of international co-operation.

The internationalization of economic activity is based on the concentration and specialization of production. In all the European socialist states large enterprises are expanding as they seek a place in the world market, and a far-reaching division of labour has been achieved in the processing of raw materials (extraction of iron ore, coal, oil and ferrous ores, oil refining and the production of coke, ferrous and non-ferrous metals, and of electric power).

Bulgaria, Hungary, the G.D.R., Poland, Rumania, the U.S.S.R., and Czechoslovakia supply each other with hard coal, coking coals, and coke. The socialist countries of Europe are supplied with oil and oil products from the U.S.S.R. and Rumania. The metallurgical works of Hungary, Poland, Rumania, Czechoslovakia, and Bulgaria are supplied with iron ore from the Soviet Union, Bulgaria, Hungary, and the G.D.R. Rumania imports considerable quantities of cast iron and rolled metal. The U.S.S.R. is the major importer of Hungarian bauxite, Polish sulphur, non-ferrous metal ores from several countries, etc. The Soviet Union, Czechoslovakia, the G.D.R., Hungary, Rumania, and Bulgaria are co-operating in the exploitation of power plant. Without continuous inter-state supply of raw materials, neither the economy of individual countries nor the world socialist economic system as a whole could function. The raw materials problem of contemporary industry can be solved only on an international scale and through the united efforts of a number of states.

Given the particularly complicated fuel and power problems, and the desirability of uniting scientific, technical, and economic forces in the socialist countries, it might be practicable, through Comecon, national planning committees, and the Academies of Science, to construct a long-term plan for the electrification of the socialist countries of Europe, on the lines of the Lenin plan for the Electrification of Russia (GOELRO). The collaboration of the socialist countries in this field could comprise geological exploration and technico-economic surveys of existing and future sources of energy ; comprehensive investigation of possible new energy sources ; modernization of existing, and creation of new, fuel and power plants ; establishment of unified power grids ; and the development and technical reconstruction of heavy electrical engineering.

The international division of labour in manufacturing — especially in mechanical engineering — has become particularly important. The exchange of machinery and equipment between the socialist countries greatly surpasses the rate of growth of foreign trade as a whole. The most efficient types of engineering plants are being set up, although they are not yet producing as quickly, or as substantially, as desired the first-rate low-cost goods suitable for the world socialist market. There are wide prospects also for closer collaboration of the socialist countries in industries producing consumer manufactures and agricultural goods.

Freight traffic is growing rapidly, and international co-operation in the use of transport is becoming essential. According to rough estimates, shipments from the Soviet Union to the European people's democracies in 1980 will be 5 times the 1960 level. The transportation of this volume of goods is clearly impossible without the construction of a traffic network of international importance. A common wagon pool has been set up to improve the utilization of rolling stock. The value of this kind of collaboration is evident from the fact that there are instances of superseding strictly national requirements in order, for purely economic and technical reasons, to promote the effective functioning of enterprises with international connections. Thus, to provide the East-Slovakian group of metallurgical enterprises with materials from the Soviet Union, it was decided to build a broad-gauge line, although standard European gauge is the norm in Czechoslovakia.

In the process of solving raw-material supply problems, increasing the efficiency of manufacturing and co-ordinating research, etc., productive forces have been created that range far beyond national borders. Among such international projects may be cited the oil pipe-line (and the oil-refining plants it supplies) installed on the territories of the Soviet Union, Hungary, Poland, the G.D.R., and Czechoslovakia. This whole elaborate production system, including oil extraction, transportation, and processing, is forced by engineering requirements to function on an international scale. No less an international undertaking is the power grid connecting Bulgaria, Rumania, Hungary, Czechoslovakia, Poland, the G.D.R., and the western regions of the U.S.S.R. Moreover, this unified power grid may be considered the forerunner of the far greater and more extensive network which will promote the efficient use of generating capacity, supply participants according to their needs, and solve fuel problems by means of power transmission over long distances. Research into the peaceful use of atomic energy requires the collaboration of the scientific resources of many countries. The financing of such work is beyond small states — hence the establishment of the Nuclear Energy Research Institute at Dubna (U.S.S.R.). Similarly, the effective inter-state specialization and co-operation of production, and the output of first-class low-priced goods were found impossible under contemporary conditions without the establishment of an international Institute of Standards.

The international enterprises which Poland is setting up with other interested countries are a form of association in which two or more together supply the capital for a jointly-managed activity ; projects include the production of steel and of roller-bearings. The undertakings operated by such associations are the property of countries in which they are situated and are chiefly concerned with the planning of investments, operational programmes, research and design.

The internationalization of productive forces, being governed by the same productive relations as at the national level, is motivated by correspondingly similar objectives for consumption and welfare and for the balanced development of production, and is promoted by specific institutions. Among these an important role is played by Comecon, established in 1949, notably by research on co-ordinating national economic plans, regulating foreign trade, and arranging the specialization and co-operation of production. The co-ordination of plans for 1966–70 is chiefly being undertaken by the joint review of investment plans. Encouragement of collaboration between the socialist countries by monetary mechanisms is, moreover, gaining importance : the International Bank of Economic Co-operation has been established, and the price system used in trade between socialist countries is being improved. Viable financing is to operate in all spheres of joint action.

The internationalization of economic life is paralleled by the equalization of economic standards. The socialist reorganization of the economy and the common objective to create the material and technical foundation of socialism are the main conditions for achieving equality in *per capita* national product and uniformity of labour conditions, and for raising living standards corresponding to the needs of the society and its national traditions. It may already be said that equality has been attained in such contributions to welfare as the social ownership of the basic means of production and of the goods produced, the right to work and be rewarded according to that work, and the provision of social consumption in such forms as education, medical services, and child care. For the equalization of economic levels, modern engineering is of primary importance. In attempting to outline this process of equalization, the development of industry in the peoples' democracies may be compared with that in the Soviet Union. Before the Second World War the industrial level of the capitalist countries of Eastern Europe lagged behind that of the Soviet Union : the rate of industrial growth in the capitalist economies of Rumania, Poland, and Hungary in the pre-war decade was from one-tenth to one-quarter that of the U.S.S.R. at the same time, while in Czechoslovakia industry did not expand at all. There was a high rate of growth in Bulgaria — though from a low starting point — but still less than the Soviet. The construction of socialism and Soviet aid since the war has changed the situation. If the Soviet rate is taken as 1, the rates of growth of industry were 1·68 in Albania, 1·27 in Bulgaria, 1·11 in Poland, and 1·47 in Rumania. The rate of growth in Hungary was higher than in the U.S.S.R. if the effect of counter-revolutionary upheaval is excluded, and only in the highly-industrialized economies of the G.D.R. and Czechoslovakia did the rates of growth of industry approximate the Soviet figure. One would expect the rates of industrial growth of the less-developed countries to remain higher than in the U.S.S.R., but the question of growth rates cannot be solved in the same manner at all times and in all places. The changes already effected in industrial structure, the present concentration of resources on the improvement of agriculture, and other factors may cause the rates of growth in different countries to vary ; moreover, once the planned growth rates have been achieved by the international division of labour, economic equalization does not necessarily entail uniform industrial production *per capita*, because territory, population, and natural endowment differ. The introduction of modern technology in the formerly underdeveloped countries, together with scientific and technical assistance and collaboration between the countries, may be regarded as the most effective means of equalizing economic development. Correspondence in techniques must precede, and contribute to, the equalization of the economic level. Industrial construction in Poland, Rumania, Hungary, Bulgaria, and Albania has benefited from equipment and expertise supplied by the U.S.S.R., the G.D.R., and Czechoslovakia. While the long-run rate of growth of inter-member commerce in Comecon has been 12 per cent per annum, trade in equipment in recent years has been rising by more than 20 per cent a year. In 1948–62 the U.S.S.R. delivered to Comecon members more than 16,500 sets of scientific and technical documentation, and obtained 8,500 in return. The exchange of scientific and technical information is also proceeding between other socialist countries. Differentials in the ratio of arable land to tractors are becoming smaller.

Closer economic collaboration between Comecon countries by no means signifies the separation of these countries from the rest of the world, for Comecon is no closed economic alliance like the Common Market. Besides trade with other socialist countries, such as Yugoslavia and Cuba, the socialist countries particularly aim to foster economic relations with former colonies which have set out on the path of socialism. The trade of the Soviet Union with the developing countries in 1953–63 has grown more than 10 times. At the onset of that decade, the U.S.S.R. had trade and payment agreements only with three countries, but today it deals with 35 countries of Asia, Africa, and Latin America, where more than 900 industrial and other projects have been undertaken with the assistance of the European socialist countries. The total sum of the credits and grants made by Comecon members for the needs of economic development of the newly-independent states amounts to 3·5 billions of rubles. The credits are granted at very low interest, free of political ties. In 1955–61 the trade turnover between Comecon countries and these states grew 3·2 times, against a 1·6 times increase in exchanges between these countries and the developed capitalist countries. The economic relationship between the socialist countries and the developing countries assists these latter to achieve economic independence, industrial progress, and a higher standard of living.

The socialist countries are also ready to expand trade and credit relationships with the western capitalist countries, but their attempts in this respect often encounter discriminatory measures, especially on the part of the U.S.A.

The world socialist economy and its market are competing with the world capitalist economy and market. History suggests that the world socialist economic system will succeed in this peaceful struggle.

Chapter 2

CHARACTERISTICS OF THE MIDDLE PHASE OF SOCIALIST INDUSTRIALIZATION

BY

NIKOLA ČOBELJIĆ and RADMILA STOJANOVIĆ
Belgrade University

A DEFINITION OF THE MIDDLE PHASE

By the middle phase of socialist industrialization we understand that phase following the period of initial rapid industrialization through which all underdeveloped socialist countries must pass. It thus begins after a country has built up the basic elements of its own productive capacities, enabling the effects of industrialization to penetrate all sectors of the economy. Four features can serve to define it more precisely.

The middle phase for a socialist country is, in the first place, one of substantial structural change : industry will already in the initial phase have gained a certain ascendency over agriculture, and during the middle phase the economy rapidly loses its agrarian features. More slowly, all forms of small-scale free-market production disappear in the economy, and corresponding changes take place in society as a whole. The socialist sector, secondly, achieves an increasing degree of homogeneity, intersectoral dependence and integration, and productive technology not only develops, but becomes more balanced in relation both to industries and to regions. At the same time, a diversification of domestic capacity necessitates a deeper integration in the international division of labour. Thirdly, the expansion of national product in the initial phase permits society during the middle phase to dispense with the exogenous elements of compulsion, previously inevitable, but which can be replaced by more suitably socialist methods of economic management. Large-scale production and the application of modern technology evoke a continuous evolution of forms and methods of economic management, and are incompatible with those used in the initial phase of socialist industrialization. This phase, put briefly, is the period of development during which the socialist society gets on its feet : its fourth characteristic is the disappearance of the marked disharmonies induced by the inadequacy of resources in relation to the needs generated by socialist productive relations. It must nevertheless be pointed out that productive relations at the initial phase have the attributes of socialism only in rudimentary socialist form.[1]

The concept of a middle phase is empirical : it follows from an analysis of contemporary socialist states and their different levels of development ; an attempt to subdivide the much longer period of the entire transition from capitalism to communism would be more complex, and, though the phase here distinguished would appear, it would not be at the mid-point. It could be singled out as that phase in which a socialist society begins clearly to emerge — by the definitive supersession of the elements of the old society and its backward economic structure. Moreover, although it is considered as a link in the lengthy historical transition from capitalism to communism, it is not monolithic, but made up of a series of transitional stages in which the old and new elements continually intermingle, but in which the characteristic features of a developed socialist society increasingly predominate.

Entry into the middle phase may roughly be seen as taking place when *per capita* national income reaches $400–$500. A country at such a stage is, on contemporary criteria, no longer underdeveloped : industry has become the leading sector of the economy, generating about 40 per cent of national product, and less than half the population is dependent on agriculture (although farming accounts for a larger proportion of the gainfully employed).[2] Rural overpopulation may prevail and surplus labour in agriculture can be of major importance. Technology is very uneven : a single plant may be equipped with both primitive and modern tools, and old and new enterprises stand side by side, but the rate of mechanization is accelerating. The pattern of exports shifts from primary products to include semi-manufactures and manufactures, and a start is made in selling capital goods. Imports consist mainly of equipment and industrial materials, for the pattern of domestic accumulation in

---

[1] The characteristics of the middle phase to some extent correspond to those of the third of four stages in Minc's classification (B. Minc, *Zagadnienia ekonomii politycznej socjalizmu* (Problems in the Political Economy of Socialism), Warsaw, 1957, pp. 318–319).

[2] The proportions of agricultural population and manpower are based on present population density.

physical terms is insufficiently diversified. The first important nuclei — large, modern enterprises in the most important industries — have been rapidly established in a relatively backward agrarian society, but the transformation of the remaining branches has still to be accomplished : patently the economy is heterogeneous in structure and transitory in character.

However fraught is the initial phase of accelerated industrialization with difficulties to be surmounted, and whatever sacrifices have been made to give the first, powerful impulses to structural change, the middle phase has, in all socialist countries, been far more complex. Economic policy and the system itself have to be rethought. The factors of production must be more rationally utilized, the choice of the pattern of development, the problems of investment efficiency and of optimal technology, and the entire planning and management system have to be reviewed. In all these fields the scientific approach, the training of highly-skilled manpower and prompt application of research and development are of great importance. It can rightly be said that in this phase science comes to the fore and becomes the leading factor of production.[1] From these many problems, this paper confines its analysis to a few major issues of the dynamics of the factors of production, and of their varying importance over time.

CHANGES IN THE RELATIVE IMPORTANCE OF THE FACTORS OF PRODUCTION

In the initial phase the organic composition of capital — the curcial element in the pattern of factor utilization — is influenced by forces acting in opposite directions — one tending to raise the organic composition of capital, the other to keep it at the existing level. The forces acting in the first direction are the increasing share in investments of capital-intensive branches ; the need to reduce the construction period of major investment projects by more mechanization ; the pressure to improve the quality of production (and the productivity of labour) to bring it nearer that in the more developed economies ; and the reduction of cumulative labour costs to increase the marginal propensity to save and, very frequently, to cut down the marginal propensity to import. Opposing forces tending to restrict the application of advanced technique comprise the scarcity of accumulation in both volume and type ;

---

[1] See S. G. Strumilin, 'The Role of Science in the Development of Productive Forces', *Voprosy filosofii*, no. 3, 1954 (reprinted in *Izbrannye proizvedeniya* (Selected Works), vol. 4, Moscow, 1964, pp. 232–250).

the limited scope, due to balance-of-payments difficulties, for increasing the real volume of accumulation and changing its physical composition through foreign trade; the necessity to delay the systematic retirement of fixed assets to ensure more resources for new capital formation (and notably in new branches); considerable pressure by the labour force, particularly pronounced in countries with surplus agrarian labour, manifested either in the presence of redundant labour in existing enterprises, or in demands for new jobs in non-farm activities.

These opposing pressures impose upon the choice of technique frequent and varied compromises between the old and the new: new technology is broadly favoured for the branches which in the long run are most important for economic development, but the scarcity of capital compels the postponement of such technology in many others.

In the middle phase, however, the factors favouring advanced technology exert more force, while the restricting factors gradually disappear (or their effect is considerably attenuated). Thus, for example, because the capital stock and the flow of production is larger and of higher quality, accumulation becomes a decreasingly restrictive factor in the choice of capital-intensity. The initial balance-of-payments disequilibria of underdeveloped countries gradually diminish as a result of changes in the volume and structure of domestic production. Delays in capital replacement, previously very pronounced, disappear completely in the middle phase. These tendencies would by themselves push technical progress into a dominant role in the middle phase as the basic dynamic factor of development, but this is reinforced by three new causes strongly favouring technical progress.

The first is the need to support by a high technical level of production the rapid initial rates of growth engendered by a virtually exclusive expansion of those branches which physically generate new accumulation. Once those industries have been set up by a concentrated mobilization of resources, the economy can develop more evenly. The accelerating effects provided by the accumulation-generating sectors can to a great extent be replaced by a higher technical level of production in all productive sectors.

In the initial stage, much of the increment in average labour productivity is achieved by a massive transfer of manpower from sectors with lower productivity (chiefly agriculture) to those with a much higher return. In course of time, however, this source dwindles or is exhausted. The second tendency is the counteraction of this phenomenon by raising the capital-to-labour ratio. This shift proceeds approximately along the following course :

Per capita National Income in Dollars	Percentage Share in the Increment of National Income	
	Employment	Productivity
Up to 200	80	20
400–600	50	50
600–800	35	65
800–1,000	25	75
Over 1,000	20	80

Once the surplus of agricultural manpower is exhausted, the volume of new employment is constrained to the current increment in the economically-active population, the growth of which tends to decrease to a very low rate.

A final reason is the accumulated needs for capital replacement, as a result of prolonged postponement of retirements and repairs in the initial period and of the readier acceptance of obsolescence, previously disregarded.[1]

THE LEVEL OF EMPLOYMENT

Although greater stress is laid on capital-intensity in the middle, than in the previous, phase, a socialist government remains under the obligation fully to employ the economically-active population. Few countries, and scarcely those with substantial agrarian over-population, will have assured full employment by the time the economy enters the middle phase ; during it, therefore, the growth of *per capita* income must be assured both by raising the productivity of workers already employed and by the transfer of agricultural manpower to higher-productivity branches. The optimal combination of each is that which provides enough capacity in one cycle of accumulation to furnish in the ensuing cycle the required employment and the equipment needed for the introduction of new techniques. The rate of accumulation in this phase is just as crucial

[1] Such policies of the initial phase distort the composition of capital in the 'old' industries, which, because the value of fixed assets is low (and often completely written-off) chiefly consists of inventories. In the middle phase increasing capital replacement and the introduction of new techniques change the structure of capital in these branches in favour of fixed assets.

for an economy having a relative abundance of labour as for an economy without any manpower surplus : in the former case it has both to stimulate technical progress and more fully to employ labour ; in the latter case, the shortage of labour must be compensated by more capital-intensive techniques and consequently also by a rate of accumulation corresponding to the desired rate of product growth.

Within any optimal relations between capital- and labour-intensive technique arises the choice between investing in new enterprises and modernizing existing enterprises. The latter kind of investment calls for very little construction work, and shortens the period from investment to operation, but, despite such advantages over new enterprises, this option is not fully open until the later stage of the middle phase. An empirical examination of both socialist and capitalist countries suggests the following rough association between *per-capita* national income and indicators of investment composition : [1]

	Per capita National Income (Dollars)		
	Up to 500	From 500–1,000	Over 1,000
Net as percentage of gross investment	70	50	40
Outlay on capital replacement and modernization as percentage of gross investment	35–40	45–55	60–65
Outlay on plant and equipment as percentage of gross investment	40	50	60 +

In the first stages of the middle phase it appears that the greater part of investment must be earmarked for new projects, since an economy, entering this phase of development, tends to have an inadequately diversified industrial structure, massive reserves of under-employment, and an uneven regional distribution of productive forces, all calling for investment in new projects. There is no inherent bias towards technical progress in building new enterprises as against modernization of existing capacities, but the former create more employment. Consequently, optimal factor proportions depend

[1] A similar relationship is presented by Krasovsky who takes growth rates of product as the independent variable (V. P. Krasovsky, 'On Proportions in Capital Investment', in *Kapitalnye vlozheniya i rezervy ikh ispolzovaniya* (Capital Investment and Reserves for Its Fuller Utilization), Moscow, 1963, p. 84).

not only on the total volume of accumulation but also on the pattern of investment in the sense just described.

A further important issue on employment is the cost of labour. If a plant is made more capital-intensive by modernization, the labour thus released is almost costless from the social point of view, if used for expansion of the branch concerned or of other branches of production : it does not call for any additional expenditure on wages, accommodation, use of public services, etc. New projects require, however, employment of additional labour involving the inevitable costs of its retraining and transfer from agriculture (except, of course, when it is available free of cost in the form of large-scale voluntary work). However, in order to make a real estimate of the effects of the transfer of agricultural manpower, it is also necessary to take into account the social benefit resulting from the increment in the average productivity of labour. As distinct from the initial phase, in which the intake of rural labour is pre-dominant, the middle phase is characterized by variations at each spiral of this phase. While some writers are of the opinion that the social costs of new labour are equal to wages paid (perhaps increased by the costs of urbanization), others consider it completely free in underdeveloped countries abounding in labour, since the volume of consumption in real terms virtually does not change. Finally, some writers discussing the volume of these social costs insist on the difference between the transfer of labour from village to town and the transfer from one industry to another, but without a change of residence.[1]

ALLOCATIONS TO 'NON-PRODUCTIVE' ACTIVITIES AND FOR REGIONAL DEVELOPMENT

The question of proportions between capital and labour un-doubtedly has a central place in economic policy, but it would be an exaggerated simplification to leave it at this and neglect problems of the allocation of the factors of production between the productive and non-productive sectors, and between regions.

In the initial phase the development of the productive and non-productive sectors does not, as a rule, proceed harmoniously and simultaneously, because, in view of the limited size of accumulation, a high priority is given to the productive sector. Restrictions in the

---

[1] Notable contributors to this discussion include Dobb, Kahn, J. Robinson, Lewis, Galenson, Leibenstein, and Sen.

non-productive sectors result in a rather lengthy postponement of investment in housing, in communal services and in educational, cultural, social, and health establishments, just as the replacement of fixed productive assets is delayed. The unsatisfied requirements accumulate, and, for reasons similar to those described above, the proportion of productive to non-productive investments changes during the middle phase in favour of the latter.

The construction of dwellings and urban amenities, which is consciously slowed down in the initial phase, is subsequently accelerated under the pressure of an ever greater volume of non-farm employment and of the necessity to improve the material and cultural conditions of town life. In capitalist countries, too, the process of urbanization is marked by considerable leaps forward from one phase of development to another, although a markedly slower, but considerably longer, process of industrialization in these countries leaves greater possibilities for a more even growth of towns. The acceleration of the rate of urbanization in capitalist countries and the degree of urbanization in relation to national income, are clearly shown in Kuznets' calculations for 44 selected countries :

| | *Per capita* National Income (Dollars) | | | |
	Over 775	351–775	151–350	150 or less
Number of countries reviewed	8	11	15	10
Percentage of population in towns of 20,000 and more inhabitants	47·4	35·9	27·9	12·4

Source : S. Kuznets, 'Consumption, Industrialization and Urbanization', in UNESCO, *Industrialization and Society*, Paris, 1963, p. 101.

It is understandable that in socialist countries the process of urbanization must be even more pronounced in the middle phase, because it was suppressed in the preceding period, so that the above Table, adjusted to conditions in socialist countries, would show greater changes in the first and second group of countries and smaller in the third and fourth.

Moreover, the middle phase calls for a definite order of changes within the framework of productive investments. An increased share is needed of 'indirectly-productive' investments (communications, ports, wharves, storage facilities, etc.), which, in the initial phase of industrialization, lag behind the rapid rise in 'directly-productive' investments. This feature of the structure of productive

24

investments is taken by some writers as an argument for the marxian Department I of national product to grow faster even after the initial construction of industry.[1] An increase in 'non-productive' investments is also postulated by the more rapid development of facilities for collective consumption, a channel increasingly predominant in the higher stages of socialist development for the satisfaction of personal needs.

It must be observed, finally, that not all regions of a country enter the middle phase at the same time. In some socialist states, deviations from the national average are so great that parts of the country retain the characteristics of the initial phase while others are well into the middle phase. Since very little can be done towards regional equalization during the initial phase, it is in the middle phase that the problem imposes itself as an urgent social obligation.

Some of our analysis for the economy as a whole can be applied to its regional features : construction of new projects, for example, predominate in less-developed regions while modernization is more frequent in developed areas. Some is applicable in attenuated form : the tendency towards an increasing share of non-productive investment is not so strong in underdeveloped regions, because of the overwhelming requirement for productive investment. And some is altogether invalid : in the choice of technique, the underdeveloped regions must be left at a lower level of technology, which would only sharpen, instead of alleviating, the regional differences.

The needs for capital-formation in the middle phase are too large for the economy to reduce the high rate of accumulation inherited from the initial phase. This is partly dictated by the urgency of society's expectations to enter the subsequent phase of highly-developed socialism, and partly by the need to deal quickly with problems, the solution of which had previously been delayed (adoption of modern technology and of a more homogeneous and complex structure of production, creation of sufficient employment, expansion of 'non-productive' branches, and attainment of regional balance). But this massive investment cannot, as in the preceding period, be effected by a reduction in personal consumption ; it must be derived from a more efficient and rational use of accumulation — implying an ever greater importance for scientific methods, and the search for economic optimality.

[1] *Cf.* A. I. Bechin, 'The Proportions of Reproduction' in *Sorevnovanie dvukh sistem — Problemy ekonomicheskoi nauki* (Competition between the Two Systems — Problems of Economics), Moscow, 1963, pp. 45–46.

CHANGE IN THE LIMITING FACTORS

Limiting factors constrain all phases of development — scarcity is inherent in economic development — but their nature changes with each stage. During the initial phase the extreme scarcity of resources exhibits itself in a very pronounced way; because the constraints are less glaringly obvious in the middle phase, it is important to recognize in time the problems they induce, to assess their relative significance, and to single out the most crucial.

A review of all the underdeveloped socialist countries in Europe in the initial phase of industrialization supports a common classification of constraints into two groups. The first group comprises sharp maladjustments resulting from lopsidedness of investment in the development of productive capacity in Department I; a relatively long period of investment gestation in new projects; temporarily idle capacities in branches of Department I; rapid increase in the capital-to-output ratio in the first phase of the investment cycle, as a direct result of the investment structure and unactivated capacity; and, last but not least, balance-of-payment difficulties (a serious limiting factor particularly in smaller countries). The other group of factors includes a dynamic rise in personal consumption insufficient to stimulate the development of Department II; and the absence of adequate incentives in the field of personal consumption to accelerate the growth of labour productivity by individual effort. These factors need be no more than listed, because many economists (Kalecki, Notkin, Sweezy, Dobb, etc.) have discussed them extensively.

Most of these factors begin to weaken, and even to disappear, in the transition to the middle phase, but some persist in a variant form, and new factors, peculiar to this phase, start to emerge. The first of the changed constraints is that of the balance-of-payments, which becomes more intimately related to investment allocations. The overwhelming stress on heavy industry, power, and transport in the initial phase had, by creating similar product-mixes in each socialist economy, limited the scope for trade. The ensuing diversification permits specialization and a wider and more rational integration within the international division of labour. Economic policy is hence faced with great responsibilities in the selection of the most suitable structure of exports and imports. Furthermore, under earlier practices scant attention could be paid to the efficiency of each importing and exporting branch : the country exported what it happened to have and imported what it could not do without. Consequently, in the middle phase, economic efficiency in external trade assumes much greater importance, since it becomes necessary continually to rank exports according to their yield in foreign exchange and imports on their domestic economies.

The major limitation in the field of labour becomes the bottleneck in highly-skilled manpower. The training of specialists requires a relatively long time, a complex system of higher education, and the establishment of specific forms of co-operation with other countries (of particular importance for small nations). Often the numerical strength and availability of highly skilled manpower inhibits the application of a specific technology and technical innovation in general. Some socialist states have even found labour as a whole a limiting factor in production. In theory, lack of manpower can be compensated by capital deepening, but this, too, reaches its limits when the rise in capital intensity, by diminishing the effectiveness of accumulation, begins to depress the rate of growth.

Factors of an organizational-technical nature also limit growth. There can still be an inordinate or increasing proportion of un-completed projects to investment and to completed projects, as in the initial phase, but in the middle phase it is no longer caused by an array of time discrepancies following imbalanced branch-allocations to investment and the lack of complementary activities, but by bottlenecks in designing, organization of construction, production of building materials and plant, and equipment for new projects. These problems are much discussed in socialist countries, because incomplete projects have run ahead of investment outlays under the influence of these organizational-technical factors.

The assertion made above, that in the middle phase labour productivity must be increasingly based on modern technology and highly skilled personnel, also implies the possibility of a shortage of supporting research and development. Scientific enquiry, the adjustment of innovations to local conditions, and efficient communication services require an extensive network of specialized institutions ; the difficulties are especially acute in the middle phase when the indispensable conditions for a systematic organization of research are only being created.

In presenting the constraints, our intention has been to indicate, rather than fully to analyse, the changes they undergo in the middle phase. In any case, we lack the perspective given by time, and the

retrospective study and quantification which is available for the
initial phase of industrialization.

INVESTMENT CYCLES IN THE MIDDLE PHASE

Economists in the socialist countries have treated the problem of
investment cycles in the socialist economy either as such or only
partially, without calling it by its name and without drawing general
conclusions on fluctuation in the economy.

The most numerous group (notably Strumilin, Notkin, and Pash-
kov) are those who try to explain the necessity of changing from
time to time the growth rates in Departments I and II. Successive
accelerations and decelerations in Department I are the result of
structural changes, caused either by rapid shifts in the rate of
accumulation or by technical progress. A spurt in Department I
is followed by accelerating production in Department II, whereafter
Department I begins again to expand rapidly, so beginning a new
cycle.[1] These deviations in growth rates in the two Departments
gradually tend to level out at higher levels of development, and are
most pronounced in the initial period of industrialization.[2] Boyarsky
has gone a step further in a mathematical model which seeks to
explain the successive changes in the rates of Departments I and II
by the variable impact of technical progress in each Department,
which affects the rate of addition to fixed assets and their transferred
value per unit of production.[3] Because he takes technical progress
as the cause of changes in the mutual relations between the two
Departments, Boyarsky does not associate this phenomenon with
rapid structural changes during early industrialization, but considers rather the more developed socialist economies, where technical
progress acts as the basic dynamic factor of development.

Among economists directly discussing the problem of cycles who
find causation in the uneven course of capital replacement,
Czechowski considers that capital replacement is always uneven,
even at a zero rate of growth.[4] He refers to Marx's concept of an

[1] See S. G. Strumilin, 'The National-Economic Balance as Instrument of
Socialist Planning', *Voprosy ekonomiki*, no. 11, 1954 (reprinted in *Izbrannye
proizvedeniya, loc. cit.*, pp. 251–268).
[2] A. I. Notkin, *Tempy i proportsii sotsialisticheskogo vosproizvodstva* (Rates and
Proportions of Socialist Reproduction), Moscow, 1961.
[3] A. Boyarsky, 'On Econometrics and the Application of Mathematics to
Economic Analysis', *Planovoe khozyaistvo*, no. 7, 1959.
[4] T. Czechowski, *Cykliczność procesu reprodukcji prostej* (The Cyclicality of the
Process of Simple Reproduction), Warsaw, 1957.

inherently uneven process of 'withering away of fixed capital'.[1] Unlike Czechowski, Lange limits the existence of reinvestment cycles solely to the period of accelerated initial industrialization, when the rapid capital formation leads to lagged replacements ; when the initial industrialization is complete, the cycles rapidly disappear.[2]

These theories of investment cycles bear some similarity to Minc's hypothesis of cyclical investment efficiency. He discerns alternate periods of growth and decline in the capital coefficient, possibly separated by periods of stability ; the slope and duration of each movement depends on the character of technical progress. Minc partly substantiates these theses by statistics for the Soviet Union and Poland.[3]

We may add that similar views have been expressed by bourgeois economists who are concerned with the comparative development of capitalist and socialist countries (Nutter and Kuznets), or who examine critically the theory of 'balanced development' (Streeten). They conclude that a high rate of expansion may require successive changes in the growth rates of individual branches (*e.g.* Nutter's 'growth cycles') or the concentration of accumulation on key branches.

Although the foregoing exhausts neither all arguments nor all their refinements, it indicates the kind of dynamics we have in mind when discussing the investment cycle : the idea of an investment cycle is not new — either in name or as an explanation of economic movements — but it has perhaps not been completely explained.[4]

By an investment cycle we understand the fluctuation of aggregate material production under the impact of structural changes caused by the rapid expansion of new techniques. During each cycle there are changes in the direction of the flows of accumulation, in the structure of material production and in the rates of growth in its

---

[1] 'Ist die kapitalistische Form der Reproduktion einmal beseitigt, so kommt die Sache darauf hinaus, dass die Grosse des absterbenden und daher in natura zu ersetzenden Teils des fixen Kapitals (hier des in der Erzeugung der Konsumtions-mittel fungierenden) in verschiednen sukzessiven Jahren wechselt. Ist er in einem Jahr sehr gross (über die Durchschnittssterblichkeit, wie bei den Menschen), so im folgenden sicher um so geringer.' (*Das Kapital*, Zweiter Band, Buch II, Berlin, 1958, p. 473.)

[2] O. Lange, *Teoria reprodukcji i akumalacji* (The Theory of Reproduction and Accumulation), Warsaw, 1961, p. 147.

[3] B. Minc, 'The Investment Coefficient during Economic Growth', *Ekonomista*, no. 3, 1963, esp. pp. 501–502.

[4] The following exposition is condensed from our article, 'A Contribution to the Study of Investment Cycles in the Socialist Economy', *Ekonomist*, no. 4, 1961 (English trans. in *Yugoslav Economists on Problems of a Socialist Economy*, New York, 1964).

basic departments ; there are shifts, too, in the organic composition
of fixed capital, in the coefficients of capital-intensity and in labour
productivity, which together bring about changes in capital coefficients. These changes follow a definite time pattern by grouping
themselves in two different phases of the investment cycle, which
appear and alternate with definite regularity. In the first phase, the
stress is on sectors producing the elements of new techniques, while
in the second, the stress shifts to the technical modernization of
Department II and the expansion of its production on the basis
of the previous increment of productive capital. The creation of
additional means of production (the material embodiment of technical progress) implies that the movement of capital formation
towards productive sectors in Department I is more pronounced,
leading in turn to further expansion of the latter. These additional
means of production are absorbed in the second stage, when the
processes described operate mainly in the reverse direction, to the
extent, and for the period, required to bring the economy into
equilibrium, but at a higher level of material production.

A simplified model may illustrate some of the movements. Let us
express the general rate of growth as :

$$r = \frac{k_0}{k_1}(1 + a - \gamma),$$

where r is the rate of growth of national product ; a the rate of growth
of accumulation ; k_0 the capital coefficient at the beginning of the
period under consideration, *i.e.* at the beginning of the investment
cycle ; k_1 the capital coefficient at the end of a period, *i.e.* at the end
of the first stage of the cycle ; k_2 the capital coefficient at the end
of the second stage ; and γ the rate of replacement of fixed assets.
Let us assume that all the material elements of accumulation are
produced in Department I, so that the rate of growth of Department
I may be expressed as

$$r_I = \frac{k_0}{k_1}(1 + a_I - \gamma).$$

Thus its rate of growth in the first stage of the investment cycle is

$$r_{I_1} = \frac{k_0}{k_1}(1 + a_{I_1} - \gamma)$$

and in the second stage

$$r_{I_2} = \frac{k_1}{k_2}(1 + a_{I_2} - \gamma).$$

By deriving the rate of growth of Department II from the general rate of growth and from the rate of growth of Department I, we obtain that in the first stage of the investment cycle

$$r_{II_1} = \frac{\left[\frac{k_0}{k_1}(1 + a - \gamma)\right] - \left[\frac{k_0}{k_1}(1 + a_{I_1} - \gamma)\right]\beta}{\rho},$$

where β is the share of Department I in total production and ρ the share of Department II in total production. In the second stage

$$r_{II_2} = \frac{\left[\frac{k_1}{k_2}(1 + a - \gamma)\right] - \left[\frac{k_1}{k_2}(1 + a_{I_2} - \gamma)\right]\beta}{\rho}.$$

The model [1] shows how, under the impact of technical progress, changes take place in the rate of growth of Departments I and II, in their rates of accumulation, and in the capital coefficients during two stages of the cycle. Because, as has already been indicated, the changes are not limited to the elements specified in the model, the concept of investment cycles can be seen as pervading the entire dynamics of the impact of technical progress, and as a permanent form of movement of the socialist economy.

In the initial phase of socialist industrialization, the rapid structural shift towards Department I and the correspondingly swift increase in the rate of productive accumulation cause the growth rates of production and accumulation in each Department to differ so considerably that the economy is at its most removed from general equilibrium, and in the acutest danger of exceeding the critical point at which, due to numerous bottlenecks, the marginal efficiency of capital declines. Cyclical fluctuation has been all the more marked in the socialist countries because they condensed their initial industrialization into a very short period. This has not been unnoticed in economic theory, and it can easily be statistically confirmed in every socialist country by the analysis of their production aggregates and key dynamic coefficients. Some economists maintain that the investment cycle tends to disappear in the course of the middle phase, as its initial causes are eliminated. But investment disequilibria of another kind appear in the middle phase — pursuant to the effort to catch up in productive and social infrastructure. Although such structural changes are less disturbing in their magnitude and consequences, they are sufficiently substantial for sporadically uneven concentrations of capital formation. This variability

[1] Further developed in our paper cited above.

may be accentuated by the inherent unevenness of technical progress, a characteristic of the middle phase and a more lasting cause of the investment cycle. The instability of the application of technology is due partly to the bunching of discoveries both over time and by branch affected. At times the bunching is so pronounced as to constitute a veritable technical revolution. A coincidence of capital-intensive innovations induces a succession of structural changes in production, which spreads to the whole of social production.

It would be thought that a developed socialist society, with a highly-organized network of scientific and research institutions, with widespread communication services and with advanced methods of planning could apply new technology in a smoother manner : it could perhaps stockpile capital goods to stabilize their production, or level out the rate of applying innovation. But if the country concerned is one of the most highly developed, inventories could only be of equipment already known and their purpose would thereby be frustrated, for they would lose their use-value as soon as new discoveries appeared. The second alternative implies that the economy would deliberately renounce for a certain time the advantages of a new technique and unnecessarily postpone their application : this can hardly be reconciled with the objectives of a developed socialist society.

We would like to point out in conclusion that it has been our intention only to outline the concept and significance of that stage of economic development which we have termed the middle phase. It is difficult to say more until more socialist countries are deeply within it : most are only entering it.

Even ten years ago it was very hard to assess the phase of initial industrialization, and to identify what was specific to that phase, and that which was a lasting feature of socialism ; to distinguish what was inherently socialistic and what were inevitable social compulsions to establish a socialist economy and society. In this respect the situation is much clearer today.

In relation to the middle phase, however, we are, as regards knowledge, just where we were a decade ago in respect of the phase now passed. This alone indicates caution in general theoretical analysis but it underscores the need to examine and compare the experience of different socialist countries ; without this, there could be neither any clear understanding of the goal towards which such societies are heading, nor any clear determination of economic goals as the objectives of long-term economic policy and planning.

Chapter 3

BULGARIAN INDUSTRIALIZATION AND FARM MECHANIZATION UNDER SOCIALISM

Bulgarian Academy of Sciences

THE ECONOMIC STRUCTURE OF PRE-WAR BULGARIA

BEFORE the Second World War Bulgaria was a backward agrarian country with poorly developed industries. Agriculture was one of the most backward branches of the economy: farms were predominantly small and yielded low incomes. The average size of a Bulgarian farm, measured by land owned, was 72·8 decares in 1897,[1] 63 decares in 1908, 57·2 decares in 1926, and 49 decares in 1934. According to the census taken in 1934, 40·2 per cent of all peasant households possessed less than 30 decares of land, and 63·1 per cent possessed less than 50 decares of land. Farms of over 200 decares (roughly 50 acres) constituted only 1·5 per cent of all farms in the country and they accounted for 8·8 per cent of the total arable land.

The development of capitalism in Bulgaria was matched in agriculture by a concentration of the land in a smaller number of farms and by growing impoverishment and bankruptcy among the poor and middle income farmers who could not obtain adequate equipment and livestock. Further contributors to this process were the limited possibilities of bringing virgin lands under cultivation, the growth of the rural population, and the contemporary inheritance laws. The number of peasant households rose from 751,000 in 1926 to 1,103,000 in 1944, and the practice of parcellation subdivided their land into 12,000,000 plots of an average size of 3·5 decares (less than one acre), making impossible the use of modern farming machinery and science. Rising rural unemployment was rapidly becoming a major economic problem.

During the entire period of bourgeois domination, Bulgarian equipment was primitive; to set against such anachronisms as the

[1] One decare (1,000 sq. metres) is approximately a quarter-acre.

33

wooden plough were a mere 3,200 tractors. Sowing was mostly done by hand, ploughs, hoes, and sickles were the basic tools. Draught animals constituted the principal source of power in agriculture. However, no less than 135,000 households had no such animal and some 100,000 households possessed only one. Given the small amount of land per household the existing draught animals were used inefficiently and the cost of agricultural produce was correspondingly high.

Each person engaged in farming produced sufficient for himself and for one other person. Bulgarian capitalism did not succeed in raising labour productivity in agriculture and ensuring its growth as did other capitalist countries. The primitive tools employed, the lack of mineral fertilizers and of irrigation facilities naturally resulted in low yields. During the 1940–44 period, for instance, average yields per decare were for wheat, 94 kgs. ; barley, 97 kgs. ; maize, 94 kgs. ; sunflower seed, 69 kgs. ; tobacco, 78 kgs. ; sugar beet, 1,384 kgs. ; and grapes, 320 kgs. The number of animals bred on the farms of the country was steadily declining during 1920–39, both absolutely and in relation to the area farmed. Average yields of milk were 450 litres per cow in 1939, of wool, 1·5 kgs. per sheep, and of eggs, 73 per hen. Low crop yields and animal productivity, and high labour inputs put Bulgaria in no position to ensure a rapid advance in agricultural output nor to satisfy the growing needs of the country.

Similarly, the typical industrial enterprise was small-scale and equipped with antiquated machines and installations, mainly of a semi-handicraft nature. The light and food industries predominated and were concentrated in a few centres. The number of industrial enterprises in 1944 (excluding handicraft and similar workshops as defined by value of output), was 4,001, employing 104,388, 95,185 of whom were workers — an average of 26 persons (23 workers) per enterprise. The food industry accounted for over 49 per cent of the enterprises and 60 per cent of industrial production in 1939. Ranking second in the volume of output was the textile industry, with 16 per cent of industrial output and 11 per cent of the total number of industrial enterprises. Consequently, these two branches alone accounted for 71 per cent of industrial production. Such potentially important branches as engineering, metallurgy, chemicals, electric power, and building materials were little developed. Their share in the industrial output of the country was only 8·4 per cent in 1939. The ratio between the manufacture of means of production,

Group A, and the production of consumer goods, Group B, was approximately 22 : 77 in favour of the latter.

The supply of agriculture with means of production such as machines, tools, semi-finished goods, raw materials, etc. depended on imports, and even coal and electricity were not available in sufficient quantities. The ratio of social product generated in industry to that in agriculture was 25 : 75.

The reference above to the comparative advance of the food and textiles over heavy industries was strictly relative : in comparison with industrial countries, even these branches were ill-developed. In 1937, for example, Austria, the population of which was equal to that of Bulgaria, produced six times as much sugar (150,000 against 28,000 tons), and three times as much cotton textiles (108 against 37 million metres). There were, furthermore, considerable disproportions within branches. The spinning industry, for instance, developed more slowly than the weaving, necessitating heavy imports of yarn. Tanneries and woollen mills worked largely on raw materials imported from abroad. This dependence of Bulgarian industry on foreign products disrupted output during the war.

Capitalism was marked by very slow rates of industrial development in Bulgaria. Industrial output rose only 2·8 times during the 20-year period between the two world wars. Industry was hence unable to absorb surplus manpower from agriculture, and unemployment grew.

Capitalist Bulgaria had almost no metallurgy of its own : there were a few small-scale enterprises of ferrous metallurgy in Sofia and Pernik, and dressing plants for zinc and lead ores in the Rhodope mining basin, and for copper ore at Eliseyna near Sofia. The poorly-developed metal-working and engineering industries had to rely on imports for most of their metal requirements.

The Second World War and Bulgarian economic links with fascist Germany brought further difficulties : industrial output was limited by lack of raw materials and semi-manufactured goods and in 1944 it was 15 per cent below the 1941 level.

In short, during its 66 years of rule, the Bulgarian bourgeoisie failed to develop the productive capacities of the country and to create a well-developed industry. Bulgarian and foreign capitalists directed investment to the least capital-intensive branches, the light and food industries. The basic branches of heavy industry were not developed ; and Bulgarian dependence on foreign capital was maintained.

POSTWAR ECONOMIC POLICY

The democratic government established on 9 September, 1944, thus inherited several thousand small industrial enterprises equipped with obsolescent machinery. Labour productivity was low, because the scale of output did not provide conditions for introducing modern equipment. The new government set itself the task of building a material and technical structure adequate for socialism : following postwar rehabilitation, to realize socialist industrialization within the shortest term possible, to transform the country from agrarian to industrial predominance, capable of producing with its own capacities all that is necessary for the technical re-equipment of the economy, and to train highly-qualified workers and technicians.

A two-year plan was drafted for 1947–48 to overcome the economic difficulties inherited from the war and to exceed the pre-war level of production in industry, agriculture, and all other branches. The development of the Bulgarian economy was for the first time set on the basis of scientific planning ; and, despite many obstacles, the two-year plan was successfully fulfilled.

The social and economic changes that were carried out during this period were conducive to the successful implementation of the plan. Industrial and foreign-trade enterprises and banks were nationalized at the end of 1947. The Soviet Union assisted implementation by supplying raw materials, and the popular democracies made a positive contribution. During the first year of the plan, industrial production rose by 15 per cent, while by the end of 1948 it was running at double the pre-war rate.

The implementation of the two-year plan completed the period of successful rehabilitation of the Bulgarian economy. It created favourable conditions for proceeding with the industrialization, electrification, and mechanization of agriculture and for the fostering of co-operatives. Two basic problems had to be tackled. First, the national income had to rise substantially to provide resources for industrialization proper and for the technical reconstruction of agriculture, and at the same time to supply the agricultural and industrial products needed to match rising consumer purchasing power at home and to yield the foreign exchange required by the import bill of industrial and agricultural development. Secondly, the surplus manpower in agriculture had to be absorbed before technical reconstruction and the establishment of a co-operative system could be seriously considered.

The nationalizations of 1947 made it possible to concentrate domestic savings and the technical and financial support of the U.S.S.R. and other socialist countries towards the creation of large industrial enterprises. The Soviet Union rendered assistance in surveying natural resources, in providing technical documentation free of charge, in training Bulgarian specialists and in sending experts, and in the supply (partly on credit) of raw materials, machinery, and equipment.

The main direction of investment was towards the utilization of natural resources — by setting up large generating plant and by expanding coal- and ore-mining. Manufacturing capacity was developed of chemicals and equipment for agricultural use. The process of creating a domestic heavy industry took account of the existing international division of labour among socialist countries within the framework of the Council of Mutual Economic Assistance.

Proportionality in economic development was ensured by directing capital investments according to plan, due predominance being given to the means of production. Their share amounted to an average of 55·2 per cent of all capital investments during 1949–60, the remaining 44·8 per cent going to the light industries, agriculture and transport, and to the building of establishments for research, education, health, etc.

Industrialization had to be accompanied by training specialists to apply the experience and research of the U.S.S.R. and the other socialist countries. The training programme involved learning the new manufacturing processes themselves ; expanding the educational system through the setting up of secondary and higher technical schools ; and exchanging experience among the socialist countries.

The balance-of-payments problem was eased by the readiness of the Soviet Union and the other countries of socialism to take Bulgarian exports in large quantities. Exports were multiplied much beyond the pre-war level.

THE DEVELOPMENT OF INDUSTRY

Socialist industrialization proceeded according to plan : during 1949–63 the five-year development plans were realized ahead of schedule. The global volume of industrial output in 1963 was 17 times that of 1939 ; the average annual increase of industrial output was 15·2 per cent during 1949–63. Today, only 18 days are necessary to produce the volume of industrial output turned out during 1939.

This increase is due to the introduction of new industrial capacities, to the improved utilization of existing plant, and to the higher productivity of labour.

The development of industrial output took place on the basis of the predominant increase of producer's goods to equip and supply the economy and to develop the economic forms of socialism. The mean annual rate of growth of this sector was 18 per cent during 1949–63, against 13 per cent for the production of consumer's goods ; the production of means of labour (*i.e.* machines, apparatus, and equipment) increased at much higher rates than the production of objects of labour (*i.e.* raw materials, etc.). This development promoted the technical reconstruction of industry and of the country's economy as a whole. By 1963 52·6 per cent of the industrial output of the country was means of production against 22·6 in 1939. These rates nevertheless assured rapid growth in light industry : textiles, footwear, and food processing (notably sugar refining and wine-making) were expanded.

The rate of growth of each group was not uniform : the highest rates for both were attained during the first five-year plan (operative for four years 1949–52). Under the second five-year plan (1953–1957) both rates declined, producer's goods falling more than consumer's goods. This was reversed during the third five-year plan, following the decisions adopted at the April 1956 Plenary Session of the Central Committee of the Bulgarian Communist Party.

The existing industrial enterprises were merged into bigger units (from 4,001 in 1944 to 1,739 in 1948), and the new enterprises were built on a larger scale of equipment, employment, and output than the old. This contributed to the 2·7 times increase in industrial labour productivity between 1948 and 1963 (of which in electric power, 4·8 times ; engineering and metal-working, 6·4 times ; chemicals, 3·5 times ; and textiles, 2·6 times).

Between 1939 and 1963 industrial production *per capita* rose 13 times, comprising an increment of 31 times in the output of producer's goods and of 8 times in the production of consumer's goods. The output of electric power rose 21 times ; of iron ore, 18 times ; of steel, 6·3 times ; of non-ferrous ores, 24 times ; of cement, 7·6 times ; and of coal, 7·7 times. There was a steady increase, though at lower rates, of the production of consumer's goods : output of cotton textiles increased 5·7 times ; of woollens, 2·9 times ; of canned goods, 2·8 times ; and of sugar, 4·4 times.

In 1963 the consumption of electric power in industry was 24 times greater than in 1939, the corresponding figures being 9 times in transport and 43 times in agriculture. Within the same period the consumption of electric power for household needs rose over 6 times. The use of electric power in industry was 1,337 kWh. per worker in 1948, 2,224 kWh. in 1952, 3,114 in 1957, and about 5,000 kWh. in 1964. This expansion is due both to the increased volume of industrial production and to the introduction of new machinery and novel technological processes (notably for non-ferrous metallurgy and for organic synthesis).

Amalgamated industrial enterprises have recently been formed of allied establishments, grouped around that which has the largest output, most efficient equipment, or best technicians. The large industrial units so organized have common management, and a single plan for industrial targets and technical progress. This organization of industrial enterprises provides for the specialization of industrial production and ensures technical progress and greater efficiency.

The rapid development of industrial production in Bulgaria called for the organization of large-scale research. A total of 115 research institutes were created to this end, with an aggregate staff of over 1,000 scientific workers and research associates. As an example, the research undertaken for the coal industry may be listed. Classification and assessment of coal reserves, on the basis of which it was possible to plan the long-term development of Bulgarian coal mining; further improvement of the systems of working existing mines and the introduction of more efficient methods, particularly in underground mines; introduction of the broad-face method of mining; creating and experimenting with new explosives and blasting appliances; development of highly-productive equipment for open-cast workings in the East Maritsa basin; comparing, from both technical and economic points of view, transport by rail and by belt-conveyors in strip-mining, with reference to both coal and over-burden; automation and control of stationary machines in coal mines; devising methods of briquetting lignite from the East Maritsa basin; studying the dressing capacity of the coals of separate basins and mines and working out new methods for the operation of existing and projected dressing plants; and improving ventilation, hygienic conditions, labour safety, and measures for combating silicosis, etc.

Ten higher schools of technology were founded in Bulgaria to meet the requirements of highly-qualified manpower for socialist industrialization. These institutions of higher learning are attended by nearly half the number of university students in Bulgaria. In the past twenty years institutions of higher learning have trained over 100,000 specialists with university education, as against 23,000 trained during the last two decades dominated by the bourgeoisie. Backward and poor Bulgaria of the past today ranks third in the world, after the Soviet Union and the U.S.A., in the relative number of university students (98 per 10,000 of the population). The 8 institutions of higher learning in 1944 (attended by a total of 15,360 students) increased to 25 in 1963 (with an enrolment of 79,250). It was in this manner that the difficulties involved in finding specialists for all branches of the country's economy were overcome. The economic, scientific, and technical assistance rendered by the Soviet Union and by the popular democracies played a great part in the solution of the problems arising from industrialization, making it possible for the latest achievements of science and technology to be rapidly applied ; a number of plants were erected with Soviet economic and technical assistance. Socialist industrialization has provided full employment for the entire able-bodied population of Bulgaria.

Future trends, underlying the directives for the development of the country's economy during 1961–80, include continued electrification, as a fundamental of general technical progress ; the extension of a sound metallurgical basis, to underwrite the further development of engineering, which, in its turn, will make possible in the not too distant future the renewal of the capital stock of the economy ; and expansion of the chemicals industry, to facilitate the application of chemicals in industry and in all other branches.

THE SOCIALIZATION OF AGRICULTURE

The second line along which the country sought to solve the economic and social problems inherited from the past was the reconstruction of agriculture. The prerequisite for this reconstruction was the pooling of farm enterprises into the larger units which could mechanize production, introduce specialization, and increase labour productivity. Farm mergers were effected by the establishment of co-operative enterprises, on the basis of Lenin's co-operative plan and of the experience of the Soviet Union in collectivization.

The co-operative farms are independent enterprises of farmers who voluntarily pool their land — which remains their own — and jointly organize production with commonly-owned equipment. In the initial stage, the retention of land ownership affected the distribution of common incomes, the dividend being calculated on the basis both of the labour contributed by the member in each year and of the quantity and quality of land which he brought in. Subsequently, when co-operatives had been consolidated, this form of land rent was abolished by decisions of the co-operative farmers ; and today dividends are calculated solely on the quantity and quality of labour contributed by each member.

The establishment of co-operative farms began immediately after the installation of people's democratic rule in Bulgaria, being determined by three main factors. In the first place, poor and middle-income peasants embraced the co-operative in their struggle against capitalist exploitation ; this was fortified by the successful example of collective farms in the Soviet Union and of several Bulgarian co-operatives founded before the War (either as independent establishments or as sections of existing consumers' co-operatives). In the second place, the Soviet Union offered equipment to newly-founded co-operative farms, an assistance which played a decisive part in the immediate organization of such farms. Finally, a process of reconstruction in farming had to parallel that proceeding in industry : and the growing needs of industry, of the urban population, and of exports could no longer be provided by the parcellated and backward farming of the time.

The process of setting agriculture on a co-operative footing was gradual. By the end of 1947, there were 575 co-operative farms embracing 4·4 per cent of peasant households and 3·8 per cent of the arable land. A turning point came in 1950 : the poor and middle-income farmers of the grain-producing regions of the country began joining co-operatives on a large scale, so rapidly that by the end of the following year the number of farms was 2,739, covering 57 per cent of households and 48·5 per cent of arable land. The process was completed during 1957–58. Within a relatively short span of time, some 15 years, Bulgarian farming became fully reorganized on socialist foundations. The socialist sector of agriculture in Bulgaria today, represented by the co-operative and state farms, unites 99·4 per cent of the arable land in the country.

After several years of operation the greater success and speedier growth of the larger co-operative farms evoked the amalgamation of neighbouring co-operatives into larger units. The enlarged farms so formed facilitated specialization. The mergers began towards the end of 1958 : the number of farms dropped from 3,290 in 1959 to 981 in 1963, and the average size of a farm increased from 10,340 decares (about 2,500 acres) to 38,000 decares (some 9,500 acres).

FARM SUPPLIES

The merging of the co-operative and state farms into bigger units inaugurated a new stage in their development. New opportunities appeared for a rapid expansion of their basis of finance and equipment, of specialization in specific products, of efficient utilization of the stock of farm machinery, and of improving the system of management. Machine-tractor stations, financially-autonomous state establishments, were set up to provide technical services to the co-operatives ; 212 had been created by 1952, but, subsequently, when farms had become further consolidated, they were disbanded and their equipment sold off to the farms.

The full socialization of agriculture opened broad prospects for the development of production on the basis of modern machinery and equipment. They could never have developed normally on the basis of the machines and equipment they inherited from the small and backward farms of the past, and it was essential that their organization be accompanied by the supply of large amounts of machinery (tractors, harvester combines, tractor ploughs, tractor seed-drills, etc.). The number of tractors (calculated in units of 15 h.p. each) rose from 5,231 in 1948 to 54,062 in 1963, viz., 1·1 tractors per 10,000 decares of arable land in 1948, against 11·4 in 1963 ; the corresponding figures for harvester combines were 0·3 in 1952 and 2·5 in 1963. About 12,000 harvester combines and many other farming machines were employed in Bulgarian agriculture during 1964. Mechanical power grew rapidly and reduced the share of draught animals in aggregate power resources : from 56 in 1952 the percentage of motive power supplied by animals dropped to 9 in 1963. Ploughing, for example, has been mechanized 93·1 per cent ; sowing, 91·4 per cent ; harvesting, 86·1 per cent ; and harrowing, 96·9 per cent. The percentages are much lower in the mountain regions, where the terrain is unsuited to the present types of farm machinery ; a very important problem in the mechanization of farming work is to devise machines for operation in mountainous areas, and a variety of new types of ploughs, cultivators, harvester combines, etc., are being evolved.

The productive assets of farms have risen from 22,132 leva per

1,000 decares (approximately 250 acres) in 1953 to 46,824 leva in 1963. Per working member of the co-operative farms, they rose from 480 to 1,232 leva respectively.

Bulgarian agriculture used almost no mineral fertilizers in the past. About 2,000 tons of such fertilizers, calculated in nutrient content, were used in 1939, against 175,000 tons in 1963. The years of people's government saw the appearance of an entire industrial branch producing mineral fertilizers. Consumption (in nutrient content) per 1,000 decares was 57 kgs. in 1948, 415 kgs. in 1952, and 3,659 kgs. in 1963 — an increase of 33 times.[1] Even so, the application of fertilizer in Bulgarian soil conditions is less than optimal, and the target for 1980 is 23 kgs. (nutrient content) per decare : production of mineral fertilizer must expand sevenfold. The use of other chemicals in agriculture is also developing, and constitutes one of the major trends of technical progress in this sector.

In Bulgarian climatic conditions, the application of fertilizer must be accompanied by an enlargement of the irrigated area. A programme in this field began in 1957 : from 4·2 million decares irrigated in that year, the area rose to 8·8 millions in 1963, a doubling over six years. New irrigation systems are under construction, and 80 per cent of the country's arable land suitable for irrigation will be covered by 1980. The rapid extension of irrigation systems requires the solution of a number of problems, notably the mechanization and automation of irrigation, the optimum conditions of irrigation for individual crops, and the agrotechnology of crop-cultivation and of fertilizer use under irrigation. The investments are very large and the goal is to maximize their economic effect.

Bulgarian agriculture achieved great successes in recent years in creating and introducing new varieties of high-yielding seed. In 1963, for instance, 97·2 per cent of the total area sown to wheat used seeds of five highly-productive varieties (301, Jubilee I and II, Akerman, and the Soviet Bezostaya I), the incremental yield of which is between 30 and 50 kgs. per decare. In 1964, 94 per cent of the area sown to maize was under hybrid seeds ; varieties have been taken from the Soviet Union, Hungary, Canada, and the U.S.A., and two-line hybrids evolved in Bulgaria (Nos. 298, 835, and 826) have given yields between 10 and 15 per cent above those of imported seeds.

Considerable quantitative and qualitative changes have been

[1] Increments of 19 times of nitrogenous fertilizer, 76 times of phosphates, and 46 times of potash.

shown in stock-breeding. Not only oxen, but 70 per cent of cows, were used as draught animals by pre-collectivized agriculture. In the big machine-run farms of today only 9·5 per cent of the cows are used for work, mainly on the personal plots of co-operative members. There has been a reduction of the share of draught animals and an increase in that of productive animals (cows, pigs, poultry, etc.) ; breeds have also been improved.

AGRICULTURAL OUTPUT

The setting up of large co-operative and state farms, the introduction of machinery and fertilizers, the expansion of the irrigated area, and the other qualitative changes have ensured a considerable growth of farm production. Average yields for 1957–63 show a 63 per cent increase compared with 1934–39 ; crop output has risen 79 per cent, and that of stock-breeding by 40 per cent. Between 1949 and 1963 the average annual rate of growth for all farm produce was 4·4 per cent (5·0 per cent for crops and 3·4 per cent for stock-breeding).

The intensification of agriculture, the increased cultivation of technical crops, vegetables, fruit, and fodder, brought an appreciable change in the structure of output : the share of grain dropped from 26·6 per cent in 1939 to 18·8 per cent in 1963, that of industrial crops rose from 6·8 per cent to 8·7 per cent, of vegetables and fruits from 19·0 to 26·0 per cent, and of fodder crops from 4·4 to 7·6 per cent. Calculated per head of the population, mean annual production of maize increased from 142 kgs. in 1934–39 to 183 in 1957–63, of sunflower seed from 23 to 37 kgs., of oriental tobacco from 5 to 10 kgs., of sugar-beet from 21 to 166 kgs., and of milk from 101 to 133 litres. Over the same period average yields per decare also increased : wheat rose from 125 to 167 kgs., barley from 130 to 193 kgs., oats from 75 to 109 kgs., sunflower seed from 83 to 126 kgs., and tomatoes from 2,367 to 2,830 kgs. The mean yield of milk per cow rose from 450 litres in 1939 to 1,330 litres in 1960. In co-operative farms yields rose from 552 litres in 1952 to 1,674 litres in 1963.

The average annual production of grain in 1957–63 was nearly one million tons more than in 1934–39 ; the output of tobacco increased 2·4 times, of sugar-beet nearly 10 times, and of tomatoes 14 times.

A great deal has been done since the war to train skilled manpower.

There were few specialists with higher education engaged in Bulgarian farming before the war, but by 1957 there were 4,655 agronomists, zoo-technicians, and veterinary surgeons, and by 1963, 7,677. A great number of technicians with secondary-level qualifications have also been trained, as have those with lower skills, such as mechanics. Hundreds of thousands of co-operative farmers attended training courses. Much attention has been devoted to the development of agricultural science and to the application of scientific achievements. An Academy of Agricultural Sciences was created, and now has 27 research institutes, 29 experimental farms, and 14 multi-purpose stations.

During its relatively brief period of development, socialist farming has demonstrated encouraging successes in increasing labour productivity compared with small-scale private farming. As has already been mentioned, a person engaged in farming in 1939 produced farm goods for only another one person, whereas in 1962 he produced for himself and for 4·2 others, under conditions of appreciably increased consumption per head of the population. The average annual income per person engaged in agriculture rose 2·6 times between 1952 and 1962.

Bulgarian farming can, however, be made still more intensive — by increasing yields per acre, by reducing the cost of production, and by raising manpower productivity, chiefly among the inherently labour-intensive crops. One of the principal tasks of the future is to accelerate the introduction of machinery, particularly in the cultivation of intensive crops. This growth should provide the means for improving rural incomes.

The problems of farming are significant for the programme in industry, since both are co-ordinated in the national plan. Socialist industrialization has already permitted the reconstruction of farming along co-operative lines and its wide use of machinery. A backward agrarian country has become an advanced industrial and agrarian economy with modern factories and large-scale farms. Based upon the public ownership of the means of production, the socialist state has opened broad prospects for the development of the productive capacities of the country.

Chapter 4

THE DYNAMICS AND PROPORTIONS OF ECONOMIC DEVELOPMENT IN SOCIALIST COUNTRIES

BY

J. SIROTKOVIC
University of Zagreb and Federal Planning Office, Belgrade

A THEORETICAL APPROACH TO THE CONCEPT OF DEVELOPMENT

THE Marxian theory of reproduction contains all the basic elements to render it comprehensive, and it may thus serve as a point of departure for a theoretical approach to the concept of development, bearing in mind that its application in practice depends on the existing national conditions. It is of particular value in studying the development problem under the Yugoslav social and economic system, where the application of the basic concepts of the Marxian reproduction theory, as well as of Marxian teachings in other domains such as the theory of the state, has provided an approach to development. Even more, it has led to the adoption of specific development policies, which — while related to the contemporary level of material production and of consequential productive relations — constitute an explicitly Yugoslav contribution to the Marxian theories of reproduction, of the state, and of self-government. Tested in practice, they entail a self-perpetuating process of development which effects the structural transformation of the economy.

According to Marx, the reproduction process is to be viewed as one which brings about that radical reform of the economy which legitimizes the socialization of the means of production. It is hence a necessary milestone on the road towards the realization of superior forms of social relationships — socialism and communism. A similar conception of the reproduction process plays a determinant role in the formulation of development objectives, and calls for recourse to methods involving a voluntary intervention of society into the course of the reproduction process. A free and direct form

46

of association in the working process, namely, the promotion of socialist relationships, and a continuously rising trend in the material and cultural welfare of the working people, are the basic aims of marxian reproduction theory, and the very foundation upon which should rest any analysis of the possibilities and methods used to achieve rapid well-balanced growth. Development on these lines is a precondition for the achievement of these objectives and requires systematic planning of all the phases of the reproduction process.

Marxian theory sets out both general laws of the process of social reproduction, and theoretical rules for economic analysis, thus facilitating a scientific approach to the reproduction process, and the discovery of fundamental and special laws and tendencies governing economic phenomena. It must nevertheless be recognised that the theory, in its general lines, cannot provide definitive recipes and schemes for a proper analysis of development, and hence serve as a practical tool for analysis and planning. The material and social conditions in which the reproduction process takes place have a direct impact on the aims and techniques of development. Social conditions determine not only the forms under which economic laws operate, but also the specific relationships between each stage of development and between each element of the reproduction process which warrants development; they also determine the methods of analysis to be used in each particular case, and the direction in which the development process will evolve.

Planning, within the framework of familiar economic laws, attempts to systematize relations between the constituent elements of the individual stages of the process to accomplish the main economic policy aims. Thus the Yugoslav planning agencies, in formulating policy for a given plan-period, should both seek to introduce those activities likely to contribute most to welfare and the establishment of socialist production relations, and to restrain those which have held back such progress in the previous plan.

THE DYNAMICS OF PRODUCTION IN YUGOSLAV ECONOMIC POLICY

As can be seen from Table 1, rapid growth has been a major characteristic of the postwar Yugoslav economy.

While the average growth rate of national income for the period as a whole, amounting to 6·8 per cent, is not in the highest range

TABLE 1

GROWTH RATE OF NATIONAL INCOME IN 1962 PRICES*

	All Sectors		Socialist Sector	
	(1)	(2)	(3)	(4)
1948–63	6·8	7·1	..	..
1953–63	9·0	8·1	10·5	10·2
1957–63	10·0	8·3	12·4	11·0

* For columns (1) and (3) the base year is 1947, 1952, 1956, while for columns (2) and (4) the base is the two-year average 1947–48, 1952–53, and 1956–57.

Source : 'Global Social Product, Social Product, National Income, Employment and Productivity in the Yugoslav Economy from 1947 to 1963', Federal Planning Office Communications, Series B, no. 29, 1964, Belgrade.

achieved by individual economies at certain stages of their development, it may nevertheless be considered as relatively high, taking into account the length of the period.

In analysing data on growth in the individual stages of the period covered, two distinct periods, with their own growth characteristics, may be distinguished. The first is between 1947 and 1952, the period of the first five-year plan and the system of 'administrative management' of the economy. During this period the national income growth rate — in view of the impact of exceptional extra-economic factors — was particularly low, amounting to a mere 2 per cent. But the investment undertaken then was to yield its results in the growth of the subsequent period. The second post-war period — 1953–63 — saw the affirmation of new social relationships based on the workers' management of enterprises, and social control in general. During this period, thanks to the introduction of a wide range of incentives, as a feature of the system of workers' management, the producers themselves were given the opportunity of deploying their initiative. From 1953 to 1957 national income growth was 9 per cent per annum, but it rose to 10 per cent during 1957–63. If observation is limited to the socialist sector of the economy during the entire decade 1953–63, the growth rate was 10·5 per cent, while during the later part (1957–63) it rose to 12·4 per cent.

The differences in the growth rates of the two main sectors of the economy — the socialist and the private — can be attributed to the considerably lower growth rate of the private sector, which, in turn, is due to the lag of agriculture. This is illustrated in Table 2, which shows the comparative development of industry and agriculture, the latter growing slowly despite the high rate recorded in its public sector.

TABLE 2

NATIONAL INCOME GROWTH RATES IN
INDUSTRY AND AGRICULTURE*

	1948–1963		1953–1963		1957–1963	
	(1)	(2)	(3)	(4)	(5)	(6)
Industry	10·2	9·4	12·1	11·7	12·3	11·0
Agriculture	3·2	2·7	6·3	4·4	6·6	3·6
Socialist sector	..	..	9·9	10·7	22·5	17·9
Private sector	..	..	5·8	3·6	5·0	2·1
(peasant farms)						

* For column (1) the base year is 1947 ; for columns (3) and (5), 1952 and 1956 ; for columns (2), (4), and (6) the base is the two-year average 1947–48, 1952–53, and 1956–57.
Source : As for Table 1.

The year 1953 constituted an important landmark, both as regards development itself and the new orientation in economic policies towards balanced growth (through the accelerated development of agriculture) and the improvement of living standards. The changes in agricultural policies were in two main directions. The first led to progress in the socialist sector of the economy, through the rapid introduction of modern technology and improved husbandry, and through better co-operation between the peasants of the private sector and the co-operatives. The second important change resided in arrangements for providing specific incentives in the field of agriculture through higher prices, higher investment, and subsidies in the form of ex-post rebates. These changes are closely related to the more general changes in the economic system through the introduction and development of a higher degree of autonomy in the management of enterprises after 1950, and more particularly after 1952. The results which have been achieved in this field, notably since 1956, can be attributed to the growth of the material basis for production and to the establishment of a new pattern of productive relations.

In 1963 the *per capita* national income of Yugoslavia was in the proximity of $500,[1] placing the country among the lower brackets of the semi-developed. During the period under consideration,

[1] I. Vinski, *Ekonomski Pregled* (Zagreb), no. 6–7, 1963.

Yugoslavia belonged to a group of countries distinguished by their accelerated rate of growth, but nevertheless still lagging behind many other semi-developed countries as regards *per capita* production of individual commodities.

Since the end of the Second World War some major qualitative changes have taken place facilitating rapid and relatively more balanced development, and eliminating structural maladjustments which were hindering further improvement. It should be emphasized, however, that the increases in production and consumption were not achieved without marked fluctuations, mostly of a short-term character, but nevertheless obstacles to normal expansion. At times this has rendered more difficult the implementation of the more fundamental economic policy aims, and has affected the harmony between production and consumption through corresponding disturbances in price relations (as shown by Table 3). Over the eleven years covered by Table 3 there was relatively stable growth of industrial production, accompanied by fluctuation in agricultural output. The unbalanced behaviour of the two main sectors of production resulted in the oscillation of overall growth, and hence in relative instability. Investment in fixed capital proceeded at a fairly regular pace, with more vigorous expansion during the later years, particularly after 1960. During those eleven years the rate of investment in social infrastructure was very intensive and faster than that of personal consumption, which from 1959 to 1963 expanded more slowly than the overall growth of the social product.

A characteristic feature of the development of Yugoslavia so far lies in the fact that the basic material factors of growth, primarily investment in fixed capital stock, enjoyed a stable and continuous development, largely thanks to the investment policies adopted. Changes conducive to growth also took place in the branch distribution of assets (see Table 4), and in the reduction both of obsolete equipment in the total stock and of fixed assets to inventories within the sub-total of productive assets. The change in the distribution of fixed capital was accompanied by a significant decline in the proportion of obsolete assets — as Table 5 shows. This was paralleled by important shifts in the ratio of fixed capital assets to working capital (see Table 6). These changes in the branch structure and in the ratio between fixed capital assets and working capital have been achieved under conditions of technical progress, as Table 7 indicates. Conditions have thereby been created for better utilization of available productive capacity and for an increase of labour

TABLE 3

NATIONAL INCOME, INVESTMENT, PERSONAL CONSUMPTION, FIXED CAPITAL ASSETS, AND PRICES

Index Numbers of Values at 1962 Prices

Previous year = 100

	National Income			Investment			Personal Consumption (7)	Fixed Capital Assets in the Socialist Sector (8)	Prices in the Socialist Sector (9)
	Total (1)	Industry (2)	Agriculture (3)	Total (4)	Public (5)	In Social Infrastructure (6)			
1953	119·4	109·4	145·2	118·9	...	163·5	102·6	106·3	101·9
1954	102·7	114·8	87·0	99·8	461·7	184·7	107·0	105·5	104·4
1955	114·1	113·8	123·7	107·5	32·5	80·1	108·9	113·6	107·3
1956	94·6	119·6	80·6	92·9	295·7	112·6	100·1	112·7	101·4
1957	123·9	117·1	144·0	107·4	123·3	150·3	114·2	111·7	102·0
1958	101·9	111·9	88·2	111·4	81·6	121·4	104·2	110·4	101·0
1959	117·5	111·6	131·2	124·2	138·0	125·9	118·1	107·4	102·6
1960	105·4	113·7	88·6	116·1	122·2	127·7	106·5	109·0	104·2
1961	105·9	106·6	98·0	106·6	68·3	112·6	111·6	112·8	108·3
1962	104·2	107·1	100·5	109·8	92·6	121·0	102·1	113·7	103·3
1963	113·2	118·6	107·2	114·2	123·0	114·7	109·1	112·4	104·8

Sources : Columns (1), (2), (3), and (9), as for Table 1 ; columns (4), (5), and (6), *Investicije 1947–1962*, Institute for Investment Economics, Belgrade, 1963 ; column (7), documentation of the Federal Planning Office, utilized for the preparation of the Seven-year Plan 1964–70 ; column (8), 'Fixed Capital Assets in the Socialist Sector of the Yugoslav Economy and in the Economy of the Component Socialist Republics', Federal Planning Office memorandum, Belgrade, 1964.

Theoretical Problems of a Socialist Economy

TABLE 4

BRANCH DISTRIBUTION OF FIXED ASSETS IN THE SOCIALIST SECTOR OF THE ECONOMY

Percentages of Total Stock Valued at 1962 Prices

	Industry	Agriculture	Building	Transport	Other
1952	44·7	4·0	2·1	43·2	6·0
1956	51·2	3·9	2·2	36·7	6·0
1963	52·3	8·9	2·9	28·7	7·2

Source : Federal Planning Office, Belgrade.

TABLE 5

PERCENTAGE OF OBSOLETE EQUIPMENT

	1946	1952	1956	1963
Industry	60·2	34·0	31·3	32·7
All branches	42·9	41·0	40·9	38·2

Source : I. Vinski, 'Fixed Capital Assets in Yugoslavia, 1947–1963', Ekonomski Institut, Zagreb, 1963.

TABLE 6

RATIO OF FIXED ASSETS TO WORKING CAPITAL IN THE SOCIALIST SECTOR OF THE ECONOMY

Percentage of Productive Assets Valued at 1962 Prices

	1952	1956	1963
(1) In total stock :			
Fixed assets	82	80	76
Working capital	18	20	24
(2) In industry :			
Fixed assets	81	78	75
Working capital	19	22	25

Source : Fixed assets, as for column (8), Table 3 ; working capital : 'Computation of Inventories and Conversion from Current Prices into 1962 Prices', Federal Planning Office memorandum, Belgrade, 1964.

productivity (see Table 8). The fall in the ratio of capital to social product is chiefly the result of a better utilization of capacity ; the corresponding increase in working capital has allowed fuller utilization of the available productive capacity.

Sirotkovic — *Dynamics and Proportions of Economic Development*

TABLE 7

INDICATORS OF TECHNICAL CHANGE IN THE
SOCIALIST SECTOR OF THE ECONOMY

	1952	1963	Index (1952=100) 1963
All branches:			
Fixed assets (billion dinars)	2,524	7,542	298·8
Number of employed (thousand)	1,387	2,772	199·9
Fixed capital assets per person employed (thousand dinars)	1,820	2,721	149·5
Industry:			
Fixed assets (billion dinars)	1,129	3,917	346·9
Number of employed (thousand)	562	1,222	217·4
Fixed capital assets per person employed (thousand dinars)	2,009	3,205	159·5

Source: As for column (8), Table 3.

Note: Values are in prices of 1962; as throughout this volume, billions are thousands of millions.

TABLE 8

RATIO OF PRODUCTIVE ASSETS TO OUTPUT IN THE
SOCIALIST SECTOR OF THE ECONOMY

At Prices of 1962

	1956	1963
Productive capital (billion dinars)	4,558·1	9,814·3
of which		
Fixed assets	3,624·4	7,542·3
Working capital	933·7	2,272·0
Social product (billion dinars)	1,476·1	3,310·0
Ratio of capital to social product :		
Productive capital	3·09	2.97
Fixed assets	2·46	2·25
Working capital	0·63	0·68

Source : Fixed assets, as for column (8), Table 3, except for 1963 data, estimated on the basis of documentation for the year 1962 ; social product, as for Table 1.

Qualitative changes — shown in Table 9 — which have taken place in the commodity pattern of exports and imports (together with a relatively rapid increase in exports) will facilitate the integration of Yugoslavia into the international division of labour with a radically different structure.

53

Theoretical Problems of a Socialist Economy

TABLE 9

VALUE OF EXPORTS AND IMPORTS ACCORDING
TO THE DEGREE OF PROCESSING

	Exports 1953	1962	Imports 1953	1962
High degree of processing	16·6	42·7	43·8	51·2
Low degree of processing	15·0	37·7	17·8	22·2
Not processed	33·4	19·6	38·4	26·6

Source : *Statistički godišnjak FNRJ, 1956* and *1963*.

Accumulation (net investment in production) had increased from a pre-war 5 per cent to over 20 per cent of national income by 1963, although at the same time non-productive investment was substantially larger; in 1948–52 the share of non-productive investment in social product was 5·5 per cent, but 11 per cent in 1963.

During the early postwar years the share of foreign resources in total accumulation was very high (34·8 per cent in 1953–56), but its subsequent decline has reduced it in recent years to less than a quarter of total accumulation (24·6 per cent in 1957–63).[1]

Since the War, output of the means of production (Department I of social product in the marxian model) has grown faster than that of objects of consumption (Department II of the marxian scheme), but this trend has been uneven in various periods, and occasionally Department II grew faster than Department I, as shown in Table 10.

During the period under review, foreign trade was the main factor inducing modifications in the structure of the disposable volume of goods, and it was trade which made production grow faster in Department I than in Department II. It must, however, be emphasized in this connexion that foreign trade has not speeded up the consumption of goods produced by Department I more than that of goods produced by Department II. An analysis of this phenomenon can easily be given : this was a period of major changes in economic policies — first, emphasis on the development of the key branches of the economy, accompanied by efforts to slow down the increase of consumption with respect to income growth, and more recently policies aimed at improving living standards, such that consumption grew as rapidly as income. A similar increase in the community's productive forces came about simultaneously with

[1] Source : 'Statistical materials and documentation for the Seven-year Plan of Economic Development, 1964–70', Federal Planning Office memorandum.

54

TABLE 10

CHANGES IN DISPOSABLE RESOURCES

	Percentage of Stated Product				Growth Rates		
	1952	1956	1960	1963	1953–1963	1957–1960	1957–1963
1. Global social product of which	100·0	100·0	100·0	100·0	9·6	12·2	10·7
2. disposable product	104·2	102·1	102·7	100·8	9·3	12·3	10·5
3. Production of capital goods (I_1) of which	100·0	100·0	100·0	100·0	8·3	15·7	13·1
4. disposable	137·1	111·6	120·5	110·9	6·3	18·0	13·0
5. Production of objects of work (I_2) of which	100·0	100·0	100·0	100·0	10·1	11·1	10·8
6. disposable	97·9	101·0	103·9	102·6	10·7	11·9	11·0
7. Production of means of production (I) (rows 3 and 5) of which	100·0	100·0	100·0	100·0	9·8	11·8	11·2
8. disposable (rows 4 and 6)	105·9	102·6	106·9	104·0	9·6	13·0	11·4
9. Production of consumers' goods (II) of which	100·0	100·0	100·0	100·0	9·3	12·4	10·0
10. disposable	102·1	101·4	97·4	96·4	8·7	11·3	9·2

Source : As for Table 1.

major changes in production relations : the share of the socialist sector in fixed assets rose from 52 per cent in 1947 to 71 per cent in 1962,[1] and in generation of national product from 66·4 per cent to 76·9 per cent.[2]

From 1952 onward the economic system was adapted to the new system of self-government, and the introduction of workers' management in enterprises gave rise to qualitatively new social and economic

[1] Vinski, *op. cit.* The private sector includes dwellings.
[2] Source: As for Table 1. Income is valued at 1962 prices.

Theoretical Problems of a Socialist Economy

relationships in the socialist sector. The decentralization which these reforms achieved in their first decade can be seen from the pattern of investment finance in Table 11. The fundamental aim of the seven-year plan for 1964–70 is to achieve a continuous and stable improvement of living standards and further devolution of decision-making. The plan recognizes the need for the increments in consumption to exceed that of national income. This projection

TABLE 11

SOURCES OF INVESTMENT FINANCE FOR FIXED CAPITAL

Percentage of Gross Outlay

	1947–52	1953–63	1963
Political-administrative agencies	98·2	62·7	56·2
of which			
Federation	69·4	36·7	29·4
Republics	20·5	7·9	7·2
Districts and municipalities	8·3	18·1	19·6
Enterprises, banks, and other institutions	1·8	37·3	43·8
of which			
Enterprises	1·8	28·9	27·8
Banks	..	2·8	9·2
Other institutions	..	5·6	6·8

Source: 1947–52, as for columns (4)–(6), Table 3 ; 1963, *Statisticki bilten*, no. 2, 1964, with adjustments made in totals of the Federation and component Republics for funds for the reconstruction of Skopje and for the underdeveloped regions.

is feasible, but with the further enlargement of investment autonomy, incentives must be provided to productive enterprises to encourage a better use of resources and to increase capital efficiency. It may be fully anticipated that during the plan period the Yugoslav economy will be as dynamic as over the past eleven years, and that this growth will comprise an increased share of consumption (more particularly of personal consumption), and a constant, or even slightly reduced, share of investment (accumulation). The analyses and projections for the plan show that this distribution should not entail a deceleration of economic growth. On the contrary, it should lead to the creation of an environment favourable to the more efficient conduct of affairs, even resulting in a more rapid rate of growth than that achieved in the past.

Chapter 5

SUMMARY RECORD OF THE DISCUSSION
— SESSION I

THEORETICAL PROBLEMS OF A SOCIALIST
ECONOMY

(In the Chair : PROFESSOR KAMENOV)

Professor Robinson opened the discussion on the first four papers of the
Conference. He began by reviewing the paper by Professor Sorokin on
rates of economic growth in Eastern Europe. He asked that the problem
of comparing rates of growth be left aside in order to concentrate discussion upon the factors generating the rapid expansion which had taken
place since the War. He found that the paper by Professors Cobeljic and
Stojanovic attributed much of the growth to the movement of labour from
low to high productivity sectors, *e.g.* from small- to large-scale industry.
This would not, however, be an inexhaustible source of growth : while it
still had great possibilities for a number of socialist countries, there seemed
to be some signs that this source was running out. A second source,
common also in capitalist countries, had been the increased participation
of women in the labour force. The problem, however, had been that as
families grew richer, the women tended to work less. Increasing productivity within specific industries had been a third source. This was
partly a result of technological progress following investment in research
and development, and partly of improvements in organization. Comparisons of technically-identical oil refineries in the United Kingdom and
the United States showed a higher employment in the British counter-
parts : clearly this differential arose from the degree of personal effort,
the level of training, and manning practices. There seemed indeed to be
in the United Kingdom a social limit to the rate of increase of productivity.
He hoped that participants would indicate whether any such limits, set
for example by industrial relations, operated in the socialist countries.
Perhaps such constraints were more flexible in socialist countries and this
contributed to their higher rates of growth.

He drew the attention of the Conference to the analyses of factors in
growth by Professor Denison : [1] to the increase in manpower, to the

[1] See Edward F. Denison, *The Sources of Economic Growth in the United States
and the Alternatives before Us*, Supplementary Paper No. 13, Committee for

change in the capital stock, to education, to research, etc. He enquired whether any similar studies had been attempted in Eastern Europe : in particular, he felt sure that interest would attach to the identification of the share in growth attributable to industrial training and to planning. He did not feel that the high level of employment in certain Eastern European countries was a significant factor in generating more rapid growth than in Western Europe, since this situation prevailed in certain Western European economies, notably that of the United Kingdom.

He noted that some deceleration had been taking place in Eastern European expansion. He wondered whether this was attributable to some limit on transfer from low to high productivity branches.[1] Capital accumulation might also be a limiting factor. At a certain stage, the proportion of capital resources needed for social infrastructure (*e.g.* housing) might have to rise at the expense of growth-conducive assets. Yet, on the other hand, increasing research and education would work in favour of faster growth.

The balance-of-payments was consistently a constraint in developing countries because of the high import content in development. The aid policy of donor states had to be formulated as a choice between two options : if the balance-of-payments deficit was proportionately higher in the earlier rather than at the later stages, short-term initial assistance was crucial. If, on the other hand, the deficits were likely to be relatively more serious at a later stage, a policy of slower development, including the creation of a domestic engineering sector, was advisable, viz. in order to substitute for later import needs, which consist chiefly of machinery and spare parts. He noted that Professors Cobeljic and Stojanovic (pp. 22–27) described an initial stage devoted to capital widening (*i.e.* equipment of a labour-intensive type), but pointed out that this was followed by a shift to capital deepening. A labour shortage could ensue from too much capital widening, as in Britain recently. The problem, then, was how to make sure that the technical designers would adjust their projects to economic needs, as defined for example by the expected rate of return. He wondered what were the channels for communicating such a 'philosophy of techniques'. He felt that the discussion could usefully concentrate on three questions raised in different manners by the four papers. First, what were the weights attributable to the various factors in development in Eastern Europe compared with those in Western Europe ? Secondly, why, after expanding more rapidly than in postwar Western Europe, were the Eastern European economies experiencing a decelera-

Economic Development, New York, January, 1962 ; and his paper 'Measuring the Contribution of Education to Economic Growth' in E. A. G. Robinson and J. E. Vaizey (eds.) *The Economics of Education*, Proceedings of a Conference held by the International Economic Association (London, 1966), pp. 202–260.
[1] See paper by Čobeljić and Stojanović, p. 21.

tion ? Thirdly, what criteria and channels of communication were, or should be, used for the choice of techniques in a socialist, as contrasted with a capitalist, economy ?

Professor Robinson concluded by observing that Professor Sorokin's paper raised questions of foreign trade and that the others dealt with investment cycles. Since these subjects could be treated in other sessions, he suggested that their discussion be deferred.

Professor Jeanneney observed that Professor Robinson had already formulated a substantial list of significant questions to his Eastern European colleagues, but felt that the influence of population growth should be added. He would have particularly desired to know whether Eastern European policy had been directed generally towards increasing or limiting family size.

Professor Grossman welcomed the questions posed by Professors Robinson and Jeanneney and commented that Eastern European economists seemed to have paid least attention, among those raised, to demographic problems. There was clearly no question of limiting population growth in so vast a country as the U.S.S.R., but elsewhere in Eastern Europe the ratio of population to resources was less favourable. He pointed out that recently there had been a sharp decline in birth rates and rates of natural increase in Eastern Europe, especially in Hungary and Czechoslovakia.

Mr. Kaser felt that the occasion was appropriate to discuss the criteria for the domestic development of a socialist state with those it adopted for planned co-operation with other socialist economies.

Dr. Hegedüs began the Eastern European replies to the questions raised by dealing with the demographic aspect. Since Professor Grossman had explicitly mentioned Hungary, he felt he should point out that the birth-rate trough occurred in 1962, and that now rates were again rising, although slowly. The causative factors were being analysed by many disciplines, notably economics, demography, and sociology. The relative homogeneity of the Hungarian population facilitated the study, and, although there were many complex influences on population movement, his own view was that two factors were more significant than others. Increasing affluence had sharply increased the demand for housing with a high level of amenity, for motor vehicles, for television sets, and similar goods. Consumers were clearly preferring the enjoyment of such goods and services to the children they would have had at lower standards of living. The second factor was the high rate of female participation in gainful employment, to which Professor Robinson had already referred. Both factors, he stressed, affected not only the urban but also the rural population ; the general level of fertility had certainly been reduced by the repeal of the former restrictions on abortion. An active debate was being pursued in Hungary on the appropriate level of family allowances. However, an increase in the birth rate depended not only on such direct measures but on the environment of the general standard of living.

Professor Stojanovic took up Professor Robinson's enquiries by pointing out that the limits to the transfer of labour from agriculture to areas of higher productivity were relative. The ratio between low and high productivity sectors was continually changing, but whenever there was a differential there would be scope for manpower transfer to reach a new optimal distribution. So far as concerned agriculture, the productivity gain decreased as the farm labour force diminished, and the re-distribution of manpower was concentrated on inter-industry transfers. Within industry particularly, the optimal rate of transfer then depended upon the differential paths of technological progress.

Professor Robinson having enquired whether there were any social limits on the introduction of new techniques under socialism, she asserted their absence. She attributed this to the higher rate of capital formation in socialist countries than in capitalist economies : the consequent expansion of employment opportunities, the reduced danger of unemployment, and the great flexibility in adjusting skill patterns to new techniques greatly diminished worker resistance to measures enhancing productivity. She readily admitted, however, that certain frictions could arise. Turning to the choice of technique, she believed that the rate of return per unit of capital was the most important, though not the only, criterion for the allocation of resources. Structural and regional considerations were also significant, and their formulation for planning purposes was already advanced.

On the balance-of-payments problem in economic growth, she stated that Yugoslav policy was that of an open economy. The socialist countries as a group had aimed at a rational division of labour involving national specialization and the exchange of technical experience, and bringing with it substantial economies of scale.

Professor Oelssner disagreed with Professor Grossman on the facts of birth rates in Eastern Europe. There had been no decline in the German Democratic Republic (G.D.R.), where the number of live births per thousand population had risen from 15·6 in 1958 to 17·5 in 1962. Since the death rate had declined over the same period, there had been an increase, though small, in the rate of natural growth. The policy of the government of the G.D.R. was to foster population growth, *e.g.* by allowing paid leave during pregnancy, by subsidizing the construction of day nurseries, and by a scale of family allowances which was progressive with the number of children.

He then posed a question to the participants from Yugoslavia on the ratio of fixed to circulating capital. The embodiment of scientific and technological advance tended to increase the proportion of fixed assets at the expense of circulating capital. In the G.D.R. strong pressures had been exerted for the past eight years or so by the Ministry of Finance to reduce circulating capital. In his paper, Professor Sirotkovic (p. 52) had noted that in Yugoslavia the share of circulating capital in total capital had increased from 18 per cent in 1952 to 24 per cent in 1963 for the economy as a whole (from 19 per cent to 25 per cent for industry alone). It was stated that this increase had made possible a better use of fixed capacity (p. 52). He wanted to know what factors conduced to the increase in circulating capital, enquiring particularly whether the constituents of the increment had been established, *e.g.* increment due to a rise in the wage bill, to the volume of materials input, or to price inflation.

Professor Domar addressed several questions to Professor Sorokin on Soviet economic growth. He asked, first, whether studies of the ingredients of economic growth had been made in the Soviet Union : he believed it important to identify the separate contributions made by capital formation, the transfer of labour to more productive sectors, improvement in the quality of the labour force, and technological progress. He enquired secondly about the causes of the slow-down of the growth of output in the Soviet Union since 1958 or 1959. Western estimates might differ from Soviet figures on the actual rate of growth, but both showed that it had fallen in recent years. Thirdly, he continued, could this deceleration be attributed to the higher level of industrialization ? Professor Sorokin's paper (p. 4) showed that Albania and Bulgaria had had the highest rate of growth of national income among socialist countries ; he had also demonstrated that among the members of Comecon only East Germany and Czechoslovakia had expanded their industrial production less rapidly than the Soviet Union (p. 15) : these, as he pointed out, were the two 'highly industrialized countries'. Did this imply that the rate of growth declined when industrialization reached an advanced stage ? He would like finally to hear comments on the observation that Soviet planning methods were obsolete at the present stage of development.

Professor Stefanov returned to the question of the interdependence of the demographic processes and economic growth, which he felt was certainly not a direct relationship. It was evident that a high birth rate could often accompany low rates of economic growth, while small increases in population were not obstacles to high rates of economic growth. The correlation was a multiple one and the fact that all socialist countries were passing through a period of extraordinarily intensive change could not fail to be reflected in the demographic processes. There had been a very high rate of internal migration in Bulgaria during the last twenty years : one million villagers had moved to the towns, that is about one-eighth of the population. This had represented a major break in the socio-economic living conditions of the people concerned and had been a powerful factor in the reduction of birth and death rates. There had nevertheless also been a decline in fertility and mortality in rural areas ;

internal migration could not in consequence fully explain the reduction.

Under Bulgarian conditions, the fundamental cause was the alteration in the social position of women. The increase in female employment and in the social activity of women had reduced the average size of family, a trend further promoted by delayed entry of young people into gainful occupation (by the extension of the period of education and vocational training) and by the attractiveness of facilities for using leisure by the expansion of cultural amenities. The reduction of the birth rate in Bulgaria, however, had been offset by a decline in mortality, particularly in infant mortality. Hence, the natural growth of population was still at a satisfactory level.

Professor Sorokin replied to Professor Domar's question on the constituents of growth, a problem on which Soviet economists were now working. Preliminary results indicated that Soviet industrial growth could in the near future be raised from its present annual rate to 9 per cent. The primary factor in this increase would be technical progress, but there was also scope for using existing capacity more efficiently ; investment would be maintained at a high level, but its share could not be raised in national product because this would conflict with the government policy of raising the level of consumption. Finally, better use would be made of skilled manpower, while the incentive effects of the wage system would be improved.

Mr. Bouska also felt that there was no direct relation between demographic and economic rates of growth. The policy in Czechoslovakia had been to foster fertility : the controlled rents of dwellings, for example, were on a sliding scale so that the marginal cost of accommodation declined with the number of children in a family ; retirement pensions for women were based on the number of children borne ; [1] and prices of children's clothing were subsidized (indeed, foreigners came to Czechoslovakia to buy such goods). Yet, factors had operated in the contrary direction to keep down family size : the proportion of women in gainful employment was high, and there was still a shortage of housing despite measures to correct this over the past eight years.

Professor Notkin directed his remarks both to the demographic problem and to points raised in the paper by Professors Cobeljic and Stojanovic. He suggested that any subjective or psychological explanation of the reduced birth rate was inadequate. He held that there were strictly objective factors in this decline so far as concerned the Soviet Union. In the first place, the war had unbalanced the sex-age structure of the population : as a result of war losses there had been in the past two decades many fewer males than females in the fertile age groups. Secondly, urbanization had raised the proportion of women in the labour force.

The delineation of stages in industrialization in the manner outlined by

[1] Thus, a woman with two children could retire at age 52 with the same pension as a childless woman at 55.

Summary Record of the Discussion

Professors Cobeljic and Stojanovic was of theoretical and practical importance for the socialist countries. The simple ratio of urban to rural population had had significance in the nineteenth century but now had little connotation. The sort of industry now developed operated with much embodied technology and a high labour productivity : in the short run, it could not absorb all of the labour force released by technical progress in agriculture. It was the analysis of industrial structure which had become today the significant indicator of industrialization.

He had been much enlightened by the discussions of planning officials from developing countries at a symposium convened by the Economic Commission for Europe under the United Nations Expanded Programme of Technical Assistance (Moscow, July 1964) [1] : the alternatives of an intitial concentration upon engineering or upon agriculture had been cogently expressed, and, like Professor Robinson, he would himself see these options in terms of the expected incidence over time of balance-of-payments disequilibrium. While import substitution was important, the high cost of autarky had clearly to be avoided, and for this purpose developing countries could advantageously combine among themselves in regional trade groups.

Professor Grossman welcomed the attention which Professor Notkin had said was being given to separating the underlying factors of growth in the Soviet economy. He feared, nevertheless, that such studies would not be comparable to similar ones made in Western countries because the latter were based on 'Western' assumptions on marginal productivity and returns to individual factors of production.

He asked Professor Sorokin how he would reconcile his forecast of accelerating over-all growth and a high rate of investment in the U.S.S.R. with the decision of its Supreme Council of the National Economy to give higher priority to the consumer-good industry and agriculture in the next five-year plan (1966–70).[2]

Professor Zakhariev rejected, from his experience of agricultural planning in Bulgaria, that the rate of capital investment was arbitrarily chosen. The share of capital investment in agriculture was determined by the national economic plan, in establishing which the objective realities of agricultural development were taken into account. The first stage was to assess the volume of work to be done and on that basis to calculate the demand for technical equipment and machinery. As Bulgaria produced only part of the machinery and equipment needed in agriculture, the second stage was to plan imports (in practice from the more developed socialist countries, and mainly from the Soviet Union). The investment of this equipment would, at the third stage, expand production in the agricultural sector. Some of the exports of agricultural produce covered

[1] Report of the United Nations Seminar on Planning Techniques, United Nations, New York, 1966 (U.N. Sales No. 66.II.B 13).
[2] *Pravda*, 2 October, 1964.

63

such imports of machinery. Investment in agriculture was thus related to output and trade.

Professor Hutira examined the factors of economic development under socialism in Rumania. The prime determinant of its development was industrialization. The creation of an advanced engineering sector was needed to supply the entire economy with modern equipment : agriculture would share in this and both cover home demand and assure exports. Industrialization had made possible the rational utilization of the country's natural and labour resources, an improved distribution of productive forces throughout the country, and an increased participation in foreign trade. It was evident that the economic growth of the socialist countries both widened their commerce with non-socialist states and strengthened their potential for mutual co-operation, on the basis of complete equality and mutual benefit. Rumania supported the establishment of normal and mutually-beneficial economic relations with all countries on the basis of bilateral agreement : these should develop free of political considerations or discrimination.

Professor Robinson asked Professor Zakhariev to expand on his paper and on what he had said about Bulgarian development, particularly about the limiting factors in a planned economy. Would the most significant constraint have been skilled manpower, the capacity of the construction industry, the rate of saving and accumulation, or the balance of payments : in the latter case had Bulgaria specifically been able to purchase, or otherwise finance, the amount of foreign machinery and equipment needed to support the domestic rate of investment ?

Professor Sorokin replied to Professor Grossman's questions on Soviet accumulation. He stated that the increasing attention being given to manufactured consumers' goods tended to increase capital productivity because the recoupment period was shorter in that sector than for producers' goods. Investment in agriculture did not, however, necessarily have the same effect, but on balance he believed that the increase in capital resources envisaged for these two sectors during 1966–70 was not incompatible with the expected rate of accumulation.

Professor Rachmuth answered Mr. Kaser's query on the use of criteria other than economic efficiency for the co-ordination of plans between the socialist countries. He said that an official declaration of the CMEA, *Basic Principles of the International Socialist Division of Labour*, sets forth as a criterion for the co-ordination of plans :

> to eliminate the disparities which have emerged between national levels of development, in the first place by industrialization in the relatively less-developed countries, and by the maximum utilization of domestic potential and of the advantages of the socialist system.

His own view was that this criterion may stand side by side with that of economic efficiency proper.

Dr. Novozámsky took up Professor Robinson's queries on the deceleration of growth and on the balance-of-payments constraint. He noted that from 1948 to 1960 Czechoslovakia had enjoyed rapid economic growth ; the decline which then set in could be attributed to the weakening of the factors which had generated postwar growth before the contribution to be expected from new methods of management [1] had taken effect. The structure of the economy inherited from the postwar plans was imbalanced, agricultural production was far below consumption, and half the value of imports was agricultural goods. Inadequate domestic resources of raw materials aggravated the balance-of-payments problem. The expansion of Czechoslovakia's major export, engineering goods, was very capital-intensive : such investments were slow to mature and required further investment in the supporting input branches. Since investment was tied up in the production of capital-intensive exports to cover imports, scant resources remained to invest in automation and mechanization. Yet, manpower resources and the utilization of fixed assets had been stretched to the limit. The Czechoslovak growth problem was hence structural.

Professor Fauvel followed up Dr. Novozámsky's observations on the lag in Czechoslovak agricultural output by suggesting that its cause might be found in collectivization. As members of co-operative farms, peasants seemed to adopt the habits of wage-earners, viz. working for an eight-hour day but preferring leisure to overtime. Because the collective dividend was much less directly related to remuneration of the member's personal effort, incentives were weaker than on a peasant farm.

Professor Zakhariev pursued the agricultural problem in the light of Professor Robinson's question. After the Second World War the decision to industrialize required a mobilization and consolidation of resources to develop industry and to support the re-organization of agriculture. The problem of surplus manpower had to be solved, for it inhibited technical progress and labour-productivity growth in farming. The nationalization of industry allowed internal accumulation to be concentrated, by the long-term and annual plans, upon the construction of large-scale enterprises. Investments were directed primarily to the exploitation of natural resources (notably coal, ores, and chemicals for fertilizer), to electricity generation, metallurgy, and mechanical and agricultural engineering. Full employment was ensured, to the extent that at present some shortages of manpower have arisen in certain branches, thereby requiring the introduction of advanced technology.

Sir Roy Harrod hoped that Professor Sorokin could elaborate on his description (p. 9) of the Soviet procedure for formulating sectoral plans. Would it be true to say that the initial stage in preparing the target for, say, the chemical industry was an over-all figure for capacity, which, as

---

[1] Reforms were introduced in 1958 in Czechoslovakia, but were only partially implemented ; discussion of a more comprehensive re-organization began in the summer of 1964 (Editor's note).

a second stage, was disaggregated to the output of specific chemicals ? Or, on the other hand, did the procedure begin with projections for the output of the major products, which were subsequently built up into a general capacity target ?

To this *Professor Sorokin* replied that for the chemical industry planning began with product outputs. These targets were then translated into requirements for new capacity. The investment demand implied was broken down into equipment and construction : the equipment component was adjusted in the light of domestic capacity in chemical engineering and likely imports ; the construction component was reviewed against the potential of the building industry to meet the specialized requirements of work on chemicals projects. Aggregate capital formation implied for the chemicals industry was also evaluated in financial terms, viz. the sum of expected self-finance in the industry (including depreciation) and the funds which could be made available as budget grants. These three limits would settle the volume of planned capacity, from which individual product targets would be derived.

Sir Roy Harrod then turned to the problem of inadequate repairs raised in the paper of Professors Cobeljic and Stojanovic. They had observed that in the early stages of industrialization new investment pre-empted some of the resources which depreciation and wear-and-tear indicated as required for maintenance and repair. The failure to make such maintenance and repair outlays increased the volume of new investment at a second stage. He was anxious to know whether the authors were describing an empirical situation, that is, an occurrence which needed correction, or a deliberate planning policy in order to concentrate resources on new investment at a stage when capital was scarcer than it would be subsequently. This led him to reflect that there seemed to be an objective basis for planning infrastructure investment in what could be termed the middle phase of industrialization. The classical economists, and an important school of contemporaries, asserted that capitalist countries at an early stage of development should give priority to infrastructure. Plans aimed at regional equality within a country also required heavy infrastructure investment. The history of developed capitalist economies showed that the initial surge of investment was geographically concentrated, and evoked substantial regional disparities in the country. Yet the plans of many virtually undeveloped countries today favoured equity in regional development from the start.

He turned finally to Dr. Novozámsky's remarks, from which he drew the conclusion of marked similarities between socialist and capitalist development. There seemed to be an objective sequence of capital formation in countries at similar levels of development. He had been struck by the parallel of the Czechoslovak case with that of Italy. In Italy the demand for food had rapidly risen as a result of the expansion of urban (industrial) employment ; this increase was not matched by the increment in agricultural output, and heavy imports of foodstuffs were needed.

Dr. Novozámsky enlarged upon the causes of the lag in Czechoslovak agricultural output. Much of the investment had been channelled into projects with a long recoupment period ; because the import budget for raw materials and foodstuffs was so large, little foreign exchange was available to purchase modern farm machinery, with serious consequential effects on the productivity of farm labour. Finally, many of the investments made in agriculture had no effect on production : thus, the formation of collective farms was followed by the construction of barns and animal shelters for crops and livestock previously kept in individually-owned buildings ; these structures had no effect on production and absorbed resources which could, for example, have been devoted to chemical fertilizers or other growth-conducive outlays.

The last contribution to the discussion was by *Professor Jeanneney*, who hoped that light could be thrown in subsequent discussions on the planning and development of the service sector. He observed that tertiary activities took an increasing share of resources as industrialized capitalist economies became more affluent. Certainly some of the tertiary expansion was specific to the capitalist system itself, *e.g.* increasing outlays on advertising, and on the continuance of retail distribution by small shops. Nevertheless, another part of the expansion was called forth by the very nature of higher standards of living, and this seemed to him to be as valid for the socialist, as for the capitalist, economies. He would be interested to know how the long-term plans of socialist countries forecast the rate at which employment in the tertiary sector would expand. Because the tertiary sector was much more dependent on skilled manpower than the primary and secondary (productive) sectors — which could rely on capital deepening — he believed that planning would have to allow for meeting the prospective shortage of qualified manpower.

THE RATE OF DEVELOPMENT AND
REGIONAL PROBLEMS

Chapter 6

PROBLEMS OF PLANNING IN SOCIALIST COUNTRIES

BY

EVGENI MATEEV

Bulgarian Academy of Sciences

THE SIGNIFICANCE OF MEASUREMENT IN PLANNING

PRODUCERS' goods by definition embody the complex inter-relationship of productive branches. The socialist ownership of such goods permits interbranch relations to be established by an *ex ante* system of balances — in precise form for the most significant goods and in a general fashion for aggregate flows. Each detailed balance exhibits availabilities and major requirements. This long-established planning practice can be described in the well-known equation, the application of which follows the work of Leontief:

$$X_i = \Sigma a_{ij} X_j + \Sigma b_{ij} X_j + Y_i$$

wherein X is the quantity of output, 1, 2, ... i, j, ... m, the different products; a_{ij} the expenditure of product i for a unit of product j; and b_{ij} production funds from product i for a unit of j. In the balance of product i, $a_{ij} X_j$ are the quantities which are allocated for use in material product; $b_{ij} X_j$ the quantities of i for fixed and working capital; and Y_i is the part devoted to consumption, to requirements other than for material production and to export. The national economic planning already practised for several decades is in fact an uninterrupted process of solving a system of equations, and the present search for better methods is essentially for refinements of the traditional solution. Four specific problems can be enumerated.

The first task is to cheapen and accelerate the solution of the complex system of equations needed for planning. It is far from being the 'technical' one it may appear to be at first sight: it is the problem of the speed of reaction to autonomous decisions of the enterprise. Technical progress or a series of other factors can disturb the pattern of centrally-planned flows, and if the plan adjust too slowly, it becomes useless. The acceleration of planning (as an uninterrupted process of solving systems of equations) and of reducing its cost is consequently an intimate part of improving its efficiency : it is more important the more complex the inter-branch relations and the higher the rate of technical progress. The means for solving this problem, the use of large electronic computers, have long been applied to certain planning techniques, and must now be applied to general planning on a nation-wide scale.

A second problem arises from the condition that different solutions to a system of equations can be derived from the same elementary technical coefficients. The possibility of structural variants requires the choice of an optimum maximizing product with given outlay, and the highest possible rate of growth of social productivity of labour with given capital formation. The rapidity of technical innovation and the increasing complexity of interbranch relations renders the problem today more urgent than before, and certainly more intricate under the purposive co-ordination of activity in the socialist countries than with spontaneous technical change. Yet, though the advantages of planning have shown themselves in high rates of economic development, they have not hitherto been fully exploited. The limit of using existing planning techniques has already been reached in this respect and the next steps must be in the direction of economic cybernetics.

A third function of planning is to provide that mix of consumers' goods — and the production underlying consumers' services — which corresponds to an incentive-oriented system of remuneration. It is particularly for this reason that planning is not, and cannot, be the work of a cabal of technocrats : it must reflect in depth the interests of millions of people, assuring (by good planning) appropriate material and moral incentives for individuals, teams, and groups. Competition has two connotations in this connexion. Consumers' goods and services do not have to be furnished by competition, that is, by a struggle of producers to make retail sales, because distribution can be assured by planning. But they have to be supplied by competition for higher efficiency, and this form of emulation not only remains but develops as the essence of socialism. In that latter field planning is faced by a complex task. In its most general aspect it is that workers, especially those employed in scientific and technical organizations, should themselves propose the most effective measures as the fundamental indicators of the plan, that they should strictly fulfil the obligations thereby assumed, and that they should be remunerated in a precise relationship with their actual contribution. There is no doubt that the successful solution of this problem creates a much more powerful and effective 'competition' than any other system.

All three tasks so far outlined converge in the fourth, and fundamental problem — that of the gauges or indicators of the plan. At first sight this may appear to be a purely 'technical' question, but it is hardly too bold to say that at a time when the common ownership of the means of production permits the successful use of planning, the many complicated and much more 'respectable' problems thereof cannot be solved until the 'humble' question of indicators is cleared up. In the first place, the national economic plan cannot — now or in the foreseeable future — practicably deal with the hundreds of thousands of equations required for disaggregation to separate products. This is not only impossible and, indeed, unnecessary, but over-centralization is harmful. If hundreds of thousands of products are to be grouped, a common measure must be found, and if the plan is to be precise, so also must be that common measure. Secondly, for a plan to be efficient, output, material and labour inputs, and capital investment must be comparable. Mensuration which inadequately reflects their real relationships confuses the information flows for planning. Correct measures are needed, as a third consideration, to compare the contributions of individuals, teams, and groups, and to remunerate them accordingly. Finally, unambiguously defined parameters are essential to any econometric programme: how could problems in modern electrical engineering be solved without such units of measure as the volt, watt, or ohm ?

It must be stressed that exact measurement in economics is wider than mere statistical observation, and is a complex and fundamental characteristic of plan technology.

THREE TYPES OF PRICE

Price is used as the universal gauge of outputs and of current and capital inputs, and hence of each individual's contribution to, and remuneration from, society, not as an abstract theoretical category but as a concrete instrument taken from existing practice.

The socialist system excludes the formation of prices spontaneously or automatically, for they are fixed by the planning organs according to certain rules or principles. But it has to be asked whether such rules permit in their practical application the measurement by price of inputs and outputs, and whether they furnish relationships which respond better to planning needs. To clear the ground for this enquiry, a classification of methods of socialist price formation may be made in three groups.[1]

The prices here termed Type I are, in existing practice, set up under the following basic rules : a certain (usually small) percentage of profit is added to the cost of production (material outlays plus labour remuneration) ; the remainder of the funds necessary for accumulation and for other social requirements are derived from a turnover tax levied at the final stage (*i.e.* on consumers' goods) ; retail price is varied in accordance with the goals of economic and financial policy. For the purposes of this study an analysis of the cost-profit principle is of especial importance.

Mathematically, this type of price can be described in abbreviated form as $p_j = (\Sigma a_{ij} p_i + c v_j)(1 + r)$, where p is the price; $1, 2, \ldots i, j, \ldots m$ kinds of commodities ; a_{ij} input of commodities i for a unit of commodity j ; c the coefficient of labour remuneration to price ; v_j the labour remuneration for a unit of commodity j, dependent in theory on the quantity and quality of labour ; and r a certain percentage of profit. For the purposes of analysis it is assumed that r is constant for all types of production.

To simplify we divide through by $(1 + r)$ (viz. to transfer the coefficient of the profit to the left) and denote $\dfrac{1}{1+r}$ by R. We obtain a determinant from this system of simple equations

$$\Delta = \begin{vmatrix} (R - a_{11}) - a_{21} & \ldots & - a_{i1} & \ldots & - a_{m1} \\ - a_{12} + (R - a_{22}) & \ldots & - a_{i2} & \ldots & - a_{m2} \\ \cdot \; \cdot \; \cdot & \cdot \; \cdot \; \cdot & \cdot \; \cdot & \cdot \; \cdot & \cdot \\ - a_{1j} - a_{2j} & \ldots & + (R - a_{ii}) & \ldots & - a_{mj} \\ \cdot \; \cdot \; \cdot & \cdot \; \cdot \; \cdot & \cdot \; \cdot & \cdot \; \cdot & \cdot \\ - a_{1m} - a_{2m} & \ldots & - a_{im} & \ldots & + (R - a_{mm}) \end{vmatrix}$$

We obtain the determinants before the unknown quantities by substituting the independent vector $[c v_1, c v_2, \ldots c v_i, \ldots c v_m]$ for the columns $1, 2, \ldots i, \ldots m$. Since c is the common factor of one and the same column for every determinant, it comes before the sign of the determinant. This cannot be applied to the coefficients of the profit r because they line up along the diagonal. Therefore the

---

[1] V. D. Belkin, *Tseni edinogo urovnya i ekonomicheskie izmereniya na ikh osnove* (Unified-level prices and economic measurement thereon), Moscow, 1963, differentiates four types, but in the present writer's view, there is no difference of principle between his third and fourth types. The book is also notable for bibliographic references on this problem.

price of each single product will be $p_i = \dfrac{c \Delta_i}{\Delta}$. The relation between

the prices of two arbitrary products will be : $\dfrac{p_i}{p_j} = \dfrac{\Delta_i}{\Delta_j}$.

Two conclusions can be drawn about the properties of Type I prices. The first is that the numerical value of each price p_i depends : (a) on the technical coefficients (including the coefficients for labour remuneration v) ; (b) on the absolute value of the profit percentage r, which is part of one of the elements of the determinant ; and (c) on the absolute value of the common factor c with which we can multiply or divide proportionally any labour remuneration. The second is that the relationship of any two prices depends on the technical coefficients and on the profit percentage r, though it does not depend on the factor c. In other words, if we multiply or divide any labour remuneration by c, any price will be increased or decreased by the same percentage, while the relation between prices does not change. But if we decrease or increase the profit percentage prices will rise or fall and alter their interrelationship : there will be both an absolute and a relative rise of the prices of commodities incorporating more material inputs.

A further factor affects prices. Let us decompose the output j into two stages along the vertical by separating one of the consecutive processes into an independent enterprise. To it is related a certain part of the general expenses, say, $\frac{1}{3}\Sigma a_{ij} p_i$, and a certain part of labour remuneration, say $\frac{1}{5} v_j$. The price of this 'new' commodity is $p^1{}_j$, wholly included in material expenditure at the last stage. Thus we obtain

$$p'_j = (\tfrac{1}{3}\Sigma a_{ij} p_i + \tfrac{1}{5} v_j)(1 + r)$$

$$p_j = (p'_j + \tfrac{2}{3}\Sigma a_{ij} p_i + \tfrac{4}{5} v_j)(1 + r).$$

Hence : $\quad p_j = [(1 + \tfrac{1}{3} r)\Sigma a_{ij} p_i + (1 + \tfrac{1}{5} r) v_j](1 + r).$

Let us repeat that before decomposing we had :

$$p_j = (\Sigma a_{ij} p_i + v_j)(1 + r).$$

Now, after decomposition, the price p_j has an additional coefficient, *i.e.* a rise.

To the properties of Type I already described may now be added that the absolute and relative prices depend on a scale of fixed sequence. From these properties three statements of economic relevance may be made. The first is that by and large labour remuneration is proportionate to the quantity and the quality of labour. In practice this is realised through a series of fluctuations around the objectively correct relationship, but each deviation generates forces which compel the planners to introduce a corrective. In the second place a given money remuneration for a unit of working time may be associated with different price levels, *i.e.* we can discard the coefficient of the money remuneration through the factor c. On that account the products cv_1, cv_2, ... cv_i, ... cv_m express in prices the direct and indirect input of labour in money units in whatever coefficient is considered necessary from any point of view. Neither the money coefficient of labour remuneration nor the factor c are of any significance so far as price ratios are concerned; there only remains the technical coefficient of the expenditure of working time (allowing for skilled labour to be reduced to simple labour). The economic nature of that factor — the direct expenditure of working time (expressed in any money unit) — does not raise any problem. A third, but more complicated, conclusion concerns the economic nature of r. With given technical coefficients and a given factor c, let us increase the value of r. The sum total of the prices (*i.e.* their average level) will increase, and the relations between them will change. We can restore the average level through a corresponding decrease of c, and only the changed relations will remain: commodities with a greater share of material input will become more expensive, and the commodities with a greater share of labour remuneration will become cheaper.

The technical norms which express material inputs have not been altered, and hence price changes under the influence of r have nothing to do with outlay viewed as expenditure of working time or of materials, with a constant stock of capital. Neither change of r nor its contribution, which has the indicated chain effect on prices, are concerned with the inputs.

Material inputs $\Sigma a_{ij}p_i$ have two elements. The first, a_{ij}, is the technical coefficient expressing the indirect inputs. The second, p_i, is the price itself. Hence the deformation of price relations under the influence of r distorts material inputs, and, because the ratios of such coefficients play an important role in the material balances of planning, distortion of Type I price reduces the precision of planning. Productive assets are also expressed in prices and the participation of r in price relatives distorts capital–output ratios. If different prices can appear when cumulative inputs are identical, price is no adequate measure thereof. Other fortuitous elements in price relatives are introduced by the sequence of price formation, which appears to be quite unrelated to inputs, and by the different values of r for the several branches.

The turnover tax on consumer goods is a further problem connected with Type I prices, which will not be dealt with here. It results in two sets of price ratios and has been the fundamental cause of the pricing difficulties for farm produce.

The prices of Type II based on the principle of the 'production price' are of great theoretical and practical importance. In this type profit is added to cost of goods in proportion, not to the cost itself, but to the fixed and working assets engaged in its production, viz.

$$p_j = \Sigma a_{ij} p_i + cv_j + rK_j$$

where K_j is the full value of productive assets for a unit of output j (for the sake of brevity designated here as 'specific funds'), and r is the profit percentage related to the specific funds. Productive assets are assumed to have been valued according to procedures of the same price type on either their initial cost or their replacement value.

The analysis may first be made with capital at original value. The determinant of the system in this subtype is a matrix which includes only the technical coefficients. The independent variables are cv_j and rK_j, which take their place in the column with the determinants before the unknown quantities $p_1, p_2, \ldots p_i, \ldots p_m$, and each determinant Δ_i separates into Δ'_i and Δ''_i. In Δ'_i, cv_i takes its place in the respective column, and c is brought before the sign. In Δ''_i, rK_i takes part and r is also brought before the sign. Thus we obtain :

$$p_i = \frac{c\Delta'_i + r\Delta''_i}{\Delta}.$$

The ratio between any two prices will be :

$$\frac{p_i}{p_j} = \frac{\Delta'_i + (r/c)\Delta''_i}{\Delta'_j + (r/c)\Delta''_j}.$$

Hence absolute and relative prices depend : (a) on the technical coefficients (expenditure of labour and materials in a physical dimension) ; (b) on the relative size of the productive assets (the elements $K_1, K_2, \ldots K_m$ taking part in the second determinants) ; and (c) on the value of the profit percentage r at a given price scale c.

Type II price formation indicates automatically the efficiency of capital investment.[1] But the elements K_i turn out to be a Trojan horse, because commodities involving identical inputs from the application of identical productive assets will differ in price if the values of r vary, despite the fact that the value of r has nothing to do either with the inputs or with productive assets engaged, and this is, of course, because assets are expressed in prices. If a relatively greater quantity of assets are engaged in branch i, product i will grow more expensive with the increase of r. But if at the same time its assets in turn consist of products with a low capital intensity, they will be cheaper and the index of the 'specific funds' in i will be distorted.

This coefficient is logical in the context of private capitalist enterprise. The capital has its 'price' in terms of profit: productive assets may be either 'expensive' or 'cheap' to the capitalist in terms of the relative levels of profit and the rate of interest. In such a system the structure of primary distribution affects the cost of each commodity to the enterprise, but not to society. To apply Type II prices to a socialist system would require that a relative share increase in social expenditures (*e.g.* on medical care or education) which raises the coefficient would make capital-intensive commodities more expensive than others, a result which would be patently false.

The analysis can next be undertaken with capital at replacement cost, that is, when the value of the stock of assets is a function of current price, p_i. Productive assets differ from other producers' goods by entry as capital consumption, determined by the period of amortization for the fixed assets and by the velocity of circulation for working capital. For any year this term is the reciprocal of asset life (or, for working capital, of the times circulated within a year), and is here denoted as d_i, whence

$$K_j = \Sigma a_{ij} d_i p_i$$

$$p_j = \Sigma a_{ij} . p_i + c v_j + r\Sigma a_{ij} . d_i p_i = \Sigma a_{ij}(1 + d_i r)p_i + c v_j,$$

wherein d_i is the turnover term. We denote $1 + d_i r = R_i$. In this system of equations the determinant will contain as its elements the products $a_{ij} R_i$, with $(1 - a_{ii} R_i)$ along the diagonal, and it will not be possible to bring R_i before the sign of the determinant. The determinants before the unknown quantities are obtained by substituting the independent vector $[c v_1, \ c v_2, \ ..., \ c v_j, \ ... \ c v_m]$ for the respective column. The common factor c is brought before the sign, but the element r remains in the matrix. The relative price, *i.e.* the

[1] See Belkin, *op. cit.*, p. 278.

ratio between any two prices, therefore, depends (a) on the technical
coefficients a_{ij}, (b) on the turnover term d_i, (c) on the profit norm r,
and (d) on labour input v_i. If the sum of the prices (*i.e.* their
average level) is to be constant under a varying r, the factor before
the sign of the determinant c must change in the opposite direction.
The relative value of r hence also plays a part under replacement
value and, again, it merely expresses the proportion of primary
distribution, its economic significance coinciding with that under
original cost.

In price formation of Type III profit is added to cost in proportion to labour remuneration, viz.

$$p_j = \Sigma a_{ij}p_i + cv_j + rcv_j = \Sigma a_{ij}p_i + (1 + r)cv_j.$$

Two factors stand before the independent variable, each identical
for each equation, and hence substitutable. In other words, the
arbitrary factor before c is given a definite meaning, namely, the
percentage of profit to wages (a measure of the quantity and quality
of labour). The determinant of the system is solely the technical
coefficients — with $(1 - a_{ii})$ along the diagonal, and those before the
unknown quantities p_1, p_2, ..., p_m are obtained by substituting
$[(1+r)v, (1+r)v_2, ..., (1+r)v_j, ..., (1+r)v_m]$ for the respective
column. The common factor comes before the sign. We therefore
obtain :

$$p_i = \frac{(1+r)\Delta_i}{\Delta}; \quad \frac{p_i}{p_j} = \frac{\Delta_i}{\Delta_j}.$$

Since r does not take part in either matrix Δ_i and Δ_j, the system
acquires a highly important characteristic : price relatives depend
exclusively on labour and material inputs, not on the profit norm ;
material inputs $\Sigma a_{ij}p_i$ are equivalent to the indirect expenditures of
working time expressed in a money unit. Absolute price depends
on the full inputs of working time and on the money coefficient
which defines the scale of prices. When r rises under a constant v_i,
the level increases while the ratios remain the same. If the level is
restored by introducing a correcting coefficient c, we shall obtain the
same prices (in absolute value) as those prior to the change of r.
In other words, the proportion of primary distribution is excluded
from price formation.

Type III prices hence also define material inputs as technical
norms, and 'specific funds' as the type and quantity (in value) of
the equipment and inventories to which labour is applied.

Whichever of the three types are adopted for price formation, certain common factors induce a deviation of price from value over a long or short period. Such divergencies are crucial to the operation of the market in a capitalist economy. Under socialism they can serve as the economic instrument regulating the financially-autonomous enterprise within a national plan which need specify only the most significant inter-branch flows.

But to speak of a deviation the standard must be known, and the need for deviation is no argument for inconsistency in price formation. Long-term deviations may be tolerated when some commodity is continually in short supply (*e.g.* timber), or when a special policy is pursued in the sphere of consumption (*e.g.* tobacco and spirits on the one hand and children's necessities on the other). A short-term price increase may be justified for novel consumers' goods, while output is adjusting to the new pattern, but — save in special circumstances — the normal price should be achieved as soon as possible because it is a sign and measure of maximum flexibility and efficiency in a planned economy.

PRICE TYPES AND CAPITAL EFFICIENCY

These three systems of measuring output, input, and capital may now be examined in relation to the efficiency of investment, in which two aspects may be distinguished — differentials in 'specific funds' by branch and by project.

In branch i output costs $q_i p_i$ units and derives from $q_i K_i$ productive assets, the capital–output ratio K_i at given prices uniquely depending on the technical features of output, an examination of which is, for present purposes, irrelevant. Nor is it germane to consider the relation of direct to indirect capital inputs, since only cumulative 'specific funds' are in issue.

Obviously, it is to choice of project that efficiency analysis must be applied, and from this point of view all technical variants of a given branch fall into two types, viz. those in which both current inputs and non-recurrent investments in one (here termed iII) are smaller than in another (here termed iI). This type can be called 'one-direction variants': no problems of economic comparison arise, for if the common unit of measure is accurate, the advantages of iII are irrefutable. If an appropriate unit has been provided by economists, the choice is wholly that of the design engineer. In variant iII current expenditures are lower, but non-recurrent investments are higher than in iI — a type which can be described as 'different-direction variants'. The designer has already done as much as he can and choice devolves on the economist and planner.

In branch i the ratio between operating expenses saved and the additional capital investment can be written as $e_i = \dfrac{{}^1f_i - {}^2f_i}{{}^2K_i - {}^1K_i}$, denoting, for the time being, outlays by the 'neutral' symbol f, because a money value depends on the type of price formation; e_i is the coefficient of efficiency (the reciprocal of the period of recoupment).

For each branch, the coefficient e_i has no meaning, but a comparison of e_i with e_j demonstrates whether in i variant II is more or less effective than in j. Similarly, we may posit a normative coefficient of efficiency e_n, such that variant iII would be accepted if $e_i \geq e_n$. A small transformation brings us to the choice between the variants :

$$ {}^1f_i + e_n{}^1K_i \geq {}^2f_i + e_n{}^2K_i $$

and from this point the value of the formulae depends on the meaningfulness of the units.

We may now proceed to identify the 'neutral' f with each of the three types of price distinguished above. If it represents Type I prices the formula is useless, for e_j is formed by factors that are fortuitous with regard to capital efficiency. Both current expenses and investment in a given project are related only to the last stage of production.

With Type II prices the formula is suitable for efficiency comparisons under capitalism if, as Belkin assumes,[1] the normative coefficient is equal to the profit percentage, *i.e.* $e_n = r$. Relative investments are elements of price and that variant of production is more effective which provides for lower prices ; because the cost of output takes account of K, the full 'specific fund' influences choice, not merely that at the last stage. In the socialist system, however, Type II price formation does not require that relative prices correspond to relative costs, which are affected by the introduction of the proportion of the primary distribution therein. It does not, moreover, follow — as Kantorovich also assumes [2] — that $e_n = r$. It does not even follow that such an equation is practically possible. A discussion of the nature of normative efficiency is made below, but here it is

[1] *Op. cit.*, p. 278.
[2] L. Kantorovich, *Ekonomichesky raschet nailuchshego ispolzovaniya ressursov*, Moscow, 1959 (English trans. *The Best Use of Economic Resources*, Oxford, and Cambridge (Mass.), 1965).

enough to remark that if, by way of example, society decides relatively to increase expenditure for consumption free of charge, hence raising r, this does not mean that normative efficiency is not improved ; if incomes are relatively increased — raising labour remuneration and reducing r — society, on that account alone, cannot be satisfied with a lower normative efficiency.

It is Type III pricing which furnishes a completely adequate expression of the direct and indirect expenditures of labour and of capital : direct and indirect inputs of working time and turnover time are affected uniquely by technical conditions. Industries can be ranked by investment efficiency, and, if this ranking is employed to invest a given value of capital funds, the largest possible volume of net output will be obtained. The distribution of this output, at the primary stage between v and m, and then in redistribution to derive the final funds of consumption and of accumulation, is a separate question which does not affect the efficiency criterion. Theoretically, it is necessary to substitute the full incremental investments for the direct ones, but in practice one or two iterations suffice.

Only one normative coefficient of efficiency (or recoupment period) is necessary and sufficient for a solution. In our view, the need for the sectoral coefficients which Belkin describes [1] arises in Type III prices only when the efficiency problem has been wrongly formulated, that is, by seeking to evaluate the efficiency of the existing branch-structure of the capital stock rather than the return to new investment according to the balance of inter-branch relations.

PLANNING PROBLEMS ARISING IN CAPITAL-EFFICIENCY COMPARISON

It has already been pointed out that no formula is strictly needed to choose between 'one-direction variants', but it might be desirable for a rigorous system to allow for such relationships. The introduction of the normative coefficient e_n makes this possible, for, since it has been given that $^2K_j < {}^1K_j$, we can change their places in the denominator

$$e_j = \frac{^1p_j - {}^2p_j}{^1K_j - {}^2K_j} \geq e_n$$

whence $\qquad\qquad {}^1p_j - e_n{}^1K_j \geq {}^2p_j - e_n{}^2K_j.$

In the 'different-direction variants' the sign is negative.

In many cases the output of two variants is not homogeneous but

[1] *Op. cit.*, pp. 281–283.

differs in quality : there are the same 'one-direction variants' (jII yields an output which is both cheaper and of higher quality) and 'different-direction variants' (in jII the output is of a higher quality but it is more expensive). Evidently, concern is with the latter. For producers' goods the problem is simply of derived demand, and quality in branch j can be defined by the value of its output as input to branch k.

We would have : $e_k = \dfrac{{}^1p_n - {}^2p_n}{{}^2K_k - {}^1K_k} \geq e_n$, wherein ${}^2p_k$ will reflect the current economies upon the exploitation of production jII.

It often occurs that price-control authorities try to allow for such quality differentials among producers' goods by adjusting the price of jI by the difference in the effect of jII. But it is fallacious to express use value on the sole basis of cost (*i.e.* that incurred in jI). Even the Austrian School could not fulfil its threat to connect price with use value, and despite the lamentations of Liefmann it had to turn to cost in the form of opportunity cost. It may be added that quality can embrace a wide range of technical variants of buildings, of technology, of design, and of materials, alternative location and broad characteristics in the field of aesthetics, hygiene, and consumer welfare.

The quality of consumers' goods raises further considerations. When a new variant of a consumer good jII is designed (embodying a higher quality) it is frequently the case that, at least for a time, costs are greater than for the lower quality product and that a price is established above that indicated by its value as a Type III price. The task of the plan is to reduce the temporary price back to the normal one within the shortest possible term. Under capitalism the deviation of the market price measures the 'efficiency' of a new commodity, as much for consumers' goods as for producers' goods ; from the point of view of society, however, this deviation is not a measure of utility but the protective screen for a disproportion. Strumilin and Konius proved from Marx's theory of value that maximum satisfaction of consumer requirements is achieved when supply and demand are balanced on the basis of a price coinciding with the value. A plan is hence more effective, from the point of view of consumption, the quicker the price of a new consumer product is reduced to its value (an exception being deliberately prohibitive prices, *e.g.* those of alcoholic drinks and tobacco), and the designer's work on a consumer product is more effective if the relative share of the new product is larger than that of the old when prices and values coincide and when supply and demand are balanced. Such shares depend both on utility and cost; the pre-ferences of the consumer are the criterion of efficiency, and it is there that we should look for it.

The definition of comparative efficiency also arises when an asset with a remaining physical life and not yet amortized is replaced by reason of obsolescence; by definition any such retirement must provide the equivalent of the capacity scrapped and some more intensive use of resources. The capacity newly installed must therefore exceed the undepreciated part of that scrapped (at replacement cost).

We may, in conclusion, discuss the factors that determine the normative efficiency e_j, which plays an essential role in investment selection.

We assume that the aggregate investment for a given period is fixed, depending on the volume of national income and on the proportion of accumulation to consumption; we assume also full employment. In such a situation capital formation must be directed to an intensive expansion of production. But there are more efficient projects than there are the means available for their realization. Obviously, the more effective ones have to be chosen. The cut-off point in the descending rank order of efficiency coefficients depends for its numerical value on those of the projects submitted. The more efficient the work of research and development the higher will this point be. It also depends on the rate of increase of the labour force and the average age of the capital stock. The normative so determined is unrelated to the rate of profit r, although, as technical progress tends to increase the normative — as just stated — the higher rate of growth which could thereby be expected could lead to an enlargement of the share of consumption and hence to a decrease of r. Vice versa, at certain values of investment returns an increase of the accumulation fund (by raising r) may become neces-sary, allowing more capital formation to take place, that is, with a lower normative. Planners should not confuse the normative and the rate of profit, but should appreciate that their economic nature frequently causes their negative correlation.

THE INFORMATION REQUIREMENTS

It has already been pointed out that the drafting of a plan by the traditional balance-method is a solution of a dynamic system:
$$X_i = \Sigma a_{ij}X_j + \Sigma b_{ij}X_j + Y_i.$$

84

Present-day electronic computers are in a position to solve this problem (expressed in the necessary mathematical form) quickly and inexpensively if the independent variables and the technical indices are known. That is why, in our opinion, the major obstacle to advance in the technology — and, indeed, more than the pure technology — of nation-wide economic planning is the provision of suitable information along these two lines. In its most complicated form, the conditions of this problem may be expressed as those for drafting a plan for the period $t_1 \ldots t_n$ in period t_0; it is simpler when, being in t_1, the first year of an established plan for $t_2 \ldots t_n$, a prolongation is to be drafted for $t_n + 1$. In all cases the application of electronic computers would follow present practice in drafting a plan by stages, but these stages would be reached more quickly.

At the first stage of computing, the dynamics of Y_1, Y_2, $\ldots Y_m$ are given and the curve of the consumption fund Y_i is estimated on the projection of past trends adjusted for likely change. Within aggregate consumption, family-budget data on the elasticity of demand and, for longer periods, nutrition norms, etc., are used to project trends for specific product-groups and certain major projects. Doubtless a specialist applied science of consumption will soon emerge. If the second question, that of determining the technical coefficients, is solved, the system is ready for programming.

It should be noted that, in the conditions stated, the system can only have a unique solution : at the given values of Y_1, Y_2, $\ldots Y_m$ and of a_{ij} and b_{ij} no other structure is possible. Projected consumption ΣY_i is next compared with the estimate of net output, $\Sigma(\Sigma b_{ij} X_j + Y_i)$, the dynamics of each being expressed by their logarithmic derivatives.

The interpretation of the ratio between the two calls for the analysis not only of economic, but of broader social, historical, and political, criteria. A high constant rate of growth of output may support an increasing share of consumption (at the expense of a diminishing share of accumulation) if the technology introduced by the coefficients a_{ij} and b_{ij} is highly effective. It is possible that the given growth of ΣY_i may lead to a deceleration of output if more consumption has been drafted than is justified by the capital stock and technology. Appropriate corrections can be introduced at this second stage, and those technical variants selected which ensure that relationship of labour-intensive and labour-extensive projects dictated by manpower resources. It is at this point that Engels' view of communism can be expressed, when society is in a position purposively to combine the interests of the present with the interests of its development.[1]   Of course, this combination is not arbitrary, but is the result and expression of objective social processes and laws, and is far superior to the blind forces of the market mechanism which determines the fate of society in the capitalist system.

The use of the mean technical coefficients and manpower inputs for a branch of industry means that one figure can represent many thousands of input coefficients in separate enterprises and numerous different patterns of the output so grouped.   Leontief's assumption of linearity was doubtless appropriate to capitalism, since the input–output table would be used for formulating economic policy to influence spontaneous development.   But it is unacceptable in planning a socialist economy, wherein the main task of the plan is to maximize capital efficiency.   To extrapolate the past is merely 'academic' planning from the armchair.   Frisch has demonstrated the very complicated functional relations underlying the technical coefficients, which not only affect inter-branch relations but are determined by them and by the rate of expansion (viz. by the share of accumulation).[2]   To optimize by central planning requires an enormous and practically impossible concentration of information about primary indices.   Such concentration is, however, possible if optimization is provided beforehand in the input information itself : electronic equipment can solve the system of m equations and of as many unknowns.   The primary technical coefficients change only under the effect of technology, and their dynamics will be determinate if enterprises during the 'base period' for the plan have been constrained to exclude all investment of an efficiency less than the normative.   By the same constraint no more capital formation will be planned than the investible resources arising from the implementation of projects.   Use of Type III prices is assumed. The system solved on this basis now leads to a definite value of X_i, by virtue of which a part of the initial suggestions are eliminated or new ones are added.   A further stage of computing begins with these average values of a_{ij} and b_{ij} now closer to reality, and two or three iterations should be enough to achieve final balance.   The same iteration establishes the exact value of the normative, as the balancing of capital investments proves.

---

[1] F. Engels, *Dialektik der Natur* (1873–82 ; First edn., Moscow, 1925), Bulgarian trans., Sofia, 1950, p. 40.

[2] R. Frisch, *A Survey of Economic Forecasting and Programming* (Memorandum of the Institute of Economics, University of Oslo, 13 May, 1961).   See also E. Mateev, *Perspektivno planirane* (Long-Term Planning), Sofia, 1963.

The sources of the primary information are the technical designs for establishing new or developing existing enterprises. These designs hence become a form of constant technical creative work and economic management, and in this field also computers can automate the plan information sent by the enterprise to the centre.[1]

The fact that planning is recurrent and continuing further supports the need for electronic computers to assure quick reaction in changing the plan in the light of new phenomena. A cybernetic system can operate by the rules of inverse relations in a previously-programmed manner to react to unforeseen signals from its environment. Adequate inventories are essential to implement the activity undertaken in response to the change and to permit a balance to be struck between an optimum mobility and an optimum stability of inter-branch and inter-enterprise relations. Such stocks can be held by the producer, by the consumer, or by some central agency ('deep' reserves); or in the form of reserve productive capacities in the branch concerned. Stock ratios can easily be subject to automatic control and an optimum achieved in a purely empirical way. Information on inventories and the degree of capacity use to the computing centre constitute as important data as orders from consumers.

Uninterrupted planning of this automated nature also solves the problem of iteration. The daily processing of the input information (suggestion) into output information (acceptance or rejection of the suggestion), allows current adaptation of the determinant parameters (proportion of accumulation, rate of growth, and normative efficiency). The inadequacy of price as a measure of efficiency inhibits the disaggregation of these parameters into branch groups, and this has led in the past to resort to detailed orders to branches by the central authorities (introducing, as they see it, 'discipline' into planning). Improving the apparatus of measurement makes it possible to subordinate choice of the degree of centralization to the technical establishment of inter-branch relations. A higher degree of decentralization is admissible and sufficient in the initial stages of planning, so that relations between primary units are established at such points as involve the least expenditure of time and money. Their co-ordination can be achieved partly along central channels — and this concretely for the most important products — and partly by decentralization for other elements in synthesized groups.

---

[1] A. I. Berg, A. I. Kitov, A. A. Lyapunov, 'The Automation of Economic Management', *Problemy kibernetiki*, no. 6, p. 96.

The scope of this paper is not intended to cover incentives, but their improvement is of course closely related to the problems here discussed of precise indicators. The prospects of better national planning by modern cybernetics are not to be relegated to the distant future : all the conditions for application are immediately at hand in the socialist countries. The grounds for optimism lie in the fact that social prerequisites are of decisive significance : the advantage of public ownership is self-evident, and to it must be added the absence from a socialist society of the social forces whose interests could obstruct such developments. But its application will not be brought about without discussion by a broad circle of economists, who are able to pin down the details of their essentially technical problems, and who could advise on their realization without sudden disruption of current procedures.

Chapter 7

RATES AND PROPORTIONS OF THE ECONOMIC DEVELOPMENT OF THE SOCIALIST COUNTRIES

BY

A. I. NOTKIN

Institute of Economics, Moscow

THE PROBLEM OF THE RATE OF DEVELOPMENT

THE rate of economic development represents one of the most important internal problems facing the socialist countries. On it depends the speed with which their economy can be transformed on socialist principles, and the course of their economic competition with the developed capitalist countries. The consolidation of economic and political power within states and of their international potential as members of the world socialist economic system is dependent upon this factor.

Progress within the countries concerned, particularly in industrial development, has been considerable : within 12 years, from 1950 to 1962, the average annual rate of the growth of industrial production in the member states of Comecon was 11·4 per cent and in the U.S.S.R., 11·3 per cent ; that in all the capitalist countries together was 4·9 per cent ; in the members of the Common Market, 7·6 per cent ; and in the U.S.A., 3·9 per cent. Some western economists have sought to demonstrate that the socialist states are at a stage of industrialization corresponding to that of the now-developed capitalist countries in the nineteenth century. This contention is ill-founded : when the western capitalist economies were at the *per capita* industrial product levels of Comecon members today, they were growing more slowly (as a rule, by not more than 5 or 6 per cent per annum).

The priority given, on the basis of public ownership of all social production, to achieving the largest possible national income, allows ever fuller satisfaction of the people's needs and constantly expands both the market for consumers' goods and the means of production.

Together with the systematic planned control exercised over production, this obviates economic crises and depressions, and provides for a continuous growth of production, thus producing the higher rates of economic development characterizing socialist countries. This is not to say, of course, that there are no bounds to the expansion of production and of consumer-good markets under socialism. The limits of the extension of production are determined at each given stage by the real resources for accumulation — the natural endowment, the stock of material assets, and manpower — and the efficiency of their utilization. The limits thus formed on the supply side and those correspondingly set by the size of the domestic market may be widened by foreign trade, on the basis of the international socialist division of labour and the co-ordination of the national plans of separate countries. Plan co-ordination provides specialized and concentrated production in certain countries with a stable market in the world socialist economic system; given that this production is efficiently managed in respect of costs, capital is recouped earlier, and production is cheapened or its quality enhanced. This collaboration naturally provides another factor in maintaining the high rates of economic development in socialist countries. The exploitation of natural resources and of achievements in science and technology in the interests of the whole world socialist system is of no less importance. Thus, the combination of iron ore in Krivoi Rog and coking coals in Upper Silesia enabled Poland and Czechoslovakia to develop their own blast-furnace production on a large scale. It is clear that combining the natural resources of various countries can accelerate growth only to the extent that profits so derived exceed transport costs, and when other methods of solving the supply problem of raw materials are not appropriate.

RATES OF DEVELOPMENT AND THE OPTIMUM OF ACCUMULATION AND CONSUMPTION

Although rates of economic advance play a great role in the development of the socialist economic system, they should not be considered as an end in themselves. They cannot be regarded independently of their contribution to satisfying the needs of the population, and of the influence they exercise on the proportion between productive and non-productive investment and current consumption.

It is a commonplace that the economic development rates depend both on productive manpower and its productivity, and on capital assets and their utilization. In the national income the fund of productive assets on which the growth of employment and labour productivity primarily depend counterbalances the consumption fund. Therefore, the influence of development on the improvement of welfare may be estimated through analysing the proportion between productive accumulation and consumption at different rates of growth, and thence choosing the optimal combination of accumulation and consumption. Under socialism the optimum ratio of productive accumulation and consumption has to ensure, within a certain period, not only high rates of the gross national product and the national income, but also the maximization of consumption. In this connexion, the problem of the period used for maximization is of great importance, and has not yet been completely solved. A possible solution might be reached by determining the period of the 'reproductive cycle' of the whole national economy from the date of opening up raw material and fuel deposits to the output of consumer goods — a period, in the U.S.S.R., of between 9 and 10 years. Proceeding from this it is possible to work out a number of variant patterns of economic development in which the endogenous dependence of productive accumulation, on the one hand, and the aggregate of consumption (including non-productive investment), on the other hand, could be clearly distinguished. In order to find this dependence we may limit ourselves to three simplified types of economic development : (I) based on a rising rate, (II) based on a constant rate, and (III) based on a decreasing rate of productive accumulation. In all these, the national income in the initial year is taken as 60,000 million (60 billion) rubles, of which 20 per cent is devoted to productive accumulation. The coefficient of this accumulation in terms of product is assumed constant at 0·4 ; the latter does not include non-productive accumulation, which is counted in the consumption fund. The rate of increase of the national income is determined by the rate of productive accumulation under, and the capital coefficient of, three variants. These are shown in Chart 1, viz. with an additional one per cent of national income added annually to productive accumulation (I), with a constant allotment to accumulation (II), and with one per cent of national income deducted each year from accumulation (III). The annual rate of growth of national income in variant I rises to 11·6 per cent by the tenth year, in variant II remains at 8 per cent, and in variant III falls to 4·4 per cent in the tenth year. For the first six years the consumption return is greatest in variant III : the aggregate for those years is 355 billion

CHART 1

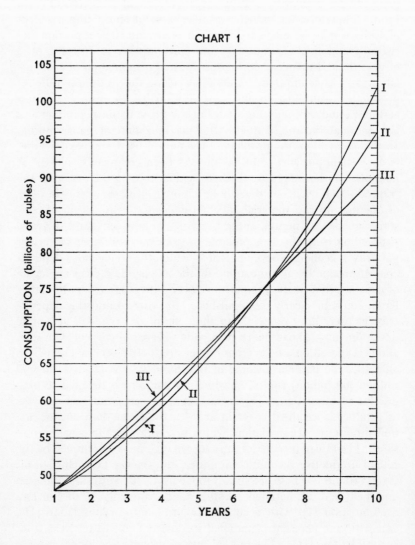

rubles, against 352 billion in variant II and 348 billion in variant I. Hence, if it is desired to achieve the largest consumption fund in the shortest period, economic development on the basis of a decreasing rate of productive accumulation is most effective. Variant III, with a rising allotment to productive accumulation, is obviously disadvantageous. The amount by which the volume of the consumption fund (which, it may be recalled, includes non-productive accumulation) under variant III exceeds that in variant I is greatest in the fourth year, and disappears after the sixth year. After the seventh year variant III becomes increasingly disadvantageous from year to year. In the seventh year the consumption fund in variant I amounts to 400 million rubles more than in variant III, and in the tenth year to 11 billion rubles more. For the whole ten years calculated, the volume of the consumption fund is equal to 700 billion rubles in the first variant, 695 in the second, and 687 in the third variant. Thus variant I produces 13 billion rubles more for the total ten-year consumption fund than does III, and 5 billion rubles more than does II. In other words, maximization of the consumption fund for the whole calculation period is given by variant I with a gradually increasing rate of production accumulation, while in variant III this maximization can be obtained only in the first six years.

This demonstrates the well-known contradiction between long-term and current interests of a socialist society, which must be continuously controlled, taking into account the stage of social development reached : at some stages preference is given to productive accumulation (*e.g.* in the years of the first five-year plan in the U.S.S.R.), at others to the acceleration of the rise of consumption. However, socialism entails the need to provide for the absolute growth of the consumption fund in aggregate and *per capita* even under conditions of very intensive accumulation. In the first place, this is a consequence of the rise in employment and productivity associated with the growth of income and, secondly, of the need for an increase in consumption *per capita* as incentive for both urban and rural labour. Therefore, in socialist countries the growth of the accumulation fund is usually accompanied by a more rapid expansion of the consumption fund than of population. As the following table shows, in the U.S.S.R. in 1959–62, when the share of productive accumulation was rising, aggregate personal consumption increased by 16·5 billion rubles, *i.e.* by nearly 19 per cent, and the population increased by 10·8 million, or 5·1 per cent.

The Rate of Development and Regional Problems

	1959	1960	1961	1962
Percentage of national income devoted to productive accumulation	19·9	20·1	22·1	22·5
Personal consumption (billion rubles)	88·0	93·9	96·7	104·5
End-year population (millions)	212·3	216·1	219·7	223·1

In Poland in 1955–62 the annual volume of capital investments into the socialist sector increased by 76 per cent, and the consumption fund increased by 51 per cent, the total increase of the national income being 54 per cent. In the G.D.R. the percentage of the national income devoted to accumulation increased from 8·4 in 1950 to 20·4 in 1962, and aggregate consumption increased from 26,300 to 60,300 million marks, *i.e.* nearly 2·3 times.

A correlated rise in the share of accumulation and in the volume of consumption is the problem of the continuity of systematic socialist development. One of the most important tasks of socialist planning is permanently to ensure not only intensive accumulation and high rates of reproduction, but also a more rapid growth of consumption to keep pace with population increase.

However, the fact that *per capita* consumption increases does not alone signify the achievement of a socialist economic optimum, which requires the maximization of consumption over the period defined. In determining this optimum, a socialist society naturally cannot ignore the fact that for the long period the highest increase of consumption *per capita* is ensured by an initial increase in the rate of productive accumulation. To find the most favourable combination not only of productive accumulation and consumption but also of current interests and those for the whole calculation period, a developed socialist society should, it would seem, resort to a settlement by compromise. If, as in the case of a developed economy, the share of productive accumulation is of the order of magnitude chosen for the numerical example above, a constant share (variant II) has two advantages. In the first place, such a policy avoids the strain on the national economy associated with increasing the rate of accumulation, which requires the incorporation of considerable additional natural and labour resources into the economic process. Nor does it, secondly, involve losses in the national economy which could arise from decreasing the rate of accumulation (*e.g.* incomplete utilization of capacities in the capital-good and building industries and unemployment).

In the example given above the mean coefficient was assumed to be constant. If a change operates equally in all the variants the efficiency of accumulation with respect to the volume of consumption will not of course be affected. There are circumstances, however, in which the coefficient may be altered by the rate of growth of investment.

As just mentioned, an increasing share of accumulation requires the incorporation of considerable additional natural and labour resources into the economy. There is no reason why this should affect the quality or conditions of extraction of natural resources : for example, in the eastern areas of the U.S.S.R. the quality and conditions of extraction of coal are superior to those in the old Donbas coalfields. The same can be said of oil, the extraction of which at present in the new Volga-Urals oil deposits is cheaper than in Baku. Nevertheless, a rapid expansion of the volume of productive accumulation and production often necessitates the exploitation of less-effective natural resources, requiring more capital investment and higher production costs. With a slower rate of investment, there is a greater possibility of selecting the natural resources most suited for immediate exploitation, and deferring use of others until technical progress permits their more efficient employment.

With an increasing rate of accumulation there may be a tendency to encourage capital investment in developed regions, which often do not dispose of the most valuable resources, and into existing enterprises of which the reconstruction and expansion may not provide the best economic indices (for example, the Cherepovets iron and steel works).

THE RELATIONSHIP OF THE OUTPUT OF CAPITAL GOODS TO THAT OF CONSUMERS' GOODS

The proportion between production and productive accumulation, on the one hand, and non-productive accumulation and current consumption, on the other, is based (in a closed economy) on the proportion between the growth of output of capital and consumers' goods. The more the production of capital goods exceeds the retirement and wear of fixed assets, the higher evidently is the rate of reproduction. According to the classic concept, the preferential development of the output of the means of production is conditioned by technical progress, by the mechanization of manual labour, and by the supply of energy per worker. The industries needed to embody technical progress, to substitute capital for labour, and to develop energy production are hence crucial to the process of growth.

Technical innovations and discoveries, especially in the present scientific and technical revolution, constantly promote further automation, and the more rapid replacement of obsolete equipment.

The experience of the Soviet Union and other socialist countries shows that the preferential development of the output of industrial producers' goods is necessary to accelerate the growth of those sectors, but that when a modern industrial structure has been achieved, it is readily feasible to align more closely the rates of growth of producers' and of consumers' goods. The trend towards more efficient use of capital and of current inputs permits a high rate of growth to be maintained with a lower proportion of net investment. Technical progress, moreover, tends more frequently to substitute for labour than for capital, and the priority growth of the output of means of production hence retains its significance even in a developed industrial society.

Sometimes it is considered that a policy according faster than average growth for the means of production prevents the organization of production in the interests of expanding consumption. This might be a valid viewpoint if it were merely a convenient theory : it is, however, a reality which must be taken into account when planning the development of a national economy : indeed, far from inhibiting a rise in welfare, it creates the material prerequisites for it. It is demonstrable that the greatest amount and widest variety of production and consumption of consumers' goods *per capita* have been achieved in precisely those countries in whose output producers' goods bulk heavily, not in those with a one-sided dependence on the branches producing consumers' goods. The ratio of the output of means of production to that of consumers' goods is not in itself of significance for the optimal combination of production. The desirable pattern of output depends on the type of producers' goods, that is, on their different productivities and on the national preference between the highest absolute increase of consumers' goods immediately and in the period of calculation, which, in turn, is part of the question (discussed above) of the compatibility of accumulation with the maximization of consumption. Furthermore, since the greater part of the means of production are intermediate goods, their specific weight tends to rise during a period of technical innovation. Producers' goods, moreover, are not only required for the production of other producers' or of consumers' goods, but also for defence. At present in the U.S.S.R., when a high level of the output of means of production has been reached, means of production produced in ever-increasing quantity should serve directly or indirectly to the development and expansion of consumer-good production. If in the U.S.S.R. it has not yet been possible to bring together the rate of growth of producers' and of consumers' goods, as envisaged in the seven-year plan for 1959–65, this is due not to the law of the preferential growth of output of the means of production but to certain exogenous conditions.

In recent years the stock of fixed assets has increased more rapidly than gross national product and the national income ; *i.e.* capital–output ratio rose and the gap in the rate of increase of the output of producers' and of consumers' goods has remained rather considerable. This excessive gap was aggravated by the insufficient development of the raw materials forming the basis for the industrial production of consumers' goods — agricultural produce, synthetic fibres, artificial leather, plastics, etc.

The following factors seem significant if the growth of production of consumers' goods in industry is to be accelerated to parity with that of producers' goods. First, the reduction of the capital–output ratio, particularly by progressive improvements in the branch structure of production ; second, the development of the basic raw materials for agriculture by intensifying agricultural production and by increasing the material incentives for higher production ; third, the acceleration of growth in the chemical industry, supplying agriculture with mineral fertilizers and other chemical means of production, and the production of consumers' goods in industry using all types of modern chemical raw materials ; fourth, the full utilization of productive capacity for consumers' goods in both light and heavy industry ; and fifth, the expansion of the output of equipment for agriculture and for those branches of industry which produce consumers' goods.

Engineering, with its high share in industrial production (about one-fifth) has, and will have in the immediate future, the strongest influence on the preferential growth of the output of producers' goods. Its more rapid expansion is necessary for the replacement of outworn and obsolete equipment, and for the complex mechanization and automation of a number of processes in all branches of the national economy, for the development of the chemical industry and other producers' goods and for the intensification of agriculture. The alignment of rates of growth of producers' and consumers' goods should contribute to the speedier establishment of the material and technical basis of communism and to a more rapid rise in urban and rural living standards.

The existence of the world socialist economic system also has some bearing on the action of the law of preferential growth of the output of means of production. When industrialization is being carried out in a single socialist country and heavy industry is being developed, the priority growth of the output of means of production is inevitable. On the basis created by industrialization, the problem of which branches it is expedient to develop faster in any country should be solved in the light of the economic advantages available through the international socialist division of labour. The necessary systematic proportionality of the development of social production is hence to be ensured on the scale of the entire world socialist economic system.

Chapter 8

PROBLEMS OF REGIONAL PLANNING IN CZECHOSLOVAKIA AND OF RESEARCH INTO REGIONAL MODELS

BY

J. FERIANC

Higher School of Economics, Bratislava

THE NEW CONCEPT OF REGIONAL DEVELOPMENT POLICY

INTEREST in regional planning and the location of production has greatly grown throughout the world in the last decade. Apart from the concern with regional economics which follows from the increasing study of economic development, this enhanced attention may perhaps be attributed to the possibility now opened of solving complex problems of regional development with the use of mathematical models employing contemporary computer technology, and of deriving therefrom new conclusions permitting the elaboration of a theory of regional economic growth. This paper deals with these developments as they can be applied to socialist conditions.

Development under capitalism has tended to be regionally unequal, growth being concentrated in some areas, the labour force and population of which expand and enjoy higher standards of living, while other regions lag behind and even retrogress. Marxist-Leninist analysis recognizes unequal political and economic development as a logical concomitant of capitalism and suggests that the differentiation of personal consumption increases with time. Certainly this was the case in inter-war Czechoslovakia.

Since the War, with the start of a socialist economy, the backwardness of economic regions has begun to be overcome; regional consumption levels have tended to converge more rapidly than those of production by virtue of an increased centralization of income distribution. In barely twenty years Slovakia has changed from a dominantly agricultural to an industrially developed region, while its agriculture, transformed into socialist units, has enlarged output

99

by more than 40 per cent. The same trend towards equality can also be discerned among the eleven administrative regions into which Czechoslovakia is divided.

This is not of course to say that economic equality has been achieved and that problems do not still remain : the concentration of the fuel and power sector and of raw-material extraction into certain zones and the inadequate division of labour with other socialist countries have resulted in great differences in regional production and *per capita* income. The effect of the first of these factors can be attenuated by the reduction of transport costs under new techniques of shipment and transmission. Electric power, crude oil, gas, and other products can now be carried efficiently over thousands of kilometres and regions are no longer as dependent on nearby sources of energy as they were in the past. The present development of the chemical industry — in Czechoslovakia, as in the other socialist countries — permits the exploitation of raw materials in regions which do not have the resources for the industries which hitherto were at the core of development. The extension of higher specialized and general education, the dispersion of scientific and research institutions and of cultural amenities, and the broad improvement of labour skills have formed the foundation for regional equality.

At the same time, the microeconomic conditions which supported regional dispersion in the past — the small-scale processing of local materials — have yielded to large-scale production intricately dependent on resources farther afield — at home or abroad. The increase in these direct and indirect dependencies has posed the problem — new for Czechoslovakia — of assuring the proportionate location of a multitude of specialized branches and of optimizing their interdependence both within a region and on a national scale. A quite different type of region has to emerge in such circumstances, which assures the intensification of specialization, co-operation, and concentration in production. The old concept of helping backward at the expense of developed regions is no longer tenable : the progress of the former is intimately linked with that of the latter and can only be achieved by integrating regions. Producers of goods and services within such a region would have inward and outward flows both within and outside its region ; these flows will increase relatively to value-added but neither intra- nor inter-regional transactions would be *prima facie* preferable. This applies also to the highest stage of this interconnexion of regions — flows across the frontiers of individual countries in international integration. Bilateral and multilateral co-operation is fostering such exchanges among economies of the socialist system, and can be used to promote changes in the economic structure of backward regions. Slovakia is a case in point, for the iron and steel industry being built up in the East-Slovakian region serves markets abroad, while irrigation is being developed to intensify agriculture for home consumption.

THE MEASUREMENT OF REGIONAL DEPENDENCE

The degree of intra- and inter-regional dependence may be determined from the technical coefficients of specific branches in regional input-output tables. The relevant Czechoslovak work is not yet complete, and, for the present, examples must be taken from other countries. Thus, regional input-output tables (of 250 branches) for each of the three Baltic Republics of the U.S.S.R. showed a higher degree of dependence in Estonia and Latvia — the two more-developed republics — on the group of three than in Lithuania. These two republics also had a higher dependence on the other regions of the U.S.S.R. than had Lithuania. The State of California in the U.S.A., Lorraine in France, and the Stockholm region in Sweden are similar examples in other countries.

Regions thus integrated with others enjoy the economies of scale of regional specialization, which may be carried to the point of determining the character of the entire region. This concentration has long been the case in Czechoslovakia, in the North-Moravian and the North-Bohemian regions, and similar effects are to be seen in developing regions — on metals in the East-Slovakian region and on chemicals in the West-Slovakian region : it is shown in higher inter-branch and inter-regional flow coefficients and bigger ratios of final product to aggregate sales.

The production economies of regional concentration are of course accompanied by diseconomies in transport costs, and dozens of optimization models, maximizing the one and minimizing the other have been elaborated : they are, however, nearly all for a single product or group of closely-connected products with a high weight-to-value ratio.

The attraction of a highly-developed region is considerable : there is an infra-structure for further industrial development and conditions of living, cultural amenities and the way of life as a whole act with magnetic attraction — and continue to do so even when their rate of production and investment is slower than that of back-ward regions. These factors must be accounted for in the optimality criteria (and the objective function thence derived) in long-run perspective planning, and will be discussed at the end of this paper.

UNRESOLVED PROBLEMS IN CZECHOSLOVAKIA

As Table 1 shows, Slovakia is more developed in relation to the Czech lands than it was just before the War : it has, moreover, a number of industrial branches with a higher degree of concentration than in Bohemia. But many unsolved problems of Slovak develop-ment persist, not only because the country as a whole has difficulty in mobilizing the means for economic development, but also be-cause regional economic theory and planning methods of regional development are deficient.

TABLE 1

PERCENTAGE OF SLOVAKIA IN SELECTED CZECHOSLOVAK AGGREGATES

	1937	1964
Population	24·5	30·8
Global industrial production	7·3	19·0
Global agricultural production	23·0	29·9
Volume of work by building organizations	28·1	30·8
Retail sales	19·7	25·4

Some Czechoslovak observers have contended that the country should hardly be concerned with regional development, which is important mainly in the so-called 'large-space economies', such as the U.S.S.R. or the U.S.A. Few economists expressed this view in writing, but it was frequently implicit in planning practice.

It is not of course easy to reconcile the objective of using the under-employed resources of a region — as expressed, say, by data on manpower (total and industrial), stock of fixed assets and personal consumption — with that of maximizing the mean national pro-ductivity (minimizing production and transport costs) within a specific horizon. That the solution has not yet been found in Czechoslovakia is demonstrable from the disparity of certain key parameters among its eleven regions. In 1964 the percentage of industrial employment in the total for the socialist sector (excluding co-operative farms) varied in the regions from 31 (Eastern Slovakia) to 57 (Northern Moravia) ; two regions had as little as $3\frac{1}{2}$ per cent of industrial employment (Southern Bohemia and Eastern Slovakia) while another had $17\frac{1}{2}$ per cent (Northern Moravia). The regional percentage shares of industrial fixed assets ranged from 3 to 19. The value of agricultural production per hectare of agricultural land (on average 6,602 Kcs.) varied by region from 3,274 Kcs. to 7,128 Kcs. A detailed analysis of the extent to which this is attributable to the natural endowment is beyond the framework of this paper.

Much greater opportunities for industrial employment in some regions have denuded others of labour — predominantly male — in branches with inferior conditions of work (agriculture, building, and transport). The regions thereby left with a work-force distorted in sex and age composition can only fully employ the remainder at a high capital-to-labour ratio, notably by modernising and reconstructing obsolete plants. At the same time, the demographic age-pyramid must be influenced by economic and organisational measures to assure the reproduction of the local working population. In other regions there is still scope for fuller industrial employment.

For several years Czechoslovakia has been investing in areas with an insufficient labour force ; since, furthermore, the less-developed regions have a more rapid growth of population, labour has been migrating to the more developed areas. Investments have, moreover, been excessively dispersed in the lower-priority sectors of industry and in agriculture. Production is scattered among many isolated plants and factories, each having too broad a product-mix. Despite some measures in the past ten years to encourage concentration, it is still the case that similar production is undertaken in most of the eleven regions, especially in electrical and general engineering, furniture-making, textiles, food-processing, consumer manufactures, and agriculture. The same is true even of weight-losing products which should be processed within the region itself (*e.g.* beet for sugar, hops for beer, etc.). Protracted and uneconomic transport — and even cross-hauls — take place of sugar-beet, timber, cellulose, glass, etc. : capacities are not harmonized or linked, such specialization as operates is irrational, and marketing is badly designed. There is insufficient co-operation between centrally-controlled enterprises and those (accounting for about one-third of production) administered by local government. Admittedly, some of the problems — notably the distribution of sugar refining, furniture-making, and many branches of engineering — are a heritage from before the war, and their solution required more investment than the country, rapidly developing as it was, could spare : reconstruction and modernization are needed for whole branches of industry, especially in consumer manufactures and food-processing. A long-run programme is necessary, if possible associated with bilateral and multilateral co-operation among socialist countries.

SHORTCOMINGS IN PLAN TECHNIQUE

Other problems have been caused by imperfect and over-simplified methods of planning. It has happened that investment projects and programmes of industrial development have, in practice, been evaluated without considering all the important regional aspects. The comprehensive economic analysis of the proportions of development of individual regions has been lacking, *e.g.* of the ratio of productive to final consumption ; of inter-branch relations in industry and agriculture ; and of the correlation between productive and non-productive activities in a region (*i.e.* of material product on the one side and health services, schooling, research, and cultural services on the other). Tables of inter-regional flows of products have been constructed for only a few products (such as building materials and electrical energy) ; there has been no investigation of the regional origin of exports or the regional end-use of imports, and only the crudest balance is available of the distribution and re-distribution of final production and income.

The methods of planning and control management used today fail to solve the problems just mentioned because they neither collect nor analyse the appropriate data. Research has nevertheless been proceeding satisfactorily in the past ten years, and models of regional and interregional relations have been elaborated. The first generation of models simply characterized (on the structural analysis method) the inter-branch flows, mainly on the basis of commercial transactions. The second generation of work used linear programming for individual, or a small group of, products. The present round of research — still only exploratory — is intended to demonstrate regional development as a whole and to find rational solutions to intra- and inter-regional flows for a large number of branches. At this point the simplification to product flows has been abandoned, and macroeconomic programmes can be set up, including the regional patterns of the distribution and redistribution of income and structural changes in personal and social consumption. Some extremely interesting models of this type have recently appeared in the U.S.S.R. capable of dynamization, and static models in other countries have been quantified. As a result of the empirical data obtained, regional development is clearly placed in the context of economic growth. What remains is to apply the knowledge of these relationships within a theory of regional economic development ; the concepts hitherto put forward do not respond to practical requirements.

Economists in the West have sought to explain regional economic development in terms either of the 'export basis' or the 'sector'. The theory of the 'export basis' ascribes the key role to export branches and services : investments flowing into export branches and activities lead to a further development of related branches and activities in the given region. The 'sector' theory, evolved from the empirical observations of Colin Clark and Allan G. Fisher, explains — in application to regional development — the causes of development as follows. The increased income per inhabitant is accompanied by a decrease in the share in labour employed in agriculture and an increase in the share of labour in the tertiary sector. The main cause of this change is found in the elasticity of income (the demand for food increasing more rapidly than income per head), and in differentiated movements of labour productivity (increasing productivity of agriculture being attained by decreasing manpower, by the use of machinery, or by the improvement of soil fertility or of farm techniques). The dynamics of economic development are thus the consequence of two changes — in income *per capita* and in productivity.

The present writer believes that these theories are only partial. That 'export basis' may be adequate when a new source of development is found in the region (the discovery of gas, oil, or useful minerals). Similarly, the 'sector' theory may explain certain aspects or phases of economic development, that, for example, industrializing a predominantly agricultural region. Neither, however, explain the dynamics of economic development in causal terms, for each lacks a social and economic basis upon which the economic development of a region is founded. They do not, for instance, answer the question of why in Brazil, for example, the industrialization programmes for several states (Santa Catarina, Rio Grande do Sul, and Paraná) remain in the formal stage or why Slovakia was, on the eve of the Second World War, behind Bohemia (according to the postwar estimates, when the industrialization programme for Slovakia was worked out) : what was the reason, in particular, for the decline of Slovak industry and for its expansion since the war ?

THE REQUIREMENTS OF REGIONAL-DEVELOPMENT THEORY

For the present writer an explanation of the economic development of a region requires, first, the analysis of qualitative production relations, viz. of the motive forces of economic development under laws of its form of production, and secondly, a disaggregation of the factors currently affecting productive forces (the degrees of convergence and integration), amplified by a quantitative expression of their dynamics in the form of an objective function, within the internal and external constraints.

The solution to these two aspects of regional development could form a theoretical basis for efficient regional planning and management : its importance will be the greater, the more convergent and integrated is the region. It would thus be more significant in an intensively-developed economy within a small territory, than in a less-intensively developed but larger area. The complex of natural, geographic, technological, economic, demographic, ethnic, and other factors which affect the dynamics of economic development cannot be solved in regional planning by the simple methods which have prevailed until now. Crude projections ignore the likelihood that these factors operate in opposite directions, the net effect of which could be exhibited by the tools of mathematical economics.

Of such instruments, multi-factor analysis offers the most scope for constructing models of regional development, but it cannot be limited to production factors, for account must be taken in its critical function of the objectives of the social system. It is precisely this aspect on which Soviet research has most to contribute. The essentials are that a complex personal and social consumption function be maximized (with spatial variants appropriately differentiated and a suitable time-preference), and that marginal social opportunity costs be fully represented. Such costs must properly demonstrate marginal scarcities within a more precise formulation of the marxist theory of value and of prices.

As the gap in fundamental theoretical research is filled, so will the two main problems of developing regional models come under real measurement and practical solution.

Chapter 9

SUMMARY RECORD OF THE DISCUSSION
— SESSION II

THE RATE OF DEVELOPMENT AND REGIONAL
PROBLEMS

(In the Chair : PROFESSOR ROBINSON)

Professor Domar opened the discussion with the hope that the foundation of goodwill laid by Professor Robinson was strong enough to stand
some stress.   His intention was not merely to report on the papers under
discussion, but to make some critical remarks about them and even to pick
a quarrel or two with the authors.

Beginning with Professor Notkin's paper, he agreed with the author's
basic assumption that consumption should be the final purpose of economic activity, while investment should be merely an instrument for
increasing future consumption.   The main purpose of the paper was the
determination of the optimal rate of capital accumulation, or, more
precisely, of the fraction of national product to be invested in productive
industry (indicated by the symbol a).   Western economic usage employed
the ratio of total investment to national product, but the difference was
unimportant for the present discussion.   This determination of an
optimum a had been a rather popular subject in economic literature,
beginning at least with the classical work of the English economist Ramsey
in 1928 ;   recently it had been dealt with by the Indian economists Sen
and Chakravarty, the American Koopmans and many others.[1]   Professor
Notkin's paper had the advantage, as compared with the others, of
simplicity, though its scope was more limited.   Professor Notkin divided
his a by the marginal capital–output ratio, which he termed capital
efficiency (indicated here by v).   The ratio a/v was the relative rate of
growth of national product which he used in his quest for the optimum

---

[1] F. P. Ramsey, 'A Mathematical Theory of Saving', *Economic Journal*, Decem-
ber 1928, pp. 543–559 ;   A. K. Sen, 'On Optimising the Rate of Saving', *ibid.*,
September 1961, pp. 479-496 ;   S. Chakravarty, 'The Existence of an Optimum
Savings Program', *Econometrica*, January 1962, pp. 178–187 ;   also his 'Optimal
Savings with Finite Planning Horizon', *International Economic Review*, September
1962, pp. 338–355 ;   T. C. Koopmans, 'On the Concept of Optimal Economic
Growth', in *Le Rôle de l'analyse économétrique dans la formulation de plans de
développement*, vol. 28, part I in the series *Scripta Varia* (Pontificia Academia
Scientarum, Vatican City, 1965), pp. 225–287.

a. This formulation would be familiar to Western economists — one of its originators, Sir Roy Harrod, was among the Conference participants. A model similar to Professor Notkin's but much more fully developed, had been published by the Soviet economist Feldman in the Soviet journal, *Planovoe khozyaistvo*, as early as 1928.[1] Feldman's work had been taken up in America, England, India, Japan, Poland, Czechoslovakia, and in many other countries, although, puzzlingly, Domar had never seen any references to him in Soviet economic literature.

Professor Notkin considered first a rising, then a constant, and finally a falling *a*, and found — again correctly — that the optimum *a* depended on the time horizon of the decision-makers. The longer the horizon, the more would a rising *a* justify itself. This treatment should be extended not only to the rate of change of *a* but to the magnitude of *a* itself. Again, the longer the time horizon, the higher would be the optimal magnitude of *a*, provided that a larger *a* did not increase *v*. It was unlikely, however, that the magnitude of *v* would remain constant irrespective of the size of *a*. Recent studies carried out in the United States by Kendrick, Abramovitz, Solow, and others had thrown serious doubt on such a simple relation between the rate of growth of output and the rate of capital accumulation.[2] Other factors, such as the growth of the labour force, changes in its quality, technological and managerial progress, economies of scale, etc. played their roles. Professor Notkin was aware of these considerations. According to his own calculations, the Soviet *v* had indeed been increasing, a characteristic confirmed by Bergson and other American scholars working in Soviet economics. Perhaps this phenomenon had been caused by too large an *a* in the Soviet economy. If so, the optimum *a* was likely to be lower than Professor Notkin seemed to suggest, but his model was too simple for the determination of the optimal magnitude of *a* under more realistic conditions.

Turning to Professor Mateev's paper, Professor Domar regretted that, although very interesting, it was rather too technical for a brief oral presentation. He would, however, seek to comment on its main ideas without excessive detail. As he saw it, the purpose of the paper was the establishment of correct prices and correct investment criteria in order to achieve an optimal allocation of resources. Professor Mateev was not concerned with the definition of the optimum itself, nor, more particularly,

[1] G. A. Feldman, 'On the Theory of Rates of Growth of National Income', *Planovoe khozyaistvo*, November 1928, No. 11, pp. 146–170 and December 1928, No. 12, pp. 151–178.
[2] J. W. Kendrick, *Productivity Trends in the United States*, New York, 1961; M. Abromovitz, 'Resource and Output Trends in the United States since 1870', *American Economic Review*, May 1956, pp. 5–23, reprinted as National Bureau of Economic Research, Occasional Paper 52, New York, 1956 ; R. M. Solow, 'Technical Change and the Aggregate Production Function', *Review of Economics and Statistics*, August 1957, pp. 312–320.

with the so-called index-number problem which was inherent in the choice of the optimum. He used the input-output method in order to find what he termed 'normative prices', and was willing to allow actual prices to deviate from them in response to supply and demand conditions. In the first part of his paper, Professor Mateev defined four value-aggregates to which a rate of profit could be applied. He rejected the calculation of profit on three of these, viz. cost of labour and materials ; cost of labour, materials, and the stock of installed capital ; cost of labour, materials, and capital, the latter being represented not by its stock but by its turnover. Finally, he applied the profit rate to labour cost only and emerged with what he regarded as the correct method because the rate of profit did not appear in relative prices (price ratios), which depended on relative cost of labour and of materials only. In evaluating his argument, it was important to note that he assumed labour to be the only primary input ; also that throughout most of his paper he treated the profit rate as an arbitrary magnitude determined by the state in response to its need for resources for capital accumulation and for the 'non-productive' expenditures (*e.g.* education, public health, etc.), and not at all as a genuine cost of capital corresponding to what was termed in the West its marginal productivity. In other words the profit rate was essentially a kind of excise tax. Under such conditions it might be just as well to keep it out of relative prices, if possible. The latter would then depend only on the cost of materials and labour and would thus equal average prime cost ratios. If the average and marginal cost were not far apart, Professor Mateev's price ratios would approximate the ratios between short-run marginal costs. With this interpretation, and, if used for this purpose, his price ratios made sense. But what about the cost of capital, including both depreciation and interest, so dear to the heart of a Western economist? Surely these should somehow enter the price ratios ; some industries might use little capital, others, a good deal. How would this difference be reflected in Professor Mateev's price ratios ? There was a well-known theorem in economics which stated that past expenditures on capital should not be included in current prices ; and even interest payments, though currently made, were irrelevant if they were independent of output. On the other hand, when decisions about future capital investments were made, all costs, including the cost of capital, should be included in the price. Now it seemed to him that Professor Mateev's method of choosing among investment projects on the basis of their internal rates of return and cutting off those with the lowest rates, for which funds were not available, should assure that a return to capital (depreciation and profit) would indeed be included in prices, provided of course that events came out as expected, or, more precisely, that realized profits were not below those planned. On the other hand, if the future turned out to be disappointing (for instance, if actual demand were less than expected), then prices should be reduced even if the expected profitability of investment was not realized, provided of course that the prime costs of output (labour and materials) were covered. After all, the main function of prices was the rational allocation of resources and not necessarily the compensation for expenditures made in the past.

In the second part of his paper, Professor Mateev had considered choices among alternative investment projects. Professor Domar welcomed his ranking of investment projects by their expected rates of return (passing over controversies in this field), from the list of which were selected the best until the funds available were exhausted. He found this similar to the technique advocated by Lange in *On the Economic Theory of Socialism*.[1] He was nevertheless surprised at the formula which Professor Mateev used to determine what he called the coefficient of efficiency, namely the well-known expression :

$$\frac{\text{Cost}_1 - \text{Cost}_2}{\text{Capital}_2 - \text{Capital}_1}.$$

This rather crude formula disregarded the time pattern of revenues and expenditures and the expected duration of the project. It was frequently used in practice to obtain a rough approximation of a project's profitability, but surely it had no place in a paper as sophisticated as Professor Mateev's.

He hoped that other interesting points raised by Professor Mateev's paper would be taken up in discussion, such as the usefulness of the input-output method based on *average* input coefficients in the determination of prices. What, for instance, happened if there were considerable variability in the costs of the several enterprises in a given industry? How would actual demand conditions be taken into account? But there were many others.

Professor Domar concluded with a review of the paper by Dr. Ferianc. Its subject was the development of backward regions, a problem common to many countries as well as to Czechoslovakia. The basic question it raised was whether capital should be moved to the backward region or whether its people should be encouraged to migrate to more developed areas, provided of course jobs for them were made available. Historically, both movements had often taken place. Because of differences between private and social benefits and the like, it was quite difficult to decide in practice which of the methods should be used. He took the basic purposes of regional development to be : first, to remove non-economic obstacles to the rational division of labour and to the proper allocation of resources in general ; in the West this was frequently referred to as the 'Big Push' and associated with the name of Rosenstein-Rodan after his classic article of 1943 ; [2] second, to maximize the output of the whole economy

[1] O. Lange and F. M. Taylor, *On the Economic Theory of Socialism*, Minneapolis, Minn., 1938.

[2] P. N. Rosenstein-Rodan, 'Problems of Industrialization of Eastern and South-Eastern Europe', *Economic Journal*, June–September, 1943, pp. 202–211.

Summary Record of the Discussion

and to bring about greater equality in living standards, etc. Unfortunately, these objectives might at times contradict each other ; their reconciliation was as much, if not more, a political rather than a purely economic question. The author had given a number of examples of poor regional planning in his own country. Professor Domar had no basic disagreement with those ideas and wished Czechoslovakia better luck in the future.

Professor Notkin, in reply, felt that Professor Domar might have been making too much of the formula a/v : it was well known in the process of planning and he had neither made special mention of it in his paper nor assumed authorship of it. He had used it only indirectly in calculating the efficiency of accumulation. The rate of growth of national income, $t = a/v$, was solved for v, the coefficient of efficiency of accumulation $(v = a/t)$. All were rather simple arithmetical manipulations, and he could hardly believe that Sir Roy Harrod thought that his own use of a similar presentation was a significant part of his important work on the theory of economic growth. Nor, he was sure, had Feldman considered this element to be the crux of his study. He had put forward a more general formula giving the balanced equality on which the utilization of resources in a socialist economy was based :

$$ t = \frac{\phi_1 \beta_1}{\phi \beta} = \frac{\rho_1 \gamma_1}{\rho \gamma}, $$

where ϕ and ϕ_1 were the productive funds in the base and succeeding periods, β and β_1 were the coefficients of their utilization; ρ and ρ_1 represented the labour force in those periods; and γ and γ_1 represented the productivity of labour. For a planned economy, this formula had all the more significance because, under full utilization of resources, it was absolutely essential to balance the material and labour resources of production of development.

Professor Notkin denied Professor Domar's claim that his model neglected efficiency. There was a hypothetically constant coefficient of efficiency in the model, and, later in the paper, the factors causing a change in the coefficient of efficiency of accumulation were considered. The movement of this coefficient was related to the dynamics of national product and the connexion between the coefficients was considered in detail. Moreover, if a personal note was permitted, he had himself examined this in a paper published twenty years previously and developing the pioneering paper by Cobb and Douglas before the other studies to which Professor Domar had referred.[1]

Finally, he emphasized that, in contrast to many Western economists, he had been investigating the norm of productive accumulation, and not

[1] C. W. Cobb and P. H. Douglas, 'A Theory of Production', *American Economic Review*, March, 1928, pp. 139–165 ; A. I. Notkin, 'Technological Progress and the Growth of Production', *Izvestiya otdeleniya ekonomiki i prava Akademii Nauk SSSR*, no. 2, 1946, pp. 145–168.

aggregate accumulation, because the rate of growth depended on the former.

Professor Rachmuth took it for granted that Marxist economists were agreed on the necessity for an equalization of economic levels, both between and within socialist countries. He therefore proposed to consider those characteristics of less-developed countries which allowed them scope for more rapid growth rates than the developed nations.

He pointed first to the essential implication of under-development, viz. that the country was not fully exploiting its resources. It was hence the increased utilization of natural resources under planned industrialization which permitted the attainment of higher rates of development than in more advanced countries. Of the resources to be drawn into production, one of the crucial problems related to the use of labour. The manpower must be drawn from agriculture while assuring an increase in the productivity of farm labour. One-third of the aggregate rise in Rumanian labour productivity between 1955 and 1960 had been due to the structural change of employment. A socialist planned economy could use these transfers as a positive instrument in shaping industrialization and — replying to Professor Jeanneney's query of the day before — providing for an appropriate expansion of the tertiary sector. Finally, countries just beginning to industrialize could take over advanced technology from the more developed countries ; because their capital stock would have a much smaller share of less-efficient equipment than the developed economies they could attain higher rates of productivity growth. He felt that Rumania was an eloquent example of the use of these advantages : over the past fifteen years the capital–output ratio had been declining.

Dr. Kyn observed that Czechoslovak economists were now less concerned with analysing the factors in the very fast postwar growth of Czechoslovak industry and were more concerned with identifying the causes of the recent deceleration. Putting the problem in terms of Professor Notkin's paper, he would suggest that, of the two factors determining the rate of growth, the rate of accumulation a and the capital–output ratio v, the difficulties lay in the latter. Professor Notkin's emphasis on the influence of the rate of accumulation on growth was misplaced because the largest of investment outlays could be inefficiently spent : it was rather the capital–output ratio which demonstrated the efficiency of the allocation of investment. The majority of economists in Czechoslovakia had now come to the conclusion that the limiting factor in economic development in their country was the system of planning and management, and not the rate of accumulation. As Dr. Novozámsky had pointed out the previous day, mistakes had been made in the structural composition of new capacity. This misallocation of investment had generated the disproportions which were at the root of the slow rate of Czechoslovak growth. The trouble had been perceived for several years, but only recently had it been generally realized that the old systems of planning and management were incapable of adopting corrective measures. The reform of economic management would have to change the administrative structure, the system of information flows, and the criteria for managerial decision-making.

Mr. Nikiforov took issue with Professor Notkin's use of a reproductive cycle as the time-horizon for planning. Such a time span — Professor Notkin saw it as nine or ten years — was useful from the standpoint of the production process, for it was something like the period that elapsed between opening up new deposits of fuel and the delivery of consumers' goods based upon the engineering industry developed on the enlarged energy base. Too short a plan horizon would not allow for externalities. Nevertheless, consumers were not indifferent between a steady growth of welfare and an alternation of improvement with zero or negative gain. The use of any time-horizon was open to the maximization of consumption in the final year, followed by a possible fall in the year following. It seemed to him best if planned development aimed at a stable expansion of consumption. Since this objective would imply a projection of consumption beyond the limit of the reproductive cycle, there was no guarantee that the investment decisions now being taken would assure a long-term rate of consumption growth. This could lead planners to attempt to forecast still further ahead, but the longer the projection the less accurate was the plan.

Professor Grossman said that Mr. Nikiforov had already dealt with the point he would have made on the optimal allocation of national income between investment and consumption. He would nevertheless like to take the argument back a stage further. There was no rigorous definition of the concept of the optimum and he himself was unable to produce one. An arbitrary optimum could always be taken from a long-range target and empirically-derived coefficients which determined the required level of investment in each sub-period. Alternatively, one could proceed with Professor Notkin and attempt to determine the 'best' rate of investment over the medium term, *i.e.* nine to ten years ; again, he did not see how this could be considered an optimum. Professor Notkin's time-horizon was an instrument for measuring the weight of benefits today against benefits tomorrow, but in the last resort the ultimate decision was a political one. It was not the function of the economist to state categorically how much the present generation had to sacrifice for the next generation.

Professor Stojanovic commented that particular attention should be paid to Professor Notkin's point that optimal ratios of accumulation and consumption should not be decided on for random periods, but, rather, over a cycle of expanding reproduction or — as she and Professor Cobeljic termed it in their paper — the investment cycle. Such timing would yield optimal rates for the medium run. However, there remained the problem of finding these ratios for the long run, which could not be taken as the sum of averages for medium-term periods. She agreed with Mr. Nikiforov that optimal relations within an investment cycle would not take account of the post-horizon rate of growth. Further, she believed that the movement of these ratios during the investment cycle should be treated in relation to the development of producers' and consumers' goods, viz. Departments I and II in Marx's terminology. Since the growth of I and II might not be the same for each year in the cycle, because the incidence of technical progress was uneven, the movements of accumulation and consumption rates could not be uniform, as Professor Notkin contended. It was necessary to break up the cycle into two phases : first, the period when the stress was on the installation of new productive capacity and, consequently, the more rapid growth of Department I ; and, second, the period when the rate of growth of Department II was accelerated. The length of these periods depended on the rate of technical progress.

Professor Dupriez linked his comments on Professor Notkin's paper with those which had been made by Professor Grossman. He wondered whether Professor Notkin's dynamic stages in 'socialist transformation' were intended as the benchmarks of institutional change or simply as periods of increasing affluence. The latter interpretation implied that the optimization of accumulation to consumption was the same objective function in both liberal and socialist economies ; the divergence between systems was radical in the techniques of implementation adopted and in the principles whereby product was distributed. He noticed a similarity between Professor Notkin's 'norms' and the equilibrium level of output under full employment. This did not imply that growth had not been a preoccupation among Marxist economists for far longer than it had occupied the attention of their colleagues in the mainstream of Western thought. It had been a Marxist, Rosa Luxembourg, who had identified the problem of over-production by entrepreneurs, the 'over-capitalization' which led to imperialism as a 'higher stage of capitalism'.

He wondered, on the other hand, whether the Marxist analysis of the production boundary of national income relevant to growth was not still influenced by the views of nineteenth-century bourgeois economists. Marx, in common with our predecessors of a century ago, insisted on the productive impact of material goods ; Western economists today not only saw services as a constituent of production but as wholly new forms of consumption. Finally, he joined in the queries to participants from socialist countries on the practical utility of the concepts of 'heavy' and 'light' industry : consumers' goods were not necessarily light industry nor were producers' goods all heavy industry.

Professor Notkin termed Professor Grossman an agnostic in claiming that the economic optimum had to be selected on political grounds. It was the task of the economist to formulate the constraints within which the political authorities decided how much and what the present generation should sacrifice for future beneficiaries. The government was as much bound by economic circumstances as the professional analyst : even the President of the United States found it useful to have professional advice from his Council of Economic Advisers. Still more so had economics an important place in decision-making.

He welcomed Professor Dupriez's attempt to classify the conditions for optimization into those which were similar in the two systems and those which differed. The economist studying the capitalist system had to evolve a formula or construct an econometric model which combined growth with fluctuation ; projection for a planned economy could be limited to the factors in growth.

Mr. Nikiforov and Professor Stojanovic had argued that an objective approach was needed to define the period for which the optimum was chosen. He was happy that Professor Stojanovic had recognized the advantage of his principle of a technically-defined reproductive cycle, but he disagreed with Mr. Nikiforov that the consumption maximum for the period had to be constrained to a monotonic rate. Such a constraint was not feasible, for each maximand required entirely different movements of the norm of productive accumulation.

Professor Stojanovic had contended that, for anything like a ten- or, still more, a twenty-year cycle with a high rate of growth, there would be an initial period showing a more rapid expansion of Department I followed by the residual period in which the rate of growth of Department II would increase. This was not necessary if a highly-developed industrial structure had already been attained.

Sir Roy Harrod raised two points concerning Professor Mateev's paper, the first seeking confirmation of his interpretation of the rate of profit and the turnover tax, which he believed to be wider than that expressed by Professor Domar. Both, to his understanding, were designed to provide funds for capital accumulation and for the general purposes of government. But the profit rate also had the function of altering prices away from direct proportionality to the amount of current labour to that sum of embodied labour (*i.e.* capital) and current labour which the production of each commodity required. This appeared to him to be the relationship outlined by Marx in Volume III of *Das Kapital*. Thus, a change in the turnover tax to provide extra funds should not alter relative prices, while a change in the profit rate should, if the rate of profit were designed to achieve the purpose explained by Marx. Accordingly, among the formulae offered by Professor Mateev, one should choose that which effectively altered relative prices when the rate of profit was changed.

His second point concerned the imputation problem created by Professor Mateev in his proposal that 'workers, especially those employed in the scientific and technical organizations . . . should be remunerated in a precise relationship with their actual contribution' (pp. 72-73). This was a fine idea and presumably socialist in intention, but there were difficulties in practice. It involved 'imputing' parts of a total product to the different elements responsible for its production. Classical economists held that this could only be achieved by applying the principles of marginalism. These principles were notoriously difficult to apply in practical cost accountancy. But they might be applied indirectly by the process of trial and error. If an article could not be produced in sufficient quantities to meet consumers' desires owing to lack of specific skilled personnel, this could be overcome by bidding up the pay of personnel of that type. Equilibrium would thus be reached, the official price being somewhat raised in accordance with the high cost due to the higher pay for the special personnel. But the question arose of how quickly an adjustment was desired. This was related to the problem of long- and short-period costs, as propounded by the English economist Alfred Marshall. He believed that socialist economists tended to confine their reading of English economists to pre-Marxian authors : but Marshall was worth studying in this connexion.

Professor Domar was prompted by Sir Roy Harrod's comment to consider the place of a capital charge in price. Evidently, before the construction of a unit of capital, its value had to be included in the marginal cost, usually by the computation of an internal rate of return or a present discounted value of the project. If, after construction, expectations held during the planning stage were realized, the planned price would be charged, *i.e.* including capital cost. But, if the demand for the product should unexpectedly fall, the mere fact that a certain amount had been invested in capital earlier was not relevant to the present price. The product would be worth producing even if price covered only prime cost of labour and materials, including some depreciation due to use of the capital asset. Conversely, if demand should rise above expectations, the price should be increased even if it covered much more than the prime cost and the cost of capital. There were, of course, a number of qualifications in practice which did not need to be discussed in this context.

This did not mean that a capital charge should be ignored when evaluating the operation of an enterprise, for to do so would deprive it of the incentive to economize on capital. He believed that the absence of a capital charge in the Soviet Union conduced to an excessively high level of enterprise inventories.

Dr. Kyn said that Czechoslovak economists were vigorously debating the suitability of formulae for price formation : although there was not yet consensus, the majority had concluded, contrary to the position held by Professor Mateev, that the most appropriate was 'production price' (with rent added in the case of scarce natural resources). He would add to Professor Mateev's formulae the possibility of using dual variables (shadow prices) in an explicitly-formulated linear programming problem. In Czechoslovakia a small experimental model of linear programming had yielded interesting theoretical results. It had been found that, if the only limiting factor in the system was labour, shadow prices were proportional to values according to the labour theory of value; if the limiting factors of capital and natural resources were also taken into account, a static model yielded a monopoly price of the type analysed by Cournot; in a dynamic model of the Kantorovich type, allocating investment according to the efficiency of capital in every period, a long-term tendency emerged to equalize profit rates. This was in fact a model of the process described by Marx in Volume III of *Das Kapital*. Rent appeared with non-reproducible resources. It was interesting to note that this approach had a number of similarities with marginalist concepts.

He did not agree with Professor Mateev that the only criterion for choosing a 'normal' price was an objectively correct measurement of the results of production. In his own opinion, this criterion was quite secondary from the point of view of the choice of a type of price. It was surely necessary that a 'normal' price be an equilibrium price in the given economic system, and in this context the problem of choosing a price formula was directly related to the problem of the type of incentives used. But the problem of measuring the results of production could not be limited to the choice of prices. The ultimate measure of production efficiency was the utility of the product, viz. the extent to which it satisfied the consumer. No measure of the results of production was satisfactory without reference to consumer preferences, and hence without a theory of consumer behaviour.

Professor Mateev had raised the question of centralization and decentralization, rightly concluding that complete centralization of economic decision-making was impossible. He opposed, however, the spontaneous operation of the market mechanism, but did not make it clear where he saw a solution. He hoped that Professor Mateev's colleagues could throw light on current Bulgarian thinking on the degree of centralization.

Dr. Ophir remarked that the first part of the paper by Professor Mateev was closely related to Session V on price systems: he would hence confine himself to points already raised. He disagreed with Professor Domar's last remark about marginal costs: when the system was reasonably close to equilibrium, marginal cost was better approximated by full cost (including a charge for the use of capital) than by average variable cost (measured as the input of labour and material). He had had the same difficulty as Sir Roy Harrod with Professor Mateev's coefficient r, though he had reached a somewhat different conclusion. r seemed to be best considered a tax, and not a profit rate: Professor Mateev had assigned it the macroeconomic role of regulating aggregate consumption. Hence the comparison with capitalist enterprises (p. 78) was misleading. Professor Mateev was rightly concerned at the multiple taxation inherent in the pricing methods of type II, due to the distortion of relative prices. One solution to this difficulty, not mentioned by Professor Mateev, was the well-known turnover tax levied only at the stage of the final sale to consumers. Another solution was Professor Mateev's third pricing formula, which might be termed a tax on value added — of the type being advocated by A. Morag of the Hebrew University, Jerusalem.[1] Pricing formula III should be altered by re-defining value added to include not only labour but also the contribution of capital.

Turning to the third part of Professor Mateev's paper, Dr. Ophir found a shortcoming common to Professor Notkin's paper : in both, the concept was missing of a rate of discount (as employed in the paper by Professors Maksimovic and Pjanic). If Professor Notkin had summed over the present value of future consumption, Professor Grossman would not have looked in vain for a maximand. The coefficient of efficiency as used by Professor Mateev and others served as a surrogate for the internal rate of return in the comparison of alternatives. But it was a crude measure, and, as Professor Domar had pointed out, it could not take into account the length of asset-life and the timing of the benefit stream resulting therefrom. Dr. Ophir urged the socialist economists to accept the concept of the discount rate as one necessary for proper economic analysis and planning. He had purposely refrained from using the term 'interest rate' in order to avoid undesirable connotations. The rate of discount should be regarded as a purely formal concept which might appear as a shadow price in certain mathematical formulations, and which is necessary for the solution of economic problems.

Professor Grossman felt that it was not agnostic, as Professor Notkin had put it, to point out that the economist could not allocate between accumulation and consumption without political guidance : surely the history of the Soviet investment rate was that of political decision. The political process had something of the role of the physician in prescribing a diet restriction : the function of the economist was like that of the patient in choosing the specific foods.

Western estimates of the Soviet rate of investment showed considerable fluctuation during the decade to 1963 : it had declined from 1953 to 1955, had been rising to 1961, and had subsequently been stabilized. He believed that these changes had been made for political reasons and that the political determination of the rate could not be avoided in a socialist economy, especially in the short run. Professor Notkin's attempt in his paper to identify an optimal ratio of accumulation to consumption could not be made realistic without reference to political choice. There was a further divergence from reality in Professor Notkin's model in that he had assumed a stable capital–output ratio. This was of course appropriate for the construction of a theoretical model, but there had been substantial variations in the incremental capital–output ratio in Soviet experience : the marginal productivity of capital had, for example, halved between 1959 and 1963. This was surprising when it was realized that the rate of

[1] A. Morag, *On Taxes and Inflation*, New York, 1965, pp. 127–39.

investment remained more or less stable, that the non-agricultural labour force was rising normally, and that technological opportunities were still ample. Since capital productivity had in fact declined, he would take seriously Professor Sorokin's prognosis that the Soviet rate of growth would begin to rise in the near future, for the high capital–output ratio of recent years represented a 'reserve' for future expansion.

Finally, Professor Grossman queried the relationship which Soviet economists continued to perceive between the producer-good sector of industry and the rate of accumulation. The producer-good sector (termed Group A) was a most heterogeneous category, comprising not only capital goods but also building materials, semi-manufactures, raw materials, and fuel, all of which served either Group A or Group B (final consumers' goods). Was it really the case that Soviet planners continued to use such an aggregative category? If some disaggregated sub-groups were used, he was surprised that data had not been published on them.

Professor Notkin wished to make some corrections to Professor Grossman's statements. First, he took issue with Professor Grossman's claim that capital productivity in the U.S.S.R. had fallen by one-half. The decrease between 1958 and 1962 was only 4 per cent for industrial capital and 11 per cent for the national economy as a whole, due largely to the lag in agricultural production.[1] A number of factors had raised the capital–output ratio in the U.S.S.R., notably the reduction of working hours in industry, construction, and transport, and of the number of shifts worked. Some of the investment in agriculture had substituted for manpower transfers to other sectors. As industrial shift work again began to rise and as agriculture adjusted to a declining labour force, the strong possibility arose of stabilizing, or even reducing, the capital–output ratio.

Professor Grossman had also enquired about the use in Soviet planning of the aggregative categories of Group A and Group B in industry, believing the former to be too heterogeneous to permit a valid relationship with the rate of productive accumulation. Professor Notkin had himself repeatedly proposed the sub-division of Group A, and a step forward had been taken in computing and publishing separate output series of the 'implements of production' and the 'objects of labour', following the classical Marxist terminology.

Professor Oelssner described the reform of management and planning being implemented in the German Democratic Republic (G.D.R.) as a consequence of a government decision taken in July, 1963. It would sharply restrict direct interference in enterprise operation by central government agencies (*e.g.* the State Planning Commission, the Ministry of Finance, and regional authorities). Amalgamations of nationalized enterprises were being created to manage each branch of industry: they

---

[1] Since Professor Grossman had cited a substantial fall in the marginal productivity of capital, his statement was not inconsistent with Professor Notkin's quotation of a small decrease in average productivity (Editor's note).

would embrace only large-scale enterprises, which would remain as independent business entities, operating on the principle of cost accounting. Many enterprises would not be combined into groups, viz. those of local significance, companies in which only half the equity was held by the state, and artisan concerns. Sections would be organized by type of product, in each of which there would be a 'guiding enterprise' to stimulate technical progress, product specialization, and market research in the other enterprises.

Within the framework of a long-term plan formulated by the State Planning Commission, the amalgamation would elaborate its own plan, disaggregated for each of its enterprises. To implement such plans the amalgamation could determine the volume and structure of investment, and its marketing arrangements. It possessed the requisite financial independence for these purposes. The Ministry of Finance had in the past excessively interfered in enterprise finance : because it tended to think in fiscal rather than in economic terms, it had frequently had a negative influence on production.

Under the new system, the director of the amalgamation had complete control over four funds, viz. the 'technological fund', which was exclusively earmarked for the introduction of new techniques, retained profits, a 'credit reserve', and a bonus fund at the disposal of the director of the amalgamation. It was hoped that these funds would endow the amalgamations with considerable financial autonomy. Credit had played a tremendous role in the history of capitalism, and was an instrument to be fully exploited in the socialist system.

Turning from the future to the past, Professor Oelssner observed that economic growth had usually been associated with industrialization ; but, although Germany had long been an industrial nation, the postwar problem of the G.D.R. had been the expansion of industry. The dissolution of the historically-united German economy had left no shipbuilding and little heavy industry in a territory poorly endowed with mineral resources. The key extractive and manufacturing sectors had had first call on investment, and insufficient attention had unavoidably been paid to the other branches of the economy : thus, the sectors, such as agriculture, which had played an important role in the pre-war economy, were now the most backward. The new system had hence the goal of redressing this lag while maintaining rapid development of the major industries.

The priority until now accorded producers' goods had tended to concentrate the attention of planners and managers on their output, to the detriment of distribution and consumption. The new system tried to stress that production was completed only when output was sold, and hence put the responsibility for marketing on the director of the amalgamation.

Professor Oelssner summarized the other characteristics of the economic reform as the centring of the amalgamation and its enterprises on profitability and the consequential reform of the price structure. Wholesale prices had already been raised to cover total cost plus the mean new-investment requirement for the given branch of industry, but the changes were only the first stage of the reform. The eventual aim was a system of price formation based on the marxian labour theory of value; but the practical application was complex: one study group was, for example, trying to evolve a set of prices based upon cumulative labour inputs. A charge for installed capital was a feature of the new practice, and would be paid out of income before the calculation of the profit used as the 'success indicator' for the enterprise.

Mr. Bradistilov believed that the experience of Bulgarian planning confirmed Dr. Ferianc's views. The location of production was an important factor in economic development, and in the present round of economic reform in Eastern Europe the claims of devolution to regions had seriously to be weighed against that to industrial branches. The Czechoslovak reform, as described by Dr. Ferianc, and the changes in the G.D.R. just reviewed by Professor Oelssner, had both opted for the sector. Decentralization along these lines could obscure the economic links between regions and the intersectoral flows which could promote the formation of viable production zones.

Professor Flamant drew a parallel between Eastern and Western Europe in the emergence of regional disequilibrium. In Western Europe unequal rates of regional growth had in some countries, such as France, disrupted the former inter-areal equilibrium, while in others they had been caused by an initial maldistribution of productive resources. Dr. Ferianc's paper had shown that there was a regional problem in Eastern Europe, but neither he nor Mr. Bradistilov had defined the parameters of which regional planning had to take account. If the objective was maximal national growth, regional specialization, as Mr. Bradistilov had said, was appropriate, but it would not necessarily equalize the level of living between regions. On the contrary, pressure for intra-national migration would increase as a consequence of the wage differentials matching local labour supply with the demand under regional specialization. He wondered whether the socialist countries had made studies of the institutional structure or plan disaggregation appropriate to regional development. Had they attempted to measure the benefits of agglomeration (what Alfred Marshall had called external economies) or the costs of dispersion; were there any regional national accounts or other measures of territorial inequality?

Professor Flamant believed these points to be part of the wider field of the spatial economy. The resources of the Eastern European economies were more dispersed than those of Western Europe, as was exemplified by the 2,000-km. rail haul of coal from the Kuzbas to the industrial Urals. The problems were not only those of transport economics but also of welfare. What measure was attempted of the social cost of migration or of the posting to remote districts of highly-skilled manpower, trained in the big industrial centres ?

Professor Robinson intervened to observe that the European Centre for Development (Vienna) had taken regional problems as its main line of research and that the International Economic Association was planning to hold a conference on regional economics in the autumn of 1967.[1]

Professor Jeanneney returned to the confrontation that Professor Notkin's paper had made between capital formation and the growth of product. He found the concept of a technically-defined productive cycle meaningless, since any time-average depended upon the structure of investment chosen. Surely the choice could be made only in terms of time preference : economic calculus was no substitute for the assessment of the psychological and moral determinants. For a government-sponsored plan this implied both political choice and consultation with the electorate, the economist defining the constraints. He pointed out that the French *Commissariat au Plan* elaborated technical variants demonstrating the consumption results of each ; the choice was made, as Professor Grossman had stated, by a political organ — the government itself — after a dual consultation, one with the *Conseil économique et social*, on which the trade unions were represented, the other with the *Assemblée Nationale*, reflecting the territorial sentiment of the popular vote. This structure of choice did not eliminate the function of the market, which was the instrument for the execution of the plan, without being an objective of the plan. In this he felt Professor Notkin to have been wrong in identifying market-satisfaction as the feature distinguishing planning in the socialist countries from that under capitalism. If the objective of the plan was growth, a certain monetary and incomes policy had to be adopted to maintain global demand, expressed through the market, at a level sufficient to use the available factors of production at the rate of growth of accumulation set by the plan.

Mr. Nikiforov made a final contribution on Professor Mateev's paper. Professor Domar had interpreted the price model there set out as marginalist, but upon the assumption that the profit rate was arbitrarily determined by the state for capital and non-productive expenditure. He believed that Professor Mateev envisaged that the 'norm of surplus value' was not a fiscal imposition, but would vary with changes in prices. The different earnings of surplus value by the various branches of industry were the measures of investment efficiency : Professor Mateev did not postulate a branch rate of return but used that rate as a channel of information on efficiency.

[1] E. A. G. Robinson (ed.), *Backward Areas in Advanced Countries* (forthcoming).

THE INTERNATIONAL DIVISION OF LABOUR

Chapter 10

ECONOMIC CRITERIA OF THE INTERNATIONAL SPECIALIZATION OF PRODUCTION IN SOCIALIST COUNTRIES

BY

ZYGMUNT KNYZIAK

Higher School of Planning and Statistics, Warsaw

SPECIALIZATION THROUGH THE ECONOMIES OF SCALE

ONE of the most important ways of implementing the international division of labour among socialist countries is the specialization of production, both inter-branch and intra-branch. The erroneous view, however, still seems to persist that the inter-branch specialization of production between nations is a function of the differential natural endowment (including climate) and its suitability for specific industries (*e.g.* agriculture). Such conditions either totally inhibit the output of certain products, or render their production grossly inefficient by comparison with other countries. Obviously this cannot be the basis for the economic relations either of socialist or non-socialist countries with a complementary production structure. Applied to countries of disparate structure, it conduces to widening the gap between the industrial and the undeveloped partner. Moreover, although it has some significance in relation to raw materials extraction, agriculture, and certain sectors depending on natural conditions (*e.g.* ship-building), it cannot guide international co-operation in the case of partners in the process of industrialization — particularly intense among the socialist countries.

Specialization while each partner is expanding manufacturing industry, and thereby converging their patterns of production and exchange, can be empirically demonstrated as feasible on the basis of the advantage gained from lowering the expenditure of social labour as a result of an increase in the scale of production. This kind of specialization is such that it can only develop where it can rely on large markets; in smaller countries a growth of output based on home sales is correspondingly limited.

A widening of the market may take place by exchange with other countries. The economic co-operation of the socialist countries is developing on this principle, that is, by the renunciation by each participant of a wide variety of products in favour of increasing a series of a small number of products, and by arranging between themselves the exchanges so indicated; each country thereby obtains the appropriate economies of scale.

Such economies tend to be concentrated upon labour inputs, with the possibility that the expansion of production may evoke cost reduction in supplying sectors, and hence reduce outlays on raw materials, semi-manufactures, and components. However, even if the cost of material per unit of output is unchanged, an increased scale of production requires more inputs. Although the economy gains the benefit of reduced wage expenditure, it may have to expand its extraction of raw materials and production of other materials (or its imports thereof). The derived investment (or balance-of-trade) effects within each partner are unlikely to be the same; a similar differentiation will arise when each partner specializes in products of varying capital intensity.

It is consequently fundamental to the development of international specialization on the basis of the economies of scale that partners maintain their relative equilibrium in material structure and capital intensity of products exchanged under specialization agreements. As a rule, this condition is fulfilled in practice by specialization within the framework of the same branch. The conventional name for this kind of specialization is 'intra-branch specialization', although, in some cases, specialization of this kind may go beyond the limits of the branch as defined by the standard classification of industry. It facilitates the specialization of branches of manufacturing which have a similar structure in each partner, and it has therefore become the predominant form of co-operation between socialist countries in manufactured goods. It does not, nevertheless, exclude the implementation of 'inter-branch specialization', although it has small scope in the current conditions and development trends of the socialist countries. It is limited to the cases in which the transport cost of the imported raw material is an obstacle to the development of a certain branch of manufacturing; a high expenditure on transport may cancel out the advantages of scale, and make export unprofitable.

A NUMERICAL EXAMPLE WITH EQUAL UNIT-VALUES

The determination of rational and practical criteria for assessing the advantage gained from specialization must start from the concrete conditions in which the co-operation of the socialist countries is developing ; three features are relevant. The first is that the socialist countries engaged in this form of co-operation operate at different levels of labour productivity in comparable branches of manufacturing, the level as a rule being lower in undertakings which were developed early, and higher in those which have been recently commissioned. Cases do occur in which productivity is the same in a given industry, particularly in certain branches of engineering which have recently been developing very quickly in the socialist countries on the basis of similar technology. The economic advantages of specialization in these instances will depend on the existing relative productivities of labour.

The second characteristic is the absence of a free flow of labour and investment between the co-operating countries. This implies that the levelling-up of the productivity of social labour between countries occurs primarily on the basis of each country's internal resources. The independent nature of the economy of each country makes it necessary to observe external balance-of-payments equilibrium.

The third feature is the exchange of the products of specialization at world-market prices, and consequently at a uniform price not dependent on the expenditure of labour on the production of a given product in the individual country.

One may construct a simplified scheme of specialization which answers the above conditions, assuming, for the moment, an identical labour productivity in the several countries. For a numerical example, three countries, A, B, and C, may be taken, each producing twenty units of fifteen products ; the world price of each product separately is equal, and the output of each country at such prices is 150 units of international currency per year. Production costs, measured in working time, are also equal and are assumed to aggregate 40,000 hours per year in each country. It is further assumed that a change in the product-mix requires no capital investment. Consequent upon a specialization agreement, each country limits its range of products to one-third and triples the volume of output thereof. Consequently each participant manufactures 60 units of five products, but, as the traded prices are identical, the aggregate value of production will remain at 150 international-currency units per country. It is assumed that each country exchanges products of international-currency units in foreign trade to satisfy its consumption-mix. If the tripling of production increases labour productivity by 20 per cent, aggregate production costs will decline by 8,000 hours per participant. Each country thus receives a gain in the form of a reduced expenditure of the social labour necessary to satisfy internal requirements in the same volume and composition as previously.

In this example, the gain enjoyed by each country is equal and proportionate to the amount of external trade generated by the specialization agreement, but in practice this may not be so. Variation will mainly be caused by the pre-specialization degree of capacity use in the different countries : some may have increased output by a'fuller utilization of existing capacity, while others may have constructed new undertakings. Where new capacity has been created, the amount of capital per unit of output and its inbuilt technology may differ from country to country, depending on the availability of manpower and finance for capital formation. The more investment funds disposable, the more advanced will be the technology and the higher the labour productivity of the project. Although it is not a unique determinant — the relative level of real wages is also a factor — the gain from the economies of scale may vary in relation to the technology of new capital.

UNEQUAL UNIT-VALUES

Let us now examine a situation in which, as a result of the factors just described, country A is more industrially developed than B and C, the values of the units of production before specialization not being identical, and lowest in country A. Any attempt to obtain the lowest production expenditure in the context of the three countries would require concentrating the production of all products in A, from which B and C could import all their requirements and sell in exchange — to maintain the balance of trade — goods for which they enjoy a higher productivity of labour. Such possibilities would normally occur in branches of extractive industry (if these countries possessed reserves of cheaply-exploitable raw material), or in agriculture. It can easily be proved that this would lead to an increase in the economic inequality between these countries, because the export of raw material and agricultural produce is less effective than the export of products of manufacturing. At the same time, since this would be predominantly the export of the natural endowment, and not the result of man's labour, raw-material resources would be depleted, and the conditions for future development worsened.

But if the criterion is not absolute, but relative, gain, the international division of labour, in conditions either of different or equal labour productivity, will ensure some gain to all participants, on condition that the field and scale of specialization operate to assure a mutually-equilibrated balance of trade. The participants could accept the principle of dividing common gains in proportion to the degree of participation of each in the specialization, *i.e.* in relation to the increment of foreign trade generated by specialization ; the gain could be equilibrated by appropriate subsidies to the international accounts, or in some other way.

The criterion of absolute gain may be fully used when the economies of the separate countries form a unified economic organism in which capital finance and labour are freely mobile, or in the case of production depending directly on the natural endowment. If the extraction of some raw material is more efficient in country A than in B or C, but A can find more efficient uses for its capital investment, A could satisfy the requirements of other countries with the help of investment, or even the operation of the enterprises, by the latter. Evidently, the precise definition of the conditions of co-operation (amount of credit, the repayment period, prices of the material delivered, etc.) must be acceptable to each participant.

The gain for any one country is the difference between expenditure when specializing and expenditure when not specializing. Consequently, the concept of accounting is constructed on the premise that the growth of production is accompanied by the reduction of social labour expenditure per unit of output. In the untypical case of constant returns to scale, specialization of production will be totally ineffective, but, normally, a larger volume of production conduces to lower per-unit investment and operating costs (higher labour productivity) in association with technical progress.

MACROECONOMIC EFFICIENCY

Research into the effectiveness of specialization cannot, however, be restricted to expenditure at the level of the plant : specialization must be examined from the point of view of overall economic efficiency. The effectiveness then depends both on the reduction of production costs and on the amount of investment from which this was derived. This further term may be accounted for by adding the element of capital formation $\frac{1}{t}k$ to that of current outlays in the calculation. The symbol k represents the amount of capital (together with the value of assets retired by reason of specialization) under specialization in excess of that necessary without specialization. t is the marginal recoupment period of investment at current rates of technical progress (consequently $\frac{1}{t}$ is the standard coefficient of capital efficiency). The investment element in the calculation hence affects the result according to the degree of capital-intensity of production and the length of the marginal recoupment period t.

The increment in production due to specialization will alter the capital-to-output ratio and the wages-to-output ratio, although the materials-to-output ratio will remain relatively stable. Following current practice in Poland, we may represent the efficiency of a given variant of specialization as

$$e_x = \frac{[(1/t)k + c]b + s}{p},$$

where, in addition to the symbols just mentioned, e_x is the index of efficiency in product x; c is the annual manufacturing cost, *i.e.* excluding s, the annual cost of materials, depreciation, and repair; [1] p is annual production; and b is the 'coefficient of adjustment' which takes into account the effect of the period of operation on the efficiency of the capital investment.

Practice shows that in those branches of production where the proportion of expenditure on wages is small relative to total costs, the increase of output leads to a reduction in the capital-to-output ratio to a significantly lesser degree than the reduction of expenditure on wages, while the value of materials remains unchanged or declines insignificantly. Consequently, production costs, the incremental capital-to-output ratio, and the index of efficiency have decisive significance for schemes of specialization.

The achievement of the optimum volume of production of a given range will not always be possible in co-ordinating the output of a

---

[1] An alteration of production technology which does not increase p may change s and k.

group of countries, because the requirements of each participant for a particular range may differ. Secondly, it is in the interest of all to maximize the common gain (*i.e.* the sum of gains to individual participants) and not to maximize gains in each country separately.

THE BALANCE-OF-TRADE CONSTRAINT

The international specialization of production must be implemented in mutual trade, but, as indicated above, with the constraint of maintaining existing balances of payments. A numerical example may indicate the manner of allocating the gains arising as a result of specialization within such limits. Let us assume that country A is allotted the following programme, shown in comparison with its existing production.

	Without Specialization					With Specialization				
Product	p	k	s	c	e (Total)	p'	k'	s'	c'	e' (Total)
x_1	100	42	10	15	3,200	200	39	8	12	5,300
x_2	180	37	8	15	5,217	250	33	8	12	6,400
x_3	60	42	10	20	2,217	—	—	—	—	—
x_4	40	30	10	15	1,200	—	—	—	—	—
x_5	20	50	15	10	666	—	—	—	—	—
					12,500					11,700

The index of efficiency set out above is calculated for the entire production of a product, given, for simplification, that $b = 1$ (which corresponds to a 20-year operating period). Thus for product x_1,

$$e_{x_1} = [(\tfrac{1}{6}.42 + 15).1 + 10].100 = 3,200.$$

From the point of view of the efficiency of the directions of development of production, it appears that cessation of output of products x_3, x_4, and x_5 and transference to increased production of x_1 and x_2 is efficient since

$$\sum_{i=1}^{5} e_{x_i} > \sum_{i=1}^{2} e'_{x_i}$$

or, expressed numerically: $12,500 > 11,700$. In order further to examine the effect of specialization on trade, let us assume that the

intra-branch specialization is accompanied by the following programme of exchanges.

Product	Price of One Unit of Production at World Market Prices in International Currency	Export		Import	
		Quantity	Cost	Quantity	Cost
x_1	0,4	100	40	—	—
x_2	0,5	70	35	—	—
x_3	0,6	—	—	60	36
x_4	0,5	—	—	40	20
x_5	0,4	—	—	20	8
—	—	—	75	—	64

The trade programme indicates that exports (75) will exceed
imports (64) by 11 units of international currency, representing the
gain provided by specialization. If e_d is the index of the mean
foreign-currency efficiency of the given country, this gain will be
$11e_d$ in national monetary units. It follows that in our example the
common gain from specialization is

$$12,500 - 11,700 + 11e_d = 800 + 11e_d.$$

It may be observed that, although the capital intensity of a unit
of output in the specialization programme is lower for products
x_1 and x_2, the programme with specialization is more capital intensive
in comparison with the programme without specialization; because
of structural changes in production, it will require 16,050 units of
capital investment, whereas before specialization the programme
required 15,580. This was, nevertheless, more than compensated
by economies in current costs — without including the gains made
as a result of the positive balance of trade. Cases of complete
balancing of exports and imports as a result of specialization are
rare, and in the example just cited country A received as additional
gain the equivalent of the positive balance of trade.

The index of investment efficiency in export (or import-saving),

$$e_d = \frac{(1/t')k + c}{d},$$

where t' is the standard recoupment period and d is the net foreign
currency earnings (*i.e.* after deduction from gross earnings of the

cost of imported raw materials). The numerator is expressed in national currency and the denominator in international currency.

It is very difficult to attain the ideal state of balance-of-trade equilibrium in such international schemes, particularly when the operations constitute a significant part of the total turnover of the participants. The ideal is an important guide-line for co-ordinating plans for specialization, but some deviation therefrom must be tolerated, without prejudice to the general requirement of balancing national-currency expenditures.

A variant of a specialization scheme will be efficient if the following inequality is fulfilled (n being greater than m)

$$\sum_{i=1}^{n} e_{x_i} > \sum_{i=1}^{m} e'_{x_i} \pm q e_d,$$

where e_{x_1} is the index of investment efficiency for a given value of production x without specialization, e'_{x_1} is the index of investment efficiency for a given value of production x with specialization, q is the balance-of-payments disequilibrium arising in international currency from the trade generated by specialization, and e_d is an index of the mean efficiency of export production in the given country in terms of foreign currency investment.

It is now possible to present a general formula for calculating the relative gain obtained as a result of specialization, when $n > m$

$$W = \sum_{i=1}^{n} e_{x_i} - \sum_{i=1}^{m} e'_{x_i} \pm q e_d,$$

where W is the economic gain from specialization expressed in national currency, and the other symbols are as above. The value of the gain thus determined must be comparable with the gains obtained by the other participants in the scheme and hence defined in international currency, *i.e.* by dividing W by the index e_d.

$$W' = \frac{W}{e_d} = \frac{\sum_{x=1}^{n} e_x - \sum_{x=1}^{m} e'_x}{e_d} \pm q,$$

where W' is the gain from specialization in international currency.

Consequently the common gains from specialization will represent the sum of the gains W' of the participants; the maximization of such gains is the objective function in distributing the specialization tasks of the individual countries.

Chapter 11

THE ROLE OF ENGINEERING IN THE DEVELOPMENT OF FOREIGN TRADE BETWEEN THE EUROPEAN MEMBERS OF THE COUNCIL FOR MUTUAL ECONOMIC ASSISTANCE (CMEA)

BY

E. D. MATVIEVSKAYA

Institute of the Economics of the World Socialist System, Moscow

THE COST OF AUTARKY IN ENGINEERING

THE technological revolution required for a rapid development of productive forces is only possible on the basis of the extension of the international division of labour. Economic integration — the division of labour beyond the borders of individual states and the consequent extension of foreign trade — is essential if the technical and economic parameters of production in a broad range of industries are to be improved: an increase in the international division of labour is indeed a world-wide trend among the great industries of today. Even under capitalism, the absolute necessity of extending the international division of labour becomes increasingly obvious, although its practical realization is limited by the restriction of private ownership of the means of production, and by private appropriation of the results. It must be said that capitalist monopolies are seeking the way out of this deadlock, and striving to make this contradiction less acute. Attempts are being made to combine in international associations such as the Common Market, and to redistribute foreign markets, although these and other measures, while strengthening temporarily the position of certain monopolies, cannot eliminate the contradictions inherent in capitalism. So-called 'integration' under imperialism means the undermining, by the monopolies, of the living standards of the masses, adversely affects the economically less-developed countries, and aggravates the struggle and anarchy of the productive process.

Under socialism, however, there exist all the requisite conditions for solving the problems connected with the rapid growth of production; the international division of labour is achieved through mutual assistance, fully equal rights, free co-operation, and mutual benefit. Economic collaboration between the socialist nations results in the fuller and more rational utilization of domestic resources, in faster development of previously backward economies, in the rapid growth of production, and the increase of living standards in all the participating countries. Such collaboration promotes the creation and efficient development in each socialist state of those branches of the economy most answering the demands of technical progress and contributing to the increase of productivity. The Communist and Workers' Parties of CMEA members have declared that trends towards autarky are utterly detrimental to the national interests of each country, and to socialist collaboration as a whole.

The international socialist division of labour, the essence of which consists in specialization and consequent co-operation of production, is assuming ever greater significance in the development of the major branches of the economy of socialist countries. Extending its influence appears to be most urgent at present in the field of engineering, since the economic efficiency of engineering depends more than other industries on the scale of production. Advantage can be taken of modern technology to achieve a substantial growth of labour productivity and to reduce production costs only in conditions of large-scale serial production: often the optimal scale of output of certain engineering products surpasses the internal market capacity of individual countries. With scientific and technical progress, the number of engineering products proliferates, and their efficient supply depends on international trade. Many engineering branches are unprofitable without such specialization, but its achievement is not without difficulty. All countries with any industrial development have long striven to develop engineering, since it equips all other branches of the economy; moreover, engineering is somewhat less dependent than other industries on the availability of raw materials — metal can be supplied from scrap as well as from ore, and, in general, the primary input is low per unit of value-added.

The development of engineering is correspondingly less determined by such permanent features as the mineral endowment than by such variable factors as the technical level of equipment, the production technology in use, the degree of training of manpower, etc. Under all these influences certain types of engineering production may become less profitable in one country and more profitable in another. Hence some kinds of production in certain countries may be curtailed while in others they are being extended. Such a situation may be considered typical of the capitalist world, where factors influencing the economic efficiency of engineering function spontaneously in the process of competition, but in countries exercising the socialist division of labour this characteristic is taken into account through planning. Scientific and technical collaboration and other forms of mutual assistance permit the systematic improvement of engineering production for international sale, but the beneficiaries must be prepared to take the measures necessary to achieve the highest efficiency in the output of the products in which they specialize.

PROLIFERATION AND EXPANSION

The complexity of international specialization in engineering is enhanced by the fact that the diversity of its products has become particularly extensive, since the industry supplies with plant and equipment not only all the other branches of the economy and non-productive activity but also its own capital needs. It has been estimated that world production of engineering goods includes some 125,000–130,000 types, most of which are essential for any developed country, a diversity which on the one hand makes increased specialization more urgent, but on the other hinders it.

The general growth in production in the European members of CMEA has been reflected in the rapid expansion of their engineering : thus, in a mere decade (1950–60) the volume of engineering production grew 7·8 times in Poland, 7·2 times in Bulgaria, 5·8 times in Rumania, 4·6 times in Czechoslovakia, 3·8 times in the G.D.R., and 3·3 times in Hungary. These rates of engineering production growth have tended to exceed that of global industrial production — by 2·1 times in Poland and by 1·62 times in Czechoslovakia for example — by much wider margins than in the developed capitalist countries — by 1·38 times in the Federal Republic of Germany, by 1·15 times in the U.S.A., and by only 1·08 times in the United Kingdom.

The share of engineering in the total volume of industrial production of CMEA countries in 1960 was 28·3 per cent. Between

1950 and 1960 its percentage share grew from 20·8 to 33·7 in Czecho-slovakia, from 24·0 to 32·7 in the G.D.R., from 2·9 to 22·3 in Poland, from 13·3 to 24·0 in Rumania, and from 9·2 to 16·3 in Bulgaria. Thus, even the industrially-backward countries are rapidly approach-ing the highly industrial countries in this respect : in 1960 the corresponding percentage in the United Kingdom was 36·1, in the U.S.A. 31·9, in the Federal Republic of Germany 30·6, and in France 26·7.

Because engineering has become a major contributor to the global volume of production, international specialization in this field may well affect the development of the whole of the participating economies. The process of engineering specialization began in the countries under review virtually anew after the formation of a world socialist system, because in most of these countries engineering was established as a major industry in the years of socialist construction. In all of them, including those in which engineering developed under capitalism, a far-reaching reorientation of foreign trade relations took place after the Second World War which particularly affected the direction and composition of commerce in engineering. As a consequence, the problem of international specialization in this field is apparently more acute in the European socialist countries than in the majority of the developed capitalist countries, where such specialization has been implemented for much longer. They are nevertheless fortunate in being able to make use of an economic system on a world scale capable of the rapid rationalization of pro-duction in the interest both of each participant and of the group as a whole.

The specific features of organizing the system of engineering specialization under the international socialist division of labour are still largely determined by the state of the industry both under bourgeois rule and immediately after the revolutions. Before the Second World War, engineering was most developed in Germany and Czechoslovakia. In 1936 the share of engineering in what is now the G.D.R. constituted more than 22 per cent of industrial production, while machinery and equipment occupied a considerable place in the exports from this area. Engineering in pre-war Czecho-slovakia also enjoyed a relatively high level of development, although it lagged behind the most developed capitalist countries ; in 1937 engineering accounted for 16·6 per cent of industrial product, where-as in the majority of the developed capitalist countries it exceeded 20 per cent, and in Sweden in 1938 was as much as 33·5 per cent.

The large share of engineering products exported [1] points to the fact that Czechoslovakia, like Germany, was much involved in the international capitalist division of labour, although for the entire period of its inter-war existence Czechoslovakia was a net importer of machinery and equipment. The share of engineering products in total exports of the country in 1937 constituted only about 6 per cent.

In Poland, Hungary, and Rumania engineering was poorly developed : its share in the industrial production of these countries was about 7 to 9 per cent in 1938–39. About 9 per cent of Hungarian exports were of machinery and equipment, but their place was trivial in Polish exports (0·7 per cent) and non-existent in Bulgaria ; all three were heavily net importers.

ENGINEERING AS A LEADING SECTOR

After the Second World War the creation and development of each country's engineering industry successfully solved what was one of the key problems of socialist industrialization: a great number of large modern enterprises were established, and radical reconstruction of old plants was carried out. The expansion was most rapid in the economies in which engineering had been the most backward branch, and they came increasingly to supply their capital-good requirements from domestic production. Engineering both served as a leading sector in industrialization and recycled its output into further industrialization ; largely independent of locational ties, it could assist in improving the regional pattern of the economy.

Clearly, the expansion of engineering in relation to total output is not without limits, the chief of which is imposed by the cost of diversifying the product-mix as industrial requirements grow. This constraint can be to some extent relaxed, even in small countries, by agreements to distribute specific outputs by country. Due regard must of course be paid to relative scarcities : specialization should allow each country to develop those engineering products which are most needed in the group as a whole and in the manufacture of which it is most efficient. Obviously, the successful solution of this problem depends on a detailed assessment of the raw materials, productive capacity, skilled manpower, and standard of technological development available. The rapid advance of

[1] Between 18 and 25 per cent of the output of the metal-using industries was exported in the inter-war period.

engineering in the socialist countries has created the requisite conditions for extending the international division of labour along these
lines : that such specialization has already been taking place is
indicated by the correlation of the rise of the contribution of engineering to national product with that of its share in foreign trade.

THE PATTERN OF POSTWAR TRADE

Immediately after the War, the G.D.R. and Czechoslovakia were
the main suppliers of engineering products among the socialist
countries of Europe, and imported less than their exports (which
comprised equipment for the iron and steel industry, for fuel and
power, for engineering, and for mining). They were substantial
sellers of complete sets of plant for industrial enterprises. The
countries which then relied upon them for much of their engineering
supply have since increasingly promoted their own export products.
Thus as far back as 1950 Hungarian engineering exports surpassed
imports, and in the following years the margin widened even more.
Towards 1960 imports similarly overtook exports in Rumania and
Bulgaria, while in Poland the export of engineering products was
rapidly increasing, and the gap between import and export was
continuously narrowing.

Between 1950 and 1960 all but two European members of CMEA
increased their gross exports of engineering goods more rapidly than
global engineering production ; in Poland the rates for each were
virtually identical ; and only Czechoslovakia saw its exports grow
more slowly than domestic output. In 1962 Czechoslovakia exported
about 23 per cent of the machinery and equipment it produced, that
is, virtually, the same share as in 1955. The G.D.R. and Hungary
on the other hand have raised their exports to about one-third of
their total engineering production. The reasons for changes in the
export share in engineering production merit detailed analysis,
and may be traced to the investment policies of the countries concerned in relation to the sales potential of the world socialist market.

From the mid-fifties it was apparent that the countries with the
smallest engineering industries were those with the most rapid
expansion of engineering exports. All European members of CMEA
raised the share of engineering in total exports during the fifties,
but their ranking in such expansion corresponded inversely with the
initial magnitude of their output. Thus, in Bulgaria between 1950
and 1960 the rise of engineering exports was nothing less than 2,800

times ! In Rumania the expansion was 13·2 times ; in the G.D.R., 9·5 times ; in Poland, 7·1 times ; in Hungary, 4·5 times ; but in Czechoslovakia, 3·8 times. Even so the Bulgarian share of engineering in total exports was in 1961 the lowest of the group (15·7 per cent) and that of the G.D.R. the highest (47·9 per cent).

From 1955 to 1960 the shares of Bulgaria, Poland, and Rumania in the aggregate exports of the CMEA countries have increased, while those of the U.S.S.R., the G.D.R., and Czechoslovakia have fallen within a general rise in the total volume of exports of machinery and equipment and the continuance of the engineering industry as a leading sector of the economy. Simultaneously with the rapid growth of engineering exports, the European socialist countries as a group have enlarged imports of engineering products, which have come to occupy a larger share of total imports. Only in Poland has the machinery and equipment share of imports been slightly reduced between 1950 and 1961.

THE URGENT NEED FOR FURTHER SPECIALIZATION

The changes in the pattern of foreign trade have demonstrated the results of extending the international socialist division of labour in engineering.

It did not, however, develop until the end of the policy of self-sufficiency, prevalent in the early years. The objective of that period — to create in each country an engineering industry with widest possible product-mix — underestimated both the economic potentialities of the countries concerned and the advantages of international collaboration for meeting their own needs in engineering products. This produced parallelism in output and a superfluity of goods manufactured on a small scale. As a consequence, the G.D.R. and Czechoslovakia, according to some studies, manufacture today 70 to 80 per cent of all types of machinery and equipment produced in the world. In some defence of this policy, it must be realized that many socialist countries were establishing engineering almost from nothing, and that the import demand of socialist countries in engineering products was rapidly growing and not always fully satisfied. Many essentials were lacking for the rapid implementation of extensive international specialization.

However, the development of engineering in socialist countries has now created such conditions, while the necessity for specialization has become ever more urgent. It became particularly clear that many new enterprises cannot function with sufficient economic efficiency at their present small production capacities. The problems posed by international production specialization are in fact more complicated than could have been supposed at the beginning.

During the past decade much attention has been paid in the CMEA countries to the gain in efficiency to be derived from the international division of labour. Currently about 1,200 groups of engineering products have been the subject of specialization agreements, 525 types having been recommended for specialization during 1962 and 1963 alone. There is still, however, much room for improvement : the recommendations adopted mainly ratify the distribution of production already established, and are directed not to the rational reduction of product-mix produced in individual countries, but rather to its future limitation. The volume of specialized production in total engineering output of machinery and equipment is at present only 2 to 6 per cent according to country : in Poland, which has concluded specialization agreements for about 300 kinds of machinery and equipment, a mere 6 per cent of the total volume of production at the enterprises of the Ministry of Heavy Engineering was affected in 1964. It is hence that the CMEA countries derive their determination to extend international specialization in engineering.

Preliminary data on their long-term plans to 1980 predict more rapid rates of growth for engineering than the average for industry, and it is expected that the enterprises established will secure an optimal scale of production, at lower unit costs than now ruling, by trade in engineering products not only among themselves but also with other countries ; specialization in engineering production will become widespread, with especial emphasis on co-operating in the manufacture of components within individual branches. This intra-product specialization has as yet barely started, for most agreements have hitherto been on entire products (*e.g.* on machine tools between Poland and Czechoslovakia, on ship-building between Poland and Bulgaria and between Poland and Rumania). The advantages of international specialization in components are greatest in those branches of engineering characterized by a large product-mix, and with each kind and size of item produced only on a small scale. The co-operation of Poland, Czechoslovakia, and the G.D.R. in the field of electronic-tube production can serve as a shining example, and possibilities of similar development are offered in the field of bearings and fittings.

International specialization in engineering can help any country, but it is of especial value to the smaller country with an internal market of no great capacity, for it can obtain a secure place in that of the others participating in the programme.

Experience has shown that smaller countries tend to export a greater share of their production than do larger ones. Thus in 1958 the U.S.A. exported 8·2 per cent of its gross machinery production, France 13·9 per cent, Czechoslovakia 18·1 per cent, and the G.D.R. and Hungary about one-third. Small countries have in general a higher volume of trade, as exemplified by Czechoslovakia where commodity trade *per capita* is higher than in the U.S.A., France, and the Federal Republic of Germany.

The development of specialization significantly enhances both the export availability and import demand of each partner. This in turn becomes instrumental in further intensifying specialization, for trade expands both by the sale of specialized products, and by the purchase of raw materials and other goods which were formerly produced either only on a small scale or not at all.

PROBLEMS IN PROSPECT

This is not to say that trade cannot in certain cases retard the development of production and specialization. The balance of trade, the comparative profitability in terms of foreign exchange of the export of certain goods, the price level of imported goods, and many other factors may foster or hinder the process of international specialization.

Detailed study of the factors underlying foreign trade must reveal the trends in each country, and suggest solutions to the crucial problem of how to extend specialization in engineering on the basis of economic efficiency. CMEA members in this regard are endeavouring to improve their techniques of foreign trade, but some problems are not of organization alone, and it is essential also to analyse the functioning of the law of value in the sphere of foreign trade.

As time passes it is becoming more and more urgent to establish a scientific foundation for the international division of labour and systematically to measure the mutual gain from trade. No one contests the need to base the division of labour on the voluntary effort of the sovereign socialist states, which themselves decide to what degree and in what form they participate in the programme.

All, furthermore, support the requirement that the further international specialization of any branch in each country must bring rewards to each participant through the branch concerned, and must contribute to a balanced and comprehensive development of each country as a whole. Socialist collaboration is inspired by the desire unswervingly to realize this concept in practice.

In addition to the statistical year-books of the countries concerned, the following sources were used for the data cited in this paper : T. Kiss, *A socialista országok gazdasági együttmukodése* (Economic Co-operation among Socialist Countries), Budapest, 1961 (Russian trans. *Ekonomicheskoe sotrudnichestvo sotsialisticheskikh stran*, Moscow, 1963, pp. 139, 356, 361–362, 438, and 442) ; N. Kaspar, *Postaveni C.S.S.R. v svetovém strojirenstvi* (The Place of Czechoslovakia in World Engineering), Prague, 1962, pp. 11, 18, and 59 ; A. K. Kozik, *Razvitie promyshlennosti Polski* (The Development of Polish Industry), Moscow, 1950, p. 375 ; A. Vanek, *Ekonomicky a politicky vyznam vyvozu strojirenskych vyrobku* (The Economic and Political Significance of the Export of Engineering Products), Prague, 1960, p. 36 ; T. Zhivkov, 'Central Committee Report', in, *VIII s"ezd Bolgarskoi kommunisticheskoi partii* (Eighth Congress of the Bulgarian Communist Party), Moscow, 1963, p. 99 ; *III s"ezd Rumynskoi rabochoi partii* (Third Congress of the Rumanian Workers' Party), Moscow, 1961, p. 203 ; *Ekonomika stran sotsialisticheskogo lagera v tsifrakh* (The Economy of the Socialist Camp in Figures), Moscow, 1962, pp. 24 and 35 ; *Cisla pro kazdeho* (Figures for Everyman), Prague, 1962, p. 151 ; ' The Development of the Economies of the Socialist Countries', Supplement to *Byulleten innostrannoi komercheskoi informatsii*, no. 5, 1963, p. 74 ; *Planovoe khozyaistvo*, no. 4, 1964, p. 5 ; *Polsky eksport-import*, no. 1, 1964, p. 29 ; *Társadalmi Szemle*, no. 1, 1963, p. 21.

Chapter 12

THE DEVELOPMENT OF THE INTERNATIONAL DIVISION OF LABOUR BETWEEN COUNTRIES AT DIFFERENT ECONOMIC LEVELS

BY

J. NOVOZÁMSKY

Research Institute of National Economic Planning, Prague

UNITY AND CONTRADICTION IN INTERNATIONAL SOCIALIST RELATIONS

THE present paper is devoted to one of the most important categories of international economics, the division of labour as applied to the commonwealth of socialist countries. The international division of labour embraces both aspects of production: productive forces and productive relations. As Marx put it, this division is to be seen as a productive force in its co-ordination of producers, and a productive relation in the resultant activity of producers.

Two distinctive features make such co-operation between socialist countries a new type of the international division of labour. The first is the preclusion of exploitation by the equality of economic rights of each country, and the second is the fact that this division of labour is purposively planned. The basis of the first characteristic is the nationalization of the means of production on the territory of each state, and consequently also of the sum of goods there produced. In this sense, all countries within the world socialist system enjoy, in equity, an identical position. In relation to the other countries, each country is a monopolist over the goods made on its territory, and, being economically independent, it sells its products to another only in the form of a commodity, that is a world commodity moving in international trade. Any other form of the international movement of products would be contrary to the position of a country as a monopolist owner, and would diminish the economic independence of the countries. The international

144

movement of products within the world socialist system consequently abides by the law of value, the traded commodities having
an international value. The productive relation existing within the
world socialist system is thus a commodity relationship, and the
individual countries of this system act towards each other as producers of commodities. Nonetheless, the international productive
relationship within the world socialist system is neither a perfect
nor pure commodity relationship, because the products themselves
have not been generated in a strictly commodity-oriented system.
Non-commodity elements are introduced by the nature of the
domestic economies of the partners.

In each partner, as a second characteristic, economic development
is pursued in a planned manner: the system provides for the
purposive proportionality of economic activities. Such planning
implies a corresponding establishment of proportions at the international level, operating in a scheme of division of labour. The
absence of international proportions evolved by planning diminishes
the orderly nature of economic development within each partner,
since its productive process comes under the influence of international proportions established spontaneously.

The planned nature of economic development is thus introduced
on to the international scale as one of the conditions of planning
within the socialist countries. On the scale of a world socialist
system, conditions have not, however, been yet set up for the full
implementation of the planned nature of economic development.
Production on an international scale has not been made sufficiently
collective to make possible the fully-planned establishment of
international proportions. With economically-independent countries, the conditions for planned economic development on an
international scale will continue to be incomplete. The degree of
completion is a function of the rate of the collectivization of activity
within this system.

It is precisely this planned character which is the new feature
acquired in the world Socialist system by international productive
relations, and which is the attribute of the non-commodity — indeed,
the communist — aspect of the relations. The international commodity relationship within the world socialist system is linked by a
certain degree of planning (albeit only emergent), and is thereby
modified. It is not a pure, but a modified, commodity relationship,
and the categories and laws arising therefrom are correspondingly
altered.

The contemporary relationship hence has features both of unity and of contradiction : it entails commodity and non-commodity (*i.e.* planned) flows ; it is transitional and subject to constant change. Its determinant dialectic is that the non-commodity element and the communist relationship are gaining ground. This is accompanied, while the international socialist division of labour evolves, by another connected contradiction, which is a corollary to the generation, under certain social conditions, by the domestic division of labour of divergence between the collective and individual interests of producers. Within the world socialist system these contradictions, arising from the division of labour itself, take the form of a non-antagonistic conflict of national interests, *i.e.* between the interests of individual countries and the collective interests of the countries of the world system as a whole.

THE SIGNIFICANCE OF LEVELS OF DEVELOPMENT

It has already been pointed out that the members of the system enjoy equal status : this equality, however, is attenuated by their differences in degree of economic development.

There are wide differences in the economic levels of the socialist countries, historically originating in the pre-socialist period. A number of the countries which separated themselves from capitalism after the Second World War had a very low level of development and an economy based on backward agriculture. The Asian socialist countries—China, Korea, and Vietnam — were of the considerably backward group ; Mongolia, too, was underdeveloped. Even among the European countries which then began to build socialism there were striking differences in economic standards. Bulgaria, Rumania, and Albania were predominantly agricultural. Poland, Hungary, Yugoslavia had some, but relatively little, industry ; only the Soviet Union, Czechoslovakia, and the territory of the present German Democratic Republic (G.D.R.) could be ranked as countries with a more advanced industry.

In the twenty years since the end of the Second World War the socialist countries with lower levels have developed more rapidly than the economically more advanced countries. Among the socialist countries themselves the similar positive correlation of growth with initial backwardness has not yet eliminated the striking differences in individual economic levels. Thus, the *per capita* net material product of Hungary and Poland is roughly two-thirds, of

Bulgaria and Rumania one-half, and of Albania one-third, that of Czechoslovakia or the G.D.R. The *per-capita* industrial output of the Chinese People's Republic is approximately one-tenth, and of the Korean People's Democratic Republic two per cent, that of the Soviet Union. The differences in the economic levels of the socialist countries are clearly still vast; particularly great differences exist between the economic level of the European and the Asian socialist states.

Although different economic levels generate variant interest, the countries of the world socialist system are jointly interested in gradually eliminating the gap between their economic standards. Perpetuation of the deep-rooted differences between them would inhibit the long-run optimization of growth for the world socialist system as a whole, and consequently also for each member. The interest of countries with higher economic levels for their own growth lies in their participation in the international socialist division of labour, but the degree of this involvement depends on the increased participation therein of countries at lower economic levels. If the propensity to trade increases with rising production, an interdependent system such as the socialist group unites the interest of all in expanding trade. As the level of the less-developed rises, so there are more trade opportunities for the more developed, and each member of the world socialist system benefits from the gradual elimination of differences in their economic standards.

Variant economic levels have, however, engendered divergent production structures. The developed economies exploit more fully their natural resources and manpower, have more diversified output, and are objectively interested in pursuing international specialization in a wide range of industries, *i.e.* in 'opening' their production complex. Countries at a lower economic level, on the other hand, are objectively interested in completing their production complex, and in introducing new industries, that is, 'closing up' their production complex. This is what can lead to a conflict of interests.

The varying degree of complexity prevents the incorporation of the less-diversified in some international specialization schemes (for example, in components for the electronic industry), because such countries do not yet possess conditions requisite for the industry involved (sufficient skilled manpower, adequate research facilities, etc.).

Contradictions generated by aggregate and structural difference are being solved by conscientious effort, especially through the

147

Council for Mutual Economic Assistance, but effort alone does not eliminate the contradictions described. The final solution of these contradictions can be achieved only if their causes are eliminated, that is, by the gradual elimination of significant differences in the economic levels of the socialist countries. In the same way, such countries differ in their desire to achieve the international socialist division of labour in a planned manner. Here again planned co-operation will increase as the substantial differences in economic levels of these countries are overcome.

THE INTERNATIONAL ECONOMIC AIMS OF SOCIALISM

The disappearance of variant levels among the socialist states will lead to the implementation of international socialist productive relations. The status of every country within the world socialist system will be completely equal in all respects, but, because the world socialist system will thereby be completed, its integral parts will cease to exist as economically independent and relatively closed production entities. A new economic entity will emerge which will have no more internal economic boundaries as they are now understood and which impede the free international movement of the factors of production (*i.e.* of created values and of manpower). Conditions will thereby be established for the absolute implementation of Marx's 'economy of time', namely, that distribution of production corresponding to the most favourable natural conditions.

Tauchman, a well-known Czechoslovak specialist on international economies, described the relationship between equality and the economy of time as follows :

In the course of this process, international flows of productive factors and manpower will logically proceed, expand, and intensify ; the extent of such movement will exceed that achieved within the world system of capitalism, but this will be only the first stage. As soon as a group (and ultimately the whole of the system) evens out the economic levels of its member states, that is, as soon as each enjoys equal economic conditions for production, society will minimize its collective work under unified conditions, notably by the territorial deployment of specialized production schemes in the individual social units and areas in conformity with natural endowments. Marx's general law of the economy of time will then be manifested on an international scale in an almost pure form.[1]

[1] J. Tauchman, *Teoretické základy hospodářské spolupráce socialistických států* (Theoretical Foundations of Economic Cooperation between Socialist Countries), Prague, 1964, p. 44.

Devoting at present considerable attention to the problem of phasing out these differences, the economists of socialist countries are not seeking economic justification for realizing a mere political or moral slogan calling for the establishment of roughly identical economic conditions of life in all socialist nations. Far from being only a subjective wish for the welfare of the inhabitants of all the socialist countries, it is an economic necessity and a logical development.

The narrowing of the economic differences among the socialist countries is a long-term process which has already begun. The degree of utilization of productive forces is being brought to a common standard. Although productive relations in all socialist countries are of the same nature, there are divergences in stages of progress, indicated by *per-capita* national income and national wealth. To eliminate substantial differences in *per-capita* national incomes requires the equalization of the technical equipment of production, of the qualifications of manpower, and of the level of general productivity. This chiefly involves the closing of the *per-capita* investment gap, but it is also being reflected in the increasing similarity of export structure, for the countries at a lower economic level are diversifying into manufactures. Consumption, too, is reflecting the decreasing differentials between countries.

Equalizing the economic levels of socialist countries has been made the criterion for the development of the international socialist division of labour, and consequently for the economic development of its individual participants. Justifiably, the *Basic Principles of the International Socialist Division of Labour*, approved in 1962 at a conference of representatives of Communist and Workers' Parties of the members of the Council for Mutual Economic Assistance, emphasized that

> the surmounting of differences in the levels of economic development helps to make fuller use of the advantages of the international socialist division of labour, while at the same time being one of the factors which helps accelerate the rate of economic growth of the whole of the socialist system. It helps establish optimum proportions for enlarged reproduction within the world socialist system.

Chapter 13

SUMMARY RECORD OF THE DISCUSSION
—SESSION III

THE INTERNATIONAL DIVISION OF LABOUR

(In the Chair : PROFESSOR SOROKIN)

Sir Roy Harrod began the discussion with comments on the paper by Dr. Novozámsky. He drew attention to the passage which stressed that trade between socialist countries was not only co-operative, but also planned, and that this planning was essential, since, otherwise, variations in foreign trade might disrupt domestic plans (p. 145). It might be a digression, he admitted, to say that capitalist countries should shape their own commercial policies with this in view, but it was a relevant counter to Dr. Novozámsky's contentions that there was widespread belief in capitalist countries that socialist countries were inclined to conduct their export trade in an irregular manner, suddenly dumping surpluses to suit their own convenience. He pointed out that the foreign trade of capitalist countries, although not planned, grew in a more or less regular and harmonious way, and that fears of market disruption militated against an extension of trade with socialist countries. However misplaced they might be, they were honestly entertained and it would be expedient for the socialist countries to show evidence that such fears were unfounded.

Dr. Novozámsky had stressed the inequality between the economic levels of socialist countries and suggested that the more developed economies required a higher trade dependence. He was ready to agree that countries with a more advanced technology had a greater need for international specialization and that further development of international trade could increase their growth rates. He disagreed, however, with the implied view that it was necessary for well-developed countries to find fresh markets if their growth was not to be checked. This savoured of an old-fashioned view, held by some, but not by the best, capitalist economists.

The main emphasis in Dr. Novozámsky's paper was on the need for greater equality between countries. Sir Roy Harrod agreed that this was desirable, but doubted whether it would necessarily be achieved soon : rather it would, he thought, be delayed until all countries were approaching the point of satiety in material well-being. He noted that

150

Summary Record of the Discussion

Dr. Novozamsky had postulated equality, not on moral grounds, but on economic necessity and logic (p. 149) ; on the contrary, he thought the moral ground to be valid, and noted a tendency in some socialist thinking to transfer truly moral questions into the realm of alleged logical necessity. Professor Jeanneney had spoken of the moral subsumptions of economic choice the previous day ; it was surely not out of harmony with Marx to stress moral truths.

He then turned to Miss Matvievskaya's very interesting paper, firmly based on the experience of the engineering industries. On page 142 she had observed that smaller countries often exported a larger share of their production than bigger ones ; an industrialized small country invariably had a higher foreign-trade turnover *per capita* than bigger countries. She had cited Czechoslovakia as a case where *per capita* commerce was higher than in the United States, France, and the German Federal Republic. Sir Roy Harrod pointed out that her distinction between big and small was not, of course, the same as Dr. Novozámsky's distinction between lower and higher economic levels, but he noted that Czechoslovakia was on a lower level than the bigger countries quoted and which did less foreign trade *per capita*.

He severely doubted Dr. Novozámsky's statement that countries with a lower economic level were concerned with 'completing their production complex', by introducing new industries. He recognized their need to industrialize, but disagreed with the requirement that it cover so wide a spectrum : there had possibly been a false analogy with the Soviet Union, which, by virtue of its very size, had adopted a policy of what might be called 'omni-competence'. Such an aim might well be inappropriate for smaller countries, since by wasting effort it might retard growth. He suggested that planned specialization be started by these countries before their first stage of industrialization was complete. In classical economics, specialization was governed by the law of comparative costs as developed by Ricardo. By this law, lower-level countries should export goods to the higher-level ones, even though these goods required more simple labour in the lower-level countries. The law of comparative costs was related to a momentary situation, and was valid under a system in which progress was made by small, step-by-step adjustments by a large number of traders. It was less serviceable in relation to five- and ten-year plans, because within the planned period the pattern of comparative costs might have altered, in consequence of the development process itself (following changes in the availability of skilled personnel and in capital accumulation). The likelihood of such variation should not, however, invalidate the idea that some specialization could be promoted from the start.

Socialist countries might possibly put their system to advantage in relation to this early specialization and thereby give a lead to non-socialist countries. One might think in terms of the planned purchase of goods produced under an agreed scheme of specialization over a term of years. This did not merely mean that other socialist countries, looking at their own forward plans, should guarantee to buy items which would fill some gaps in their own plans, but rather that international consultation should permit a lower-level country to develop a certain industry to the scale at which it could export (and should export to get the full advantage of mass production), the other countries deliberately modifying their own plans to make room for such imports over a period of, say, ten years.

He regretted that he had been unable to study Dr. Knyziak's paper because it was available only in Russian.

He suggested that certain problems not covered by the papers could also usefully be discussed, *e.g.* barter arrangements; the price levels in terms of which trade between socialist countries was expressed and paid for; the extent to which such trade was bilateral and the scope for multilateralism; how balance-of-payments equilibrium was achieved; the use of one currency, such as the ruble, in the manner of sterling and the dollar today, for the denomination of indebtedness and the holding of reserves; the fixing of rates of exchange between socialist countries; and credit facilities for debtors within the socialist group.

Mr. Nikiforov pointed out that the socialist states at lower economic levels had developed more rapidly than those at higher levels : the development gap had in consequence begun to close. He felt that Sir Roy Harrod's point on national self-sufficiency had been well taken. Bulgaria imported iron and steel to supply its engineering industry, from which exports were made of machinery : Miss Matvievskaya's paper had cited Bulgarian growth in this context. Similarly, coal and electricity were bought abroad partly to support the export industries ; Bulgaria could not be developing at such a rapid rate under conditions of self-sufficiency.

He accepted the moral connotation which Sir Roy Harrod had found in the socialist objective of equalizing national levels of welfare, but stressed that it was inherent in the mutual relations of the group.

Professor Rachmuth stated that socialist economies based their relations with other states on sovereignty, equality, and mutual advantage. The international socialist division of labour sought maximum efficiency and growth (through industrialization) in a planned harmonious manner in the interests of all the members of the socialist community. No narrow specialization on primary commodities was compatible with such principles, because the exploitation of all available resources was the duty of a socialist government. Any monoculture, or other one-sided development, was alien to socialism ; it could, of course, occur under capitalism. The Council for Mutual Economic Assistance hence sought to ensure industrialization and promote mutual interests, but this was not to be done by making a single plan through a single planning organ. He agreed with Dr. Novozámsky that national sovereignty had to be protected in the course of bilateral or multilateral planned co-ordination, but stressed that each participant should elaborate its plan with its own characteristics in view.

Professor Oelssner rejoined that the characteristics of the proposed seller were not the sole dictate in an international specialization arrangement. The participant which renounced the production of a certain item in favour of another should have a right to guarantees that the goods would be provided competitively and over a sufficiently long term. The G.D.R. was a case in point : its engineering covered too wide a range and attempts were being made to narrow it, but, if it specialized in certain products to gain the economies of scale, it had to ensure by long-term contract that its partners were willing to take up its exports.

The problem of mutual guarantees was much less important in a large than in a small country. A large country with a diversified natural endowment was able to furnish the raw materials for its industry and the food for its urbanized population. The G.D.R. was a small country without these resources and had to require sales to it of primary commodities as a *quid pro quo* of industrial specialization.

Professor Dupriez questioned Dr. Novozámsky's contention (p. 144) that there could be no exploitation between socialist countries because there was only a simple exchange of merchandise without the intervention of entrepreneurs, for he had at the same time claimed that relations between socialist countries ought to be based on production. Did this mean that all labour should receive the same remuneration, as was implied by the exchange of goods as an equity relationship ? If such valuation was adopted, what set of prices was used : that of one country (say, the U.S.S.R.), that of Western markets, or would it be composed *ad hoc* ?

Mr. Kaser discussed the points raised by Sir Roy Harrod and Professor Dupriez on socialist trading techniques. He hoped that an outsider might essay an answer to elicit the necessary corrections by those more knowledgeable. He believed that there was virtually no element of barter in trade between socialist countries to the extent that the prices used were those of the world market in 1957–58 (although there was a negotiable margin). *Sir Roy Harrod* interjected a question on how prices could be set for goods, such as machinery, where no world price was available. *Mr. Kaser* replied that intense efforts were made to determine a price, at least by analogy, from Western catalogues and other documentary sources. He believed that for the round of trade negotiations underlying the 1966–1970 plan co-ordination, the average of 1959–63 world prices was being used. The move away from barter had also begun with the trilateral deals in 1950 and 1954, and multilateralism was the objective of the 1963 agreement on a clearing union for members of the CMEA. Trade protocols were still drawn up annually in bilateral negotiation between members, but the scope for multilateral supplementary deals had been widened by the accounting facilities of the Bank for International Economic Co-operation, set up in that agreement. He observed that the limits on a participant's debtor balance were severer than those of the former European Payments Union.

Because prices were those of the world market, the adjustment of the terms of trade to assist the less-developed socialist countries (*e.g.* Rumania and Bulgaria) at the expense of the more developed (*e.g.* U.S.S.R. or Czechoslovakia) could only be effected by exception. Hence, the equalization of economic levels within the socialist group could take place, as Dr. Novozámsky reported Tauchman as saying (p. 148) by 'international flows of productive factors and manpower'. He took the first to mean international capital flows, and hoped that Dr. Novozámsky would expand his views on international migration, which had been hitherto very limited between socialist countries. It was sometimes said in socialist countries that differences in retail price patterns were sufficiently extreme to induce temporary or permanent emigrants to buy up commodities cheaper in the country of immigration and make personal imports of the items cheaper at home. It had been suggested that such privately-financed international flows of consumers' goods could seriously disturb domestic planning as it operated at present. Under these conditions, a substantial movement of labour could not take place until retail price patterns were reconciled.

Professor Sorokin supplemented Mr. Kaser's statement on the use of world market prices among CMEA members by the observation that the prices were corrected for cyclical and speculative fluctuations and for some market imperfections. Thus, the sharp rise in commodity prices associated with the outbreak of the Korean War had been ignored and the influence of monopolistic pricing was attenuated. Since the factor proportions underlying price formation in the socialist group differed from those on the capitalist market, the CMEA was currently studying possibilities of establishing its own price basis. Sir Roy Harrod had asked how prices were fixed when no world price existed, citing engineering goods as an example. Here prices were simply determined by negotiation between the partners.

The trade policy of each socialist state aimed at equilibrium in the balance of payments. Commercial credits were available to cover short-term disequilibria ; these arrangements would be extended in future by the operation of the International Bank for Economic Co-operation. The Bank was at the moment concerned with trading accounts, but it would subsequently play a considerable part in correcting inter-member balances. Professor Sorokin accepted the limitation of the Ricardian theory of comparative costs to the static situation : he agreed that the co-ordination of long-term plans could furnish the essential dynamic correction.

Professor Robinson wished to elaborate on the problem of planning the trade of smaller nations. He noted that a negative relation existed between the size of the country and its dependence on trade. The very large nations tended to have only a 5 per cent ratio of exports to G.N.P., whereas that for small nations was around 30 per cent : the implication was that the resources of the small nation had to be supplemented by international trade.

He felt that it was hardly axiomatic that a country should develop heavy industry before building up an area of specialization. The markets of the Asian and African countries were too small for the production of steel and machinery : similar problems must exist in Eastern Europe. Australia, Canada, and the United States all began as exporters of primary products and only later moved into heavy industry. The analysis of the 'take off' showed the importance of 'leading sectors', a concept reflected in some of the papers to the present Conference. Import substitution had begun only after a leading sector had been developed. He felt that there was some conflict between the concept of a common market — *i.e.* fostering intra-regional specialization — and the aims of the socialist division of labour, and that there was danger of the subordination of the smaller country to the larger also in the socialist world.

The infant industry problem arose too in Eastern Europe, that is to select the point at which a primary producer should create its engineering and metals industries. In Africa, experience had shown that these branches could be started either too early or too late. The conflict of the long-term and the short-term which must arise was ignored by the orthodox priority for heavy industry.

Professor Stefanov directed his remarks to Dr. Knyziak's paper, which rightly stressed that international specialization was not confined to socialism, but had of course existed under capitalism. What characterized socialism was the development of manufacturing in the process of industrialization : planned specialization assured the economies of scale to all the co-operating countries in a manner which the market mechanism did not guarantee. Specialization by product within given industries could assure mass-production conditions even to countries with an identical industrial structure.

Dr. Knyziak sought criteria to judge the absolute and relative advantages of specialization among socialist countries. Realistically, he took account of such prevailing conditions as different levels of labour productivity in manufacturing among the countries, the absence of labour or capital flows between them and their use of world market prices. Professor Stefanov would have re-formulated the last condition more generally, viz. that there was a uniform price system governing inter-member transactions. Even if the absolute labour productivity in a certain industry was the same between countries, a change in the product-mix within an identical industry would bring economies of scale. In his paper he assumed that a change in assortment could take place without new investment, and that the gain from the economies of scale would enable each country to derive a profit from specialization without changing inter-partner prices. The profitability of specialization with differing labour productivity would of course be higher. Since all countries have some absolute advantages over others, specialization could only lead to a fuller exploitation of natural resources. He had been particularly struck by Dr. Knyziak's progression from formulae for the co-efficient of investment efficiency in export promotion or import substitution to an equation determining the conditions of international specialization generally.

Professor Oelssner took up the same point in Dr. Knyziak's paper, which stated that the reduction of outlays of social labour per unit of production as a result of the economies of scale came almost entirely from the reduction of outlays of current labour, and assumed a constant ratio of capital to output. Professor Oelssner believed that, even without any change in technology, the development of series output resulted in an increase in labour productivity. Assets would be more intensively used per unit of output, and their recoupment period reduced ; materials would be more rationally used and waste products better employed. In summary, the factors, described by Marx in his well-known chapter, 'Ökonomie des konstanten Kapitals', affected large series more than small ones, and the gains from the division of labour would therefore be increased.

Professor Domar noted that Dr. Knyziak in his paper (p. 129) — and Professor Rachmuth in his comments — believed that industrial exports had a higher rate of efficiency than the products of agriculture or mining ; the same position had been strongly taken by the Argentine economist Prebisch.[1] Professor Domar was intuitively attracted to this opinion, but could not easily state his reasons. He did not see why trade in primary products involved the exploitation of underdeveloped countries by the more advanced. There were several wealthy countries, such as Denmark, New Zealand, and Australia, which lived on agricultural exports. For that matter, the United States was a large exporter of farm produce. Recent Soviet purchases of American wheat had been most welcome to the United States, but could hardly be construed as exploitation of the United States by the Soviet Union. Professor Oelssner had indicated that East Germany had to import food in order to exist : if such foodstuffs came from other socialist countries, East Germany could hardly intend to exploit them. Nor did any exploitation of the Soviet Union by Poland and other socialist countries arise from Soviet deliveries of iron ore and crude oil. Finally, the United States was a major importer of Brazilian coffee. If this involved the exploitation of Brazil, would that country be better off if the United States stopped buying that coffee ? He did not want thereby to imply that the underdeveloped countries should not foster industry. The causes of their difficulties lay in their economic structure, lack of capital, shortage of skilled personnel, etc.,

[1] R. Prebisch, 'Commercial Policy in the Underdeveloped Countries', *American Economic Review, Papers and Proceedings*, May 1959, pp. 251–273.

rather than in their exploitation by advanced countries by purchase of their raw materials.

Dr. Knyziak said that his paper had tried to identify the advantages to CMEA members of their present co-ordination of long-term, medium-term, and even annual plans. Such co-ordination required specific agreements between socialist countries on concrete measures of implementation, and it was important that negotiation begin by defining the advantages to the countries concerned. On these, there were two approaches and two criteria: first, the criterion of absolute advantage, and second, that of relative advantage. Where capital and labour did not flow freely between the partners, the most important, and at the same time the most realistic, criterion was that of relative advantage, permitting the manufacturing sector of each socialist country to develop along similar lines. The criterion of absolute advantage could be employed only to determine the division of labour among socialist countries in the production of raw materials; even then, the interests of each country had to be taken into account.

While he agreed with Professor Oelssner's remarks, he could not agree with what Sir Roy Harrod and Professor Sorokin had said about plan co-ordination on the basis of Ricardian comparison. The most that could be said was that Ricardo had to be dynamized and developed by allowing for investment effects.

He disagreed with Professor Domar, who had, he believed, missed the point of recent Danish experience. Having reached the limits both of efficiency in the export of food products and of the import propensity of the United Kingdom, Denmark had been compelled to develop exports of manufactures. His paper had not implied that the export of foodstuffs was always inefficient, but had stated that, at an advanced level of development, such exports were less efficient than those of machinery. Evidently this was not solely a matter of relative production efficiencies but also arose from the disadvantageous terms of trade facing primary producers: the assessment of the appropriate terms of trade among CMEA members should be considered as a major problem.

Dr. Novozámsky pointed out that there was no exploitation among socialist partners because exploitation arose from the ownership of factors of production and no state-owned resources in another.

Mr. Kaser had brought up the question of labour mobility. This seemed to be a matter for future decades, since conditions did not currently exist for major flows of labour. The difference in retail prices which he mentioned arose from the absence of manpower movement, but did not in itself obstruct it. He felt rather that the obstacle to labour movement to more developed areas was the realization that it would speed up their development and hinder development in the countries of emigration.

Replying to Sir Roy Harrod and Professor Rachmuth, he said that he believed that an industrial complex was needed for the full exploitation of manpower and natural resources. The creation of a multiple structure (*i.e.* comprising fuel, raw materials, engineering, and chemicals) was needed because productivity was higher in those branches than in others, and the economic policy of socialist countries rightly stressed the expansion of high-productivity manufacturing to ensure the full employment of resources.

Dr. Hegedűs emphasized the importance for Hungary of collaboration within the framework of the CMEA; foreign-trade dependence was high, more than 30 per cent of production being exported. The high level of exports did not mean that there were no problems. They were particularly difficult in engineering, as Miss Matvievskaya had discussed in her paper. Hungarian engineering production was growing more rapidly than specialization, despite substantial progress already made with the assistance of the CMEA. Its product-mix was still very large, and there was little possibility of concentrating sufficient effort on the technical progress of individual engineering products. Because costs were high, Hungarian machinery was hard to sell: an increase in production involved not only the mobilization of resources (about which Professor Notkin had spoken the previous day) but also the assurance of demand. The country experienced difficulties in marketing, even though its ratio of foodstuffs to engineering prices was wider than in any other CMEA member. Hungary had in recent years had to cut back output of machinery because unsold stocks were excessive. Many theoretical and practical problems of the Hungarian place in CMEA engineering specialization still remained to be settled.

Dr. Kyprová returned to Sir Roy Harrod's question on the prices operating between socialist partners. As Professor Sorokin had indicated, they were based on world prices. But current world prices were unsuited to the planned foreign trade of the CMEA countries, and the average prices on the main world markets over a longer period served as basis. This avoided fluctuations caused by speculative and cyclical influences. The prices so adjusted were a criterion for determining the actual prices in bilateral and multilateral trade negotiations among CMEA members. The very frequency of change in world prices accounted, *inter alia,* for the disinclination of the socialist countries to use current world prices. The level and relationship of prices on the world market reflected not only economic but also other conditions in the capitalist world. The partners in international capitalist trade could not be equal partners in a situation where prices were fixed by the leading monopolies and where price and trading conditions were instruments for deriving income from the less-developed countries in favour of the developed countries of the capitalist world.

These facts indicated that the level and price relations in trade among socialist countries could not be identical with the conditions on the world capitalist markets : the socialist countries included in their prices not only elements of costs but also social preferences which differed from those implicit in prices on the capitalist market. But this rightly posed the question why even a 'basic' world-market price should be used at all. A highly simplified answer might be that these prices, in their long-term trends, reflected the objective development of production and market conditions of the world economy, from which the socialist countries could not be and did not wish to be isolated.

The specific features of price creation were not limited to the CMEA countries. They were to be found likewise in other groups tending towards regional integration. It would be very interesting if Professor Robinson would complement his analysis of the West European Common Market in this respect.

At the conclusion of the session, *Sir Roy Harrod* made two points. In reply to Mr. Nikiforov, he stressed that his remark on moral issues did not impugn the moral standing, either in objectives or conduct, of the socialist countries. He had been referring simply to the philosophical and intellectual aspect, having observed a tendency, not only in socialist thinking, but also in the West in certain schools of sociology and logic (linguistic analysis), to whittle down the sphere of moral considerations. He believed that, if truth were to prevail, moral considerations, which, in his view, constituted a sort of 'science' in their own right, should be given their proper place.

He was pleased to find that his view that it was important to encourage the international division of labour between socialist countries even in this first phase of development was not opposed by all socialists present, but was favoured by some. He was anxious to stress that he did not wish to maintain a situation in which some countries restricted their exports to primary products. He favoured industrialization from the beginning of the process of socialist development. On the one side, Dr. Novozámsky and Professor Rachmuth claimed that all countries should start by 'completing their industrial complex' or, as he expressed it during the discussion, first establishing a comprehensive base. On the other hand, Dr. Knyziak, whose view had now been revealed in English, had given a precise illustration of how costs for each country, and thereby for the whole community of socialist countries, could be reduced, even possibly without any extra capital accumulation ; if each of three countries reduced their 'series' of production in a certain type of product to one-third, each could specialize in that third. Dr. Hegedus had affirmed that there were too many branches of engineering in Hungary. Neither Sir Roy Harrod nor Professor Robinson proposed a prolonged division between primary and secondary producers, but the access to all partners of the advantages of specialization by the co-operative forward planning of the international division of labour.

ECONOMIC RELATIONS BETWEEN
CAPITALIST AND SOCIALIST COUNTRIES

Chapter 14

SOME PROBLEMS IN ECONOMIC RELATIONS BETWEEN SOCIALIST AND CAPITALIST COUNTRIES

BY

E. G. KAMENOV

Bulgarian Academy of Sciences

NUMEROUS problems characterize international economic relations among the countries belonging to the two systems — capitalist and socialist. Among these problems may be mentioned the prerequisites for the appearance and development of such relations; the nature of the economic ties between the two systems and the character of the economic laws and principles governing them; forms taken by these relationships; their fundamental trends and further prospects; and their economic, political, and social effects. The present paper concentrates on the first two questions.

OBJECTIVE PREREQUISITES FOR THE EMERGENCE AND DEVELOPMENT OF ECONOMIC RELATIONS BETWEEN SOCIALIST AND CAPITALIST COUNTRIES

It is a consistent policy of the socialist countries to develop their economic relations with other countries, regardless of differences in their economic and social systems. This is not a chance decision, but a reflection of the requirements of objective economic laws, but at the same time, it serves the essential and permanent interests of such countries. It arises from the applicability of the international division of labour — by the development of international trade and of other economic relations to both the capitalist and socialist economic systems.

The development of the productive forces in each system is indissolubly connected with the improvement of the forms, and the intensification, of division of labour; that is, with the further differentiation and specialization of economic activities among enterprises,

163

in branches of industry, in the economy as a whole, and on an international scale. This is not to say, of course, that division of labour proceeds in the same way under each system : there are differences in character, in its economic role, and in the social and economic effects. It does mean that both systems experience the objective necessity to develop economic ties with other countries, just as the obverse is related to the reverse of the medal.

The aims by which the socialist countries are guided support the development of these economic relations — notably the fundamental economic law of socialism postulating an uninterrupted expansion and perfecting of economic activity for the ever fuller satisfaction of the needs of all members of society, and the law on the economy of social labour, which requires the attainment of the maximum results with the minimum expenditure of social labour. By the international division of labour it is possible to expand production quicker to satisfy the needs of the population more fully, and to save more social labour than under autarky.

Furthermore, the countries concerned had active and well-developed economic relations with the other capitalist countries before they adopted socialism. The transformation of the domestic systems did not interrupt such contact, although new policies — accelerated industrialization and planning — inevitably affected the character, structure, and trends of their foreign trade and other international economic relations.

It would be completely erroneous to describe the consequences of these policies as autarkic, as do certain Western authors.[1] Autarky runs counter to the laws and principles of a socialist economy, which call rather for maximum use of the economic advantages offered by the international division of labour.

Accelerated industrialization and the harmonious and planned development of national productive forces do not contradict economic ties with other countries, for, as experience has shown, they lead to market expansion and to increased trade capacity with other countries. This is also valid for socialist industrialization : imports and exports constitute necessary elements in planned economic

[1] This characterization of the economic development and the economic policy of the European socialist countries has repeatedly been made by the authors of the annual review of the economic situation in Europe made by the Economic Commission for Europe, *cf. Economic Survey of Europe in 1954*, chap. 5, and *Economic Survey of Europe in 1958*, chap. I (respectively Geneva, 1955 and 1959). Similar views have been expressed also by Raymond Barre, *Économie politique*, Paris, 1958, tome II, p. 706, and by Wilhelm Röpke, *L'Économie mondiale aux XIXe et XXe siècles* (Geneva, 1959), pp. 39, 68, and 120.

development. Theory and practice have shown that the operation of different, and even contrary, economic laws constitutes no obstacle to the development of normal economic relations between the two systems : the objective conditions which make them possible are the conduct of transactions through commodity production, governed by the law of value and employing money, trade, credit, etc. On this, Lenin wrote : 'I see no reason why a socialist state such as ours could not have unlimited business relations with the capitalist countries. We have no objections to using capitalist locomotives and farming machinery, so why should they object to using our socialist wheat, linen, and platinum ? Has not socialist grain the same taste as any other grain ?' Here Lenin accepts the concordance of interest primarily in terms of use values, but it is also relevant that the goods exchanged have labour values. Each skill has a value determined by the quantity of standardized labour used in its production (the average socially-necessary time) and hence a common property and measure.

Money is likewise a category common to socialist and capitalist economies. There is a difference in its economic essence and its social role, since under capitalism it can be converted into capital and hence promote exploitation, whereas under socialism it serves the development of the communal economy and the realization of the socialist principles of production and distribution ; it in no way limits its employment as a link between the two systems. Under either socialism or capitalism money is a specific type of commodity which has value because it is itself the product of human labour. The gold basis of international currency under both systems is distinct from the national monetary forms which it acquires in the individual states ; its status of universal equivalent and of specific commodity by which all remaining commodities express and measure their value forms what one might call a golden bridge between the two systems.

The existence of credit systems under both socialism and capitalism permits the establishment of credit connexions, and the similarity of the productive process engenders trade. The two types of economy are based, not on manual labour and on primitive tools, but on highly-developed machines and technology (mechanization, electrification, automation, specialization, concentration, co-operation, and combination of production, etc.). The utilization of the same or similar machines and equipment fosters trade in these items between socialist and capitalist countries. Secondly, the application of highly-developed machinery and technological processes in both types of economy is conducive to a relative approximation of the value magnitudes of the goods manufactured under similar technological conditions, and this in its turn facilitates trade between these countries. Finally, the technical similarity between the two systems opens up the field of scientific and technical co-operation, which, under the present conditions of rapid technological revolution, further promotes commercial exchange.

The development of international transport and communications involves intercourse transcending the limits of an economic system. Countries are linked by an intricate world system of railways, requiring international railway conventions regulating the tariffs for passengers and goods, common rules on waggon transit through foreign territory, the acceptance on a mutual basis of tickets and transport documents, the periodic settlement of mutual accounts, the co-ordination of the time-tables, and many other details of a technical and economic nature. Both capitalist and socialist countries inevitably take part in these conventions. The development of road transport and of the international network of roads calls for co-operation among the countries possessing different social systems, *e.g.* the co-ordinated development and maintenance of roads of international significance, agreement on common traffic rules, the establishment of uniform international signs, etc. Co-operation between the socialist and capitalist countries is perfectly natural and necessary in sea and air transport, and telegraph, telephone, and radio communications. Without the international conventions regulating these communications in which both socialist and capitalist countries take part, a normal operation of these communications would be impossible.

The socialist countries see their direct interest from the expansion of economic relations with the capitalist countries in the advantages of the international division of labour and an opportunity of promoting the consolidation of world peace and understanding among peoples. These economic relations constitute an inseparable part of the policy of peaceful co-existence unswervingly followed by the socialist countries.

Such relations are also of considerable interest to the capitalist states as markets. The socialist countries comprise one-fourth of the land on the globe, one-third of the world's population, and 37 per cent of the world's industrial output. Certain companies keenly interested in the development of trade with socialist countries are vigorously opposed to the policy of restrictions and discrimination in this trade pursued by various Western governments, which limits it to a comparatively small share of the world total ; the cause is not to be found in objective obstacles related to differences in economic systems, as some Western authors maintain. They often go on to imply that trade with the socialist countries promotes an economic development which runs counter to the interests of the 'free world', and see in the strengthening of the socialist countries a threat to the capitalist system. By embargoes and restrictions on trade, they envisage inhibiting the socialist development of these countries. It is hardly necessary to point out that isolation and blockade of the U.S.S.R. during its most troubled period, the years just after the Revolution, failed to bring the young socialist state to its knees ; the blockade collapsed as, one after another, capitalist countries established trade relations with the Soviet Union (during 1921 alone the United Kingdom on 16 March, Germany on 6 May, Norway on 2 September, Austria on 7 December, and Italy on 25 December). Attempts to establish an economic blockade of other socialist countries after their revolutions also proved ineffective.

ECONOMIC LAWS GOVERNING THE RELATIONS BETWEEN THE TWO SYSTEMS

It is important both theoretically and practically to analyse the economic essence of the relations between the socialist and capitalist countries and to define the character of the economic laws governing such relations. These are obviously neither purely socialist relations of production, nor are they purely capitalist ones. They are relations which appear, if one may so put it, at the point of intersection of the two systems — relations resulting from the crossing of different (and very often contrary) trends : they are representative of something new and peculiar, and cannot be simply reduced to either type of productive relation.

Such a general finding is, of course, far from being sufficient : it is necessary to determine the essence and nature of this peculiarity, to find what happens with the economic laws operative under both systems, to establish whether they lose their validity under these relations, whether they undergo any changes in the character, degree, and range of their effect, or whether there appear new laws inherent solely in this new type of economic relations.

One may begin by dismissing the possibility that economic

relations appearing between the capitalist and socialist countries constitute a new type, for this implies the appearance of new forms of ownership, of new social classes and groups, and of a new manner of distribution. The new economic relations which appear as the contact of the two systems are not independent, because they neither belong to an independent mode of production nor form the basis for a particular social superstructure. A more rewarding analogy is offered by the transition period of the socialist countries from capitalism, that is in the emergence of a dual-sectoral economy with relations representative of different types of production. In the conditions examined, however, the socialist sector has expanded at the expense of the capitalist by the active intervention of the state. No such superior authority is interposed between socialist and capitalist countries: their distinctive economic laws can be considered as enjoying equal positions, with neither dominant.

In this state of affairs a concrete analysis reveals that some manifestations are those which develop under capitalism, those that appear under socialism, and still others which appear under conditions of contact between the two systems. Of these, there can be differentiated economic laws specific and inherent to only one of these systems, and economic laws common to both systems.

The existence and the operation of economic laws specific to social and economic structures are invariably related to certain objective economic conditions. The basic economic law of socialism and the laws of planned, proportionate development or of socialist distribution according to work operate on the basis of public ownership of the means of production and under the conditions of the socialist method of production. These laws can have no effect where capitalist relations rule. Conversely, capitalist laws such as the basic economic law of capitalism, or the laws of capitalist competition and anarchy of production, of average profit, or of labour remuneration under capitalism lose their validity and are inoperative under the conditions of a socialist economy. Neither of these groups of laws operate outside the bounds of their system, but shared economic categories can nevertheless be found. Commodity production, the law of value, money, trade, and credit — categories to which reference has already been made — have specific features and operate differently under socialism and capitalism, but these distinctions, whenever they manifest themselves as links between the two systems, display precisely those of their features which are common to both systems.

The points made above on money, the law of value, commodity production, and credits need not be reiterated, but special attention should be devoted to the problem of value and prices on the international mixed market where the two systems meet.

Certain authors see an obstacle to the development of inter-system trade in their different procedures of price-formation. Such differences are not to be denied : under capitalism prices are determined spontaneously on the market, are affected by such factors as the ratio between supply and demand, the role of capitalist monopolies, and their power to impose their own monopoly prices under particular conditions, profiteering practices and stockjobbing, etc., as well as by business conditions. In a socialist economy much the greater part of the goods brought on the market originates in the state sector, which determines the level of prices of each good in a directive manner and according to plan.

On neither side, however, can price-formation be arbitrary. The ratio of supply to demand on the capitalist market affects the fluctuations of prices, but the basis around which these fluctuations take place remains the amount of socially-necessary labour for the manufacture of a particular type of commodity, *i.e.* its value or its production price. Under imperfect competition part of the surplus value or part of the labour production can be appropriated from non-monopolized branches, but they cannot together appropriate more value than has been produced in society. The socialist state likewise has to take value as the basis. Deviations of price from value, which are permissible in individual cases, are resorted to temporarily for encouraging or restricting the demand for a certain commodity or for obtaining certain economic, social, or other results ; here, too, the deviations from value are, and should be, exceptional and mutually-offsetting. Three conclusions follow. First, that the creation of value is determined by the conditions of the country which produces and exports the commodity concerned on the international mixed market and is therefore governed by the economic laws of that country ; secondly, that the value to the importing country is determined by the economic laws governing that system ; finally, the content of the law of value — demanding that goods be sold according to their value (*i.e.* according to the quantity of skill-standardized labour necessary for their production) — is analogous under both systems.

To these may be added a number of specific features arising from the combined operation of the economic laws of the two systems.

Where the sellers are capitalist firms and buyers are socialist countries, competition between the firms induces deviations of prices from the value, in a manner which does not arise from competition among the socialist enterprises concerned. Yet the presence of socialist countries as buyers furnishes a number of advantages for their capitalist partners : they operate according to plan and offer more certainty to their partners in the capitalist countries ; they are reliable clients with guarantees of commercial integrity, promptness, and solvency. Such factors reduce the risk which can accompany trade among private capitalist enterprises, and is an important new aspect of commerce between capitalist and socialist countries.

Where the sale is by socialist to capitalist countries, a foreign-trade enterprise which has specialized in the particular type of goods in each socialist country appears as the only or almost only partner. For instance, capitalist firms seeking to buy tobacco from Bulgaria will approach Bulgartabak, buyers of attar of rose will get in touch with Bulgarska Rosa, while those seeking machinery will contact Machino export.

To those who are accustomed to see in competition between sellers the sole guarantee against any arbitrary rise in prices and the unique instrument of their approximation to the level of value, these conditions may seem fraught with danger and uncertainty. They might accuse socialist trade of leading to high monopoly prices. This would probably be the case if under these conditions the operation was not of socialist but of capitalist monopolies. In reality, however, socialist foreign-trade enterprises, just as all socialist enterprises, are alien to any spirit of profiteering and to the desire to exploit the needs and difficulties of their partners. These conditions do not in the least involve the dangers referred to by certain authors in the West — dangers which would have been real ones if it were a matter of capitalist enterprises. Moreover, the fact that the capitalist firms could try to obtain the goods not only from the international mixed market but also from the international capitalist market opens the channel to a certain influence of the one market over the other and inhibits any trend towards monopolistic pricing. Conditions are absolutely free, as regards competition among the buying firms, since the socialist enterprises are guided by their desire to sell under the most advantageous conditions.

A new law is actually obtained from this combined operation. The prices of the goods exported by the socialist countries are determined according to plan, though deviation is allowed mainly to adjust to competition between capitalist buyers and in reflection of the international capitalist market.

As regards price-formation for goods exported by the capitalist countries on the international mixed market, the deviation of their prices from the value occurs under the effect of the correlation between supply and demand, though competition among buyers is restricted and it has a small effect on the process of price-formation ; the operation has also restricted such factors manifested on the capitalist market as profiteering and cyclical fluctuations. Monopolistic effects, though not eliminated, are weakened by the energetic opposition, and the growing influence, of the socialist countries.

An analogous picture is obtained under the other forms of economic relations among the countries of the two systems. Thus credit relations between capitalist and socialist countries contain aspects which are realized under capitalist conditions and are governed by capitalist laws and principles, other aspects which make themselves manifest under the conditions of a socialist economy and develop according to the operation of the laws inherent in that economy, and common elements which permit the flow of credit between them. But the socialist character of the economy and government precludes the imposition of any condition on the offer of credit which would infringe sovereignty or economic and political independence (*e.g.* earmarking specific state revenues or property as security or control by representatives of the creditor on the manner of disbursement). The socialist state which owns both the means of production and the finished products of the majority of productive enterprises guarantees the strict and prompt implementation of the obligations assumed by foreign-trade and other enterprises. It has no desire to encroach on the economic independence of other countries by onerous and enslaving conditions nor to use the credits to interfere in domestic affairs. Foreign loans extended by socialist countries are characterized by favourable terms for recipients. Such conditions are easiest for credits given by socialist countries to the developing states at low rates of interest, for long periods, and under acceptable terms of payment (usually in traditional export goods, and often through the export of goods produced by the machines and equipment delivered on credit).

Socialist relations of production thereby set their imprint on international credit relations, placing them within certain limits and making them compatible with the principles and laws of socialist economics. However, despite the elimination of certain features of capitalist credit, the relations between socialist and capitalist countries retain characteristics such as guaranteed reimbursement and payment of a reasonable and normal interest. Although this form of commercial credit is not widespread in the internal credit system of the individual socialist countries, it is employed both with capitalist and among the socialist countries.

The exchange of experience in science and technology is of notable significance at the present stage of the economic development of the socialist and capitalist countries. An objective basis of this form of exchange and co-operation is both the similarity, already referred to, in the material and technological conditions of production under both systems and the scientific and technological revolution now under way in both socialist and capitalist countries. The development and application of scientific and technical knowledge in the economies of both systems are, however, realized under different conditions. A large part of research in the developed capitalist countries is done in the private laboratories and enterprises of the big monopolies, under the domination of the patent system, and the greater part of technical innovations and scientific discoveries are in the hands of these monopolies. The rights over these important scientific and technological achievements become a significant object of trade, while the sale of licences and patents turns into a major source of super-profits for the monopolies.

There can be no conflicting interests among the separate socialist enterprises under the conditions of socialism. There can be no production secrets among them and all scientific and technical achievements are popularized and introduced in an orderly manner. Scientific and technical co-operation takes place on a large scale when one socialist country informs another free of charge about its scientific and technical achievements.

In the relations between socialist and capitalist countries in this field, there is no place for the application of the socialist principles of communicating scientific and technical achievements free of charge : the interests and aims of socialist and capitalist enterprises do not coincide, and socialism is incompatible with private ownership of the achievements of science and technology. For these reasons the socialist countries co-operate with the capitalist partners on the basis of capitalist methods of sale of patents and licences. Of course, once these patents and licences are ceded, their use is determined by the economic laws and principles inherent to the system in which they are applied. The pattern of other forms of economic relations between the two systems is similar : transport and communications, international insurance, international fairs, international tourism, etc.

CONCLUSIONS

The economic relationship between countries (or enterprises) belonging to the two different social systems is complex and composite : that part which originates under socialism is governed by the objective economic laws of socialism, and that part which is generated under capitalism operates within the economic laws of capitalism, while the two systems are manifest at the point of transfer. But although the activity of socialist enterprises in foreign trade or producing for export is governed by the economic laws of socialism (including the law of planned and proportionate development of national economy), it is affected in relations with capitalist countries by elements of uncertainty, for its activity must be forecast rather than founded on the obligatory dispositions usual for socialist enterprises. An enterprise producing for export to capitalist countries must take into account certain specific conditions and requirements of the capitalist market, just as do capitalist enterprises in assessing the export market in socialist countries. In short, the operation of laws specific to each of the two systems is restricted to the conditions of the respective system, but the establishment of a connexion evokes the operation of common principles.

Chapter 15

SUMMARY RECORD OF THE DISCUSSION
— SESSION IV

ECONOMIC RELATIONS BETWEEN
CAPITALIST AND SOCIALIST COUNTRIES
(In the Chair : PROFESSOR DUPRIEZ)

Professor Jeanneney began by stating his agreement with Professor Kamenov's conclusion that international trade between socialist and capitalist countries was both desirable and feasible, although it was distinguished by certain characteristics from commerce within each system.

Professor Kamenov emphasized in his paper three similarities which facilitated trade between members of different groups, viz. first that the process of production was technically the same under each system, the scope for trade arising from the differential combination of factors in that process between any two partners ; second, that the requirement that price remunerate cumulative labour outlays under each system established a set of minimal price relations operative within each economy ; and third, that transactions were effected by foreign exchange based upon a gold parity. The fundamental characteristic distinguishing inter-system from intra-system commerce was the state monopoly of trade and production in the socialist group and private-enterprise competition in the capitalist group. As a consequence, the socialist state exercised direct control over production and transactions, while the capitalist state set no more than the framework within which private trade operated (*e.g.* by customs tariffs, quotas, and other financial conditions). In addition, non-economic considerations had arisen to inhibit certain flows of trade between countries of different systems for strategic reasons. The asymmetry of decision-making in each group did not preclude the generation of trade flows between each under market conditions, that is, by the interaction of supply and demand.

Professor Jeanneney added to Professor Kamenov's list the observation that, although each socialist state was a monopolist or monopsonist for the goods in which it transacted (implying a greater bargaining power than that possessed by any capitalist firm short of a cartel), its position was attenuated by the existence of many socialist states and by the fact that on the international market the socialist state was in competition with many private buyers or sellers. He did not think that market traders derived much benefit from the theoretical possibility of competition among socialist exporters : in general, socialist countries rarely exported the same product as each other (machine tools from Czechoslovakia were not similar to Soviet ; Poland sold steam coal while the U.S.S.R. offered anthracite). Plant co-ordination and specialization within CMEA should further differentiate products.

As long as the socialist state held only a small percentage of the international market, it had to align its prices with those of the market or even offer at some discount. Price leadership by socialist countries could be dangerous for the capitalist economies if they sought to maximize the advantages of their position. It was partly this fear which led Western enterprise to advocate a limitation on imports from the socialist group. He recalled that Soviet oil sales below the cartel price had been necessary to gain a foothold in Western Europe. This sort of market disruption was highly desirable on welfare grounds among Western European consumers, since it remedied market imperfection and limited the demands on Western enterprise of Middle Eastern governments.

On a second characteristic of East-West trade, however, Professor Jeanneney felt that the interests of Western producers and consumers were at one, that is, on the instability of the East as a client. He could not agree with Professor Kamenov's contention that a planned economy was by definition a stable buyer or seller on capitalist markets. Sir Roy Harrod had already mentioned this problem, but he would like to set it out in more detail. In the first place, Eastern purchases in the West tended to vary from year to year because they were used to make up fluctuations from plan in the domestic economy. This was exaggerated by the instability of agricultural output in the socialist group : because grain purchases made up a substantial part of sales by capitalist countries, harvest fluctuations had a major impact on East-West trade. In the second place, the socialist countries tended to prefer large, but discrete, purchases — the commissioning of complete plant was an example. It was no counter-argument to state that the socialist countries were prepared to undertake long-term commitments — and it was fair to say that such commitments were also scrupulously honoured — because such contracts could just as easily be negotiated between Western corporations.

A final constraint on the part of Western enterprise was the inability to reply in kind to potential Eastern techniques of marketing. Thus, if the British Motor Corporation were to open a price war on the French market, Renault and Citroen could respond by dumping in England : in fact the freedom of entry, subject to tariffs, prevented such a confrontation. But if a Volga car were sold below cost in France, the French competitors had no possibility to sell their products in the U.S.S.R. Nor could one capitalist country as such gain a dominant position on the market of another because, some exceptions apart, there were many enterprises exporting from the given country. On the other hand, the monopolistic position of the socialist exporter could lead to the dependence of a small capitalist country on a single socialist state.

Again, like Sir Roy Harrod, he wanted to stress his desire for the expansion of East-West trade, but its promotion should be undertaken within a framework which took appropriate account of realities.

Professor Grossman appreciated the value of Professor Kamenov's paper and Professor Jeanneney's introduction : between them they had covered the major problems of East-West trade. He wanted only to supplement their treatment by the observation that the Eastern desire for inter-governmental trade agreements was misplaced : certainly so far as concerned trade between the United States and the Soviet Union, an agreement would hinder rather than foster commerce, because intervention by the Federal Government would prejudice business with American corporations. It would, moreover, be against the interests of the socialist partners to have too high a proportion of their trade with the West regulated by long- and medium-term trade agreements, because trade with the West constituted one of their most important elements of flexibility. The Eastern economies were planned so as fully to mobilize their resources ; they had little idle capacity and few reserve stocks with which to fill sudden gaps ; and their trade among themselves (something like two-thirds) was quite rigidly planned. Thus, in the event of unexpected disturbances or deliberate and sudden changes in policy, trade with the West was a reliable channel to fill emergency needs.

Mr. Kaser believed that Professor Kamenov's paper was valuable as an examination of capitalist-socialist relations in the framework of scientific Marxism. He felt, nevertheless, that the analysis of each system in terms of productive relations implied the existence of more differences than might in fact exist.

In particular, Professor Kamenov had stated that different, and even opposite, economic laws were operative in the two systems (cf. pp. 168–169 and 171–172). If the interpretation of each system avoided reference to any imputed 'law' but relied on empirical observation, Drewnowski's contrast between a 'state preference function' and a 'consumers' preference function' might be more appropriate.[1] The one was expressed in a plan or in economic policy, and the other was demonstrated by the market. The weight accorded to the same objective might well differ in each, but the preferences revealed could in principle be similarly mapped. No

[1] J. Drewnowski, 'The Economic Theory of Socialism : a Suggestion for Reconsideration', *Journal of Political Economy*, August 1961, pp. 341–354.

'opposition' arose between one function and the other, for each represented a set of desired resource allocations.

In present circumstances the fundamental difference between the two systems was to be found in institutions and not in productive relations (since institutions under capitalism or socialism could be changed without affecting the ownership of the means of production). In the capitalist market economy, the buyer or seller faced the same price at home and abroad (subject to customs duties and transport costs), but hitherto the socialist economies of Eastern Europe had used two price sets — one domestic and the other foreign. By channelling transactions through the state foreign-trade monopoly, any profit or loss arising from the differential was absorbed by the state budget. The enterprise could not hence make rational choices between foreign and home transactors, and state policy on such decisions had to be expressed by instructions. The indirect procedures whereby state guidance was represented to market enterprises, of which both Professors Kamenov and Jeanneney had spoken, had the merit of preserving the monetary unit of decision-making by the enterprise. He saw in Hungarian and Czechoslovak measures of reform a partial solution by allowing domestic enterprises to engage in foreign trade.

Professor Dobrev could not agree with any assertion that trade with a socialist country had harmed a capitalist economy. So far as underdeveloped countries were concerned, trade with socialist countries could be a positive benefit because no socialist enterprise sought to own resources in those territories. A capitalist enterprise could have motives in its transactions with such countries which devolved from its power to possess factors of production abroad. The socialist enterprise was concerned only with mutual advantage, and could support schemes for diversifying the underdeveloped economy undeterred by the need to protect some monopoly in supply. He welcomed Sir Roy Harrod's plea for stress on the moral content of economics and believed that the disinterested trade of socialist with developing countries was a case in point.

Professor Notkin noted that some of the preceding discussion had focused attention on the restrictions and limitations allegedly created in trade between socialist and capitalist countries by the foreign-trade monopolies of the former. If discrimination were at issue, the U.S. Government should also be castigated. The evidence of one department of American government to a committee of the U.S. Senate [1] was that the discriminatory policy should be pursued in order to increase the difficulties of economic development in the U.S.S.R. Professor Grossman in a different context had claimed that some economic decisions had to be made at a political level: some circles in the U.S. Government (not paralleled in those of Western Europe) were trying to impose political

[1] United States Senate, Committee on Foreign Relations, *Hearings on East-West Trade*, Washington D.C., 1964, p. 19.

considerations on East-West trade, but such moves found little support among American businessmen.[1]

Professor Jeanneney had claimed that trade between socialist and capitalist countries was hindered by the irregularity of orders for equipment (particularly for plant), without reflecting that the same sort of contract was common between capitalist partners. The feature was typical of trade in this kind of goods — for no country bought equipment annually for the same branch of industry from any one firm, but made its purchases of equipment, as the need arose, from specialized firms. It was incumbent upon the suppliers to accommodate their capacity to this utilization by a judicious dovetailing of home and foreign orders.

Like Mr. Kaser, he welcomed Professor Kamenov's presentation of trade between two systems in the context of Marxist theory, but he had to question the contention that commodity-money relations within socialist countries were a necessary condition for the development of economic relations with capitalist states. Evidently, relations had to be grounded on some comparable basis : purchasing-power parity of the currencies employed could demonstrate the efficiency of foreign trade, but was not the only technique. Foreign trade would be possible under full communism between socialist partners where commodity-money relations had been extinguished, and between them and countries with a capitalist system.

Professor Jeanneney accepted Professor Notkin's point on the irregularity of orders for engineering goods : he would no longer consider this feature as one distinguishing socialist and capitalist countries.

Professor Oelssner criticized Professor Jeanneney's view of government trading monopolies on the socialist side facing free trade on the capitalist side. The period of free trade was over, having reached its zenith something like a century ago. Protectionism had since developed in all capitalist countries ; the simultaneous development of cartels and trusts had cumulated protection to the state-monopoly capitalism characteristic of the present century. International trade and free competition were thereby severely limited. Professor Jeanneney's hypothetical example on Anglo-French price competition in motor vehicles would lead not to reciprocal dumping, but to a tariff war. The French automobile manufacturers would merely have to influence their government to raise the duties on British cars to protect their industry and halt the dumping. A concrete example had recently occurred over the export of chickens from the United States to the Federal German Republic : when West German farmers had begun to be pressed by American competition, they had induced their government to raise import duties. Immediately the United States had announced that it would increase tariffs on West German industrial goods, and the confrontation ended in a draw.

[1] United States Senate, Committee on Foreign Relations, *East-West Trade: a Compilation of Views of Businessmen, Bankers and Economic Experts*, Washington D.C., 1964.

Summary Record of the Discussion

There were numerous contemporary examples of the important and growing role which the governments of the capitalist countries played in foreign trade. On the one hand, the government promoted trade by granting special export premia, export-credit guarantees, etc., while, on the other hand, it limited trade, particularly with the socialist countries, by imposing export prohibitions and embargoes, black-lists, and other restrictions. Often this caused friction between large corporations and the government, as the case of the embargo on the export of large-diameter steel pipe to the U.S.S.R. showed. West German firms had been willing to supply the pipe, but the Adenauer administration prohibited delivery, with the result that the orders were partly filled by other capitalist countries not subject to NATO policy and partly by the U.S.S.R. itself. The outcome was merely the loss of a good business opportunity for the West German firms.

Professor Oelssner was sure that East-West trade was less than optimal, not because commerce was monopolized in the socialist countries, but because export restrictions were imposed by the capitalist states. Curbs on trade were not peculiar to transactions with socialist countries, but operated, with as little success among the capitalist economies. There had been a serious dispute between the members of the Common Market on the number of exemptions to other members of GATT for the Kennedy Round of tariff negotiations.

Mr. Kaser had mentioned that some socialist countries, such as Hungary and Czechoslovakia, had begun to allow individual domestic enterprises to negotiate with foreign business partners : under the present reforms in the German Democratic Republic such delegation would also be made : it would not liquidate the foreign-trade monopolies, but would modify their operation.

He wanted to stress, in conclusion, that all obstacles to the development of foreign trade should be removed. Economists, for purely economic reasons, had a duty to promote free trade.

Professor Domar welcomed Professor Notkin's frank statement about American restrictions on trade with the Soviet Union ; Professor Oelssner's catalogue of American government restrictiveness could have been still further extended. The voices raised in support of such restrictions should be seen in the context of free speech : unfortunately those who deemed themselves important spoke more than others.

Soviet discussions about trade with the United States were usually associated with requests for credit, which the United States was blamed for not furnishing. But was such aid in accord with the American national interest when a former Chairman of the Soviet Council of Ministers had expressed his hope (in 1959) of 'burying' the United States ? The United States would hardly relish burial, particularly alive.

Professor Notkin was correct in recognizing political objectives in foreign-trade policies, but this was true of any country, including the United States and the U.S.S.R., for every country had the right to pursue trade policies in accordance with national interest.

On the matter of Soviet trade with under-developed countries, Neuberger had found that in the 1955–61 period Soviet imports fluctuated not less and possibly even more than those of the advanced Western countries.[1] It remained a puzzle that the Soviet Union, which took such great pride in planning, should continue to conduct its trade with underdeveloped countries in such a manner.

Mr. Kaser quoted Professor Kamenov's statement that 'the content of the law of value — demanding that goods be sold according . . . to the quantity of skill-standardized labour necessary for their production — [was] analogous under both systems' (p. 169). It had to be pointed out, however, that the criteria used for pricing on each side of the 'mixed market' were different : in Marxist terms, 'value-in-use' was included in capitalist price formation, whereas 'self-cost', *i.e.* labour value alone, was still the formal criterion employed in the socialist countries.

He felt that Professor Oelssner had minimized the problems arising in expanding commerce between market economies and state traders, and recalled the proposal that the grant of most-favoured-nation treatment or reductions in tariffs and quantitative restrictions by the former could be matched by commitments to expand trade by the latter.

Professor Jeanneney also took up Professor Oelssner on his view of the international market. No member of GATT could freely manipulate its tariffs in the way Professor Oelssner had described. It was scarcely in the interests of socialist countries to harbour old-fashioned views about capitalism. The forms of protection and of competition had greatly changed in recent decades. Competition, though not perfect, was still very much alive, although the inter-relation between government protection and free enterprise was now that of disciplined competition. The Common External Tariff of the European Economic Community was relatively low : at 15–20 per cent it was rather less than in the United States and the United Kingdom (particularly during the imposition of the 15 per cent import surcharge). Within that Tariff the Community sought to maintain competition within certain constraints.

Professor Kamenov recalled that three participants in the debate (Professors Jeanneney, Grossman, and Domar) had been concerned with the monopolistic character of socialist foreign trade. For a Marxist economist it was in the nature of a monopolistic corporation or of a capitalist state to exploit and dominate whenever possible ; if they did not so act, they would not be capitalist. When Robert Owen renounced the objective laws of capitalism, he ruined himself. But such monopolies had only the word in common with the socialist corporations : there were no cases

E. Neuberger, 'Is the U.S.S.R. Superior to the West as a Market for Primary Products?' *Review of Economics and Statistics*, August 1964, pp. 287–293.

of dumping or disloyal competition, because the socialist countries did not seek to exploit their partners.

He agreed with Professor Jeanneney that the socialist countries had to offer goods below the world price in order to break into the market : this was especially true of Bulgaria at present, because of the downward trend in primary prices. Professor Notkin had made an interesting theoretical point on the possibility of trade with capitalist countries once communism was achieved and the law of value no longer held : his own view was that trade would persist with capitalist countries and that criteria for such exchanges would be found ; his analysis remained valid for contemporary conditions.

SESSION V

PRICE SYSTEMS

Chapter 16

PRICE PROBLEMS IN YUGOSLAV THEORY AND PRACTICE

BY

I. MAKSIMOVIC and Z. PJANIC
University of Belgrade

SOME HISTORICAL FACTS

IT was long the assumption of Marxists that the economic mechanism of socialism would operate with the sort of parameters typical of the natural sciences; production units would merely be technical and organizational components of the system, and the distribution of available labour would be calculable as a technological relationship. This belief has not been borne out by the practical experience of socialist countries, which has shown that rational calculation requires a determinate system of prices; a much wider field is thus left to economic laws than had originally been thought.

The operation of market laws depends on the institutional framework of a given socialist community. From this aspect, Yugoslav postwar experience can be divided into two periods: the first comprised the early postwar years up to 1950, and the second, whose main trends began to appear during 1950 and attained comprehensive form by 1954, is still under way. The nationalization just after the War of the means of production in the leading branches of the economy created a large and potent public sector to the point that the character of the entire economic system depended on the relationships prevailing in that sector. In the first period the economy was run by state officials from one centre, the planning of production being in physical terms (as regards both quantities and assortment of goods); the role of the enterprises was confined to the execution of decisions emanating from this centre. Social outlay and accumulation were financed through the state budget by means of a turnover tax, which assumed the setting by the state of both wholesale and retail prices; the distribution system was essentially administrative. The market could hardly be said to have functioned.

Price Systems

The revolution in almost all the socialist countries came at a time when the material and technological level lagged substantially behind that in developed capitalist countries. The socialist revolutions certainly stimulated production and accumulation, but obviously not to the extent that all needs could be satisfied and products directly appropriated. Thus, around 1950 new views began to appear on the role of the economic mechanism appropriate to socialism : 'under the objective domination of relatively-backward productive forces the most general laws still remain of commodity production and commodity trade'.[1] It was recognized, however, that commodity production should continue to be based on the social ownership of the means of production ; that transactions between producers should not be subject to random movements, but operate within the framework of a social plan, which would be decisive in choosing the basic proportions of the economy ; and that investment should be allocated by, and for, the community and its dynamic social needs. Yugoslav economists at that time saw a dialectic interaction between elements of the old order — an underdeveloped material and social basis — and elements of the new, revolutionary order, which would eventually achieve the direct appropriation of goods in accordance with needs.

Three groups of prices emerged at that stage of planning — 'value' prices, 'planned' prices, and 'real' prices. 'Value' prices were intended to represent commodity value for comparison with physical indicators, expressing use value. 'Planned' prices differed from 'value' prices when accumulation generated on one product was purposively transferred to another branch of production (a reallocation made necessary by the existence of small private — and even capitalist — producers, and by the many material disproportions inherited from the pre-war economic structure of Yugoslavia). 'Real' prices were those shaped by the market, although within a planned framework.

In theory, state control was to be strongest over the prices of investment goods, less dominant over raw materials, and weakest over consumers' goods, with the impact of market forces in inverse proportion. Seen in its time component, the market was to be allowed to produce short-term effects, with the community reserving to itself the right of indirect intervention (viz. to seek desired relations between supply and demand, by using monetary or fiscal

[1] B. Kidrič : 'Economics of the Transitional Period in Yugoslavia', *Komunist*, November, 1956, p. 4.

instruments, or by inventory changes). The long-term effects were to be at the discretion of the community, but its criteria differed from those exhibited by the market, and, in the general state of the Yugoslav economy, this theoretical dichotomy never worked well.

In practice, Yugoslav price policies hardly differed from those of other socialist countries. Relatively-low prices were imposed on producers' goods, in order to promote and to encourage accumulation at the expense of personal consumption. At the same time, low prices were also set for farm products in order to utilize rural savings for industrialization, and to contain the spontaneous development of agriculture. Some of these elements can be perceived in the price policies of each socialist state, and conduced to the formulation of the theory of two price levels under socialism.[1]

The economic reform now being prepared by the Yugoslav authorities aims at a *déétatisation* involving an increased role for the enterprise in investments. This has required careful consideration of the economic situation of each branch of the economy, to find out whether the existing price relations render possible the earning of incomes proportionate to labour inputs, and whether these earnings secure sufficient amounts of resources both for investment and for worker remuneration. Interest in the so-called 'normative theory' of prices under socialism has been thereby revived, and Yugoslav and other economists have been reconsidering formulae for price determination in a socialist economy.

THE 'NORMATIVE PRICE' UNDER THE YUGOSLAV SYSTEM

A characteristic of the Yugoslav economic system is the considerable discretion over investment exercised by the enterprise, in response to which the planning authorities evolved 'normative prices' in 1950, when the new system was being devised. It was intended to set up a price system which would give producers an increasing share in income distribution — not only in theory, but effectively, that is, by assuring workers a participation in the net earnings of their enterprise. Prices had, moreover, to enable the enterprise to make a proper choice of alternatives, since it draws up its own plans on the volume and assortment of production, to maximize income, under optimal utilization of its resources.

[1] B. Minc, *Zarys teorii kosztów produkcji i cen* (An Outline of the Theory of Production Costs and Prices), Warsaw, 1958.

It was impossible to reconcile these ambitious claims, and, in the absence of a theoretical solution, price policies were essentially pragmatic. In such circumstances, theorists had to begin by defining the prices which emerged — 'normative price', 'unique price', 'normal price', and 'parity price'.

Based upon these concepts, divergent views were put forward in subsequent years on an appropriate theory of price formation — as 'value prices', 'income prices', 'production prices', 'balanced prices', or 'target prices'; various empirical lines were also suggested, including alignment to international market prices.

The broad spectrum of proposals as 'normatives' testifies to the central dilemma of Yugoslav (and not only Yugoslav) economists which still awaits solution: what are the respective limits of labour value and of commodity production in the Yugoslav model? Yugoslav opinion is divided: some economists regard the role of the law of value as essential, seeing the plan as merely an element of the law of commodity production; others see in both laws a dialectical unity and believe them to be a necessary component of the Yugoslav model; still others perceive the laws of commodity production as a function of planning, with the commodity nothing else than a form through which the random movements of the economy are purposively overcome. In the last resort, the problem of prices is reduced to the problem of the limits within which the law of commodity production operates.

'*VALUE*' *AND* '*PLANNED*' *PRICES*

In the early fifties, when the Yugoslav economic system was being radically changed, Boris Kidric, the late Yugoslav statesman and economic theoretician, attempted to define a unique criterion for the primary distribution of surplus value between socialist enterprises. Kidric saw price on the one hand as the sum of average socially-useful costs, and, on the other, as that which in aggregate yields the planned rate of accumulation: at the macroeconomic level, this would be 'value' price, and at the micro-economic level the 'planned price' which assures the planned rates of accumulation and of fiscal contributions in relation to the enterprise's assets. These rates were the instruments for the automatic distribution of global income, but, whenever accumulation was to take place in a branch other than that in which the funds would have been earned under the 'value price', a different 'planned price' had to be set. The intervention of the community in the accumulation process was thus effected by the instrumentality of price. Kidric viewed such planned discrepancies between the 'planned price' and the 'value price' as permitting the socialist sector to annul the effect of the blind forces of the capitalist law of the formation of an average profit rate, but envisaged that, within the proportions prescribed by the plan, genuine prices could be formed under the impact of the law of demand and supply. In the decade which followed, Yugoslav economic theory took little account of Kidric's ideas, either on the influence of the plan or on the principles of distribution of accumulation, but more recently they have regained some ground among economists who desire the setting of normatives for the accumulation of each branch, and of each enterprise in proportion to employment.[1] Embrace of this principle would, however, require rigorous administrative control, since accumulation proportionate to the amount of labour in individual branches could never be achieved through the spontaneous and automatic action of economic forces. Its strict observance would furthermore involve a drastic departure from the present structure of accumulation by regions, and could prejudice the present development policies of Yugoslavia.

'PRODUCTION PRICE'

More widely held is the opinion that Marx's 'production price' (adapted to contemporary social and economic relations and institutions) constitutes the most suitable category of 'normative' price for the primary distribution of newly-created values. A 'production price' takes account of both living and embodied labour, and allows the interplay of competitive forces operating in the market to compel the competitors to utilize all productive factors in the most rational manner.

But the structure of the 'production price' is not in full harmony with the new pattern of productive relationships taking shape in the Yugoslav economy: in Marx's terms the share of the workers' personal income, v, is considered more from the aspect of newly-created value, $v + m$, and less from that of the magnitude of resources engaged in production, $c + v$. v is no longer considered as a component part of cost, but as a function of newly-created values.

[1] When this sytem was applied, it was beneficial in reducing employment and in raising productivity, but it had shortcomings in stimulating the employment of a less-skilled labour force.

The capital-to-labour ratio, moreover, varies considerably between branches, and such prices would not yield adequate accumulation for labour-intensive branches unless interest were charged on fixed assets and loanable funds as a corrective to the production price.

'INCOME PRICE'

More recently another kind of 'normative price' has attracted attention, based on a concept which, on the one hand, takes into account both the laws governing commodity production under socialism and the material interests of direct producers (expressed in their desire to earn maximum incomes), without neglecting, on the other hand, the need for accumulation and for increased labour productivity, as a condition of any effort to achieve maximum incomes. 'Income price' marks up material costs by an income proportionate to an average social rate of return. The latter does not express the profitability of engaged capital assets (as would the profit rate), but the profitability of all productive factors, material and human. The basic intention of the author of the income price concept is to calculate both the general income rate of the economy as a whole and the income rate of individual branches of the economy, in order to permit a transfer of income between individual branches at the stage of primary income distribution. An analysis relating to the year 1962 showed that both the production price and the income price would substantially differ from the price formed empirically by the market mechanism and the factors of social income distribution (*i.e.* the legal provisions governing the formation and the distribution of enterprise income).

The income price concept has attracted attention as an interesting theoretical attempt to introduce a new kind of 'normative' price, but it suffers from the need to reduce all labour input to the volume of simple work furnished by an unskilled worker during a given period. It is in this way that an aggregate is obtained of newly-created values in each branch, the skill composition being converted by a coefficient for each branch. There are numerous difficulties, already much discussed, in the calculation of such a coefficient. The concept also obscures the distinction between labour remuneration and surplus value, which cannot be abandoned in the present Yugoslav model.

PRICE BASED ON COSTS

Attempts were made within the framework of purely theoretical analyses to test variants of 'normative' prices for the optimum use of productive factors at minimum costs under the conditions of a socialist economy. They indicated the inadequacy, in the Yugoslav case, of a unique price equal to marginal cost for assuring a proper distribution of primary income. Alternatively, if the distribution effect was ignored and the 'normative' price was intended to assist the maximization of the growth rate, prices were tested as those equating marginal costs with marginal incomes. This was in effect the concept of a 'normative' price based on maximum profit, viz. that price which presupposes minimum outlay (in full-cost terms) of all the factors employed by the enterprise. But in both these cases the implicit assumptions of an unhindered operation of the laws governing commodity production and of a perfect market for production factors and capital were invalid in Yugoslavia. Both, moreover, failed to satisfy the requirements of social accumulation, viz. the problem of a planned appropriation of a portion of newly-created values by incorporating a tax in production costs.

A further line of enquiry has been the determination of the 'normative' price at two levels. At the microeconomic level, price would be stable for a long period — as in the 'target price' concept of average long-run costs and a normal accumulation rate, unaffected by fluctuations of demand. At the macroeconomic level (*i.e.* that overseen by the government and the planning office), prices would be planned (by material balances) in the interests of economic development and in the light of long- and short-term price trends, of costs of the anticipated production at full capacity, and of projected investment. Such a 'balanced price' would be one of orientation only, for the accumulation implicit in its application could be distributed between individual branches, at planners' discretion. Proposals of this nature have, however, failed to make clear the functional relationship between the 'target price' of the enterprise and the 'balanced price' set by the planner.

Despite the lively discussion among Yugoslav economists described in the preceding paragraphs, a 'normative' price has still to be found which would optimize the allocation of productive factors, maximize production, and exclusively orientate the enterprise towards earning a maximum income. Nor does any solution combine the advantages of a planned economy with those offered by the market mechanism.

SOME CHARACTERISTICS OF THE YUGOSLAV
PRICE STRUCTURE

Among the many features of the Yugoslav model which affect the structure of prices and incomes, the use of the rate of interest and the concept of the 'net earnings' of an enterprise are of specific practical concern.

A rate of interest was introduced in Yugoslavia in 1954 to demonstrate that the fixed assets, the working capital, and the natural resources confided to enterprises and at their free disposal were in public ownership, and to stimulate the enterprises to their rational utilization. Since then the share of interest, repayments, and bank deposits at the disposal of public investment funds has considerably increased.

An optimal rate of interest would determine the 'yardstick for measuring the duties of the individual enterprise towards the community' and, hence, be the most important structural factor in defining the 'normative' price, but there is no consensus in Yugoslavia on the determination of such an optimum. Some understand it to be related to the maximum profit rate at the 'production' (*i.e.* the 'normative') price. For this, however, price would have to operate through the mechanism of profit maximization within the framework of the planned distribution of investment. Others avoid the initial arbitrariness of the interest rate, by separating an interest rate (always positive) which is based on the principle of the maximum profit rate, from another interest rate determined by the disparity between the level of utilization and the saturation point of capital. This, too, does not avoid a political (or extra-economic) determination of the rate of investment. Still others favour maintaining the interest rate at the level of social profitability, denying profit maximization or the price of social-resource use as criteria and pointing to the constraints of microeconomic profit and to its possible long-run cyclical variation.

In the absence of a single optimum rate, differentiated rates have been used with success in Yugoslavia (in practice between 0 and 10 per cent); the charge on individual branches and enterprises for the utilization of social resources thereby became an important factor in equalizing the conditions under which the enterprises operate.

The 'net income' of an enterprise was, like the use of the interest rate, a theoretical innovation of the Yugoslav model: its definition is close, but not identical, to that of newly-created value, $v + m$.

Maksimovic and Pjanic — Yugoslav Theory and Practice

Yugoslav practice does not distinguish wages, v, because the direct producers, exercising their right to self-government, form their own incomes from the net income of the enterprise, viz. total revenue less material costs, amortisation and various contributions (turnover tax, and contributions to the commune, republic, and federation). In 1964 the Federal Assembly recommended further decentralization of financial decision by repealing some of these contributions. Contributions by mines and on the extraordinary earnings of enterprises had been abolished in 1963, and both contributions to social investment funds and a 15 per cent tax on net incomes have been dropped.

Although the period of use of the 'net income' category is relatively short, some tentative conclusions can be drawn from the data in Table 1. The share of 'net income' in the total income of enterprises has risen while that of contributions to socio-political communities from 'net income' has decreased; funds retained for the finance of investment have increased, and more of the worker's personal income comes from distribution of 'net income'.

TABLE 1

GROSS MONEY INCOMES OF ENTERPRISES, 1957–62

(Thousand millions of dinars)

	1957	1958	1959	1960	1961	1962
Revenue						
Income derived from the sale of goods and services	4,803	5,772	6,802	8,020	9,294	10,881
Expenditure						
Expenses for the purchase of materials used in production (after allowance for inventory change)	3,555	4,331	5,104	6,034	7,006	8,231
Salaries and social contributions	405	483	630	802	988	1,102
Payments to social funds	607	666	748	889	947	1,112
Retained by enterprises	165	295	312	449	519	537

Source: National Bank of the S.F.R. of Yugoslavia, *Annual Report for 1962*, p. 47.

It is paradoxical that Yugoslav economists exhibit a lively interest in the structure of the market — particularly because they have before them a prominent example of a socialist economy in which spontaneous economic forces affect the formation of prices — but have written little about the behaviour of the market. Many analyses have been made of the number of enterprises by branch or group of branches, on the rather naïve view that this is the main competitive element. It is true that danger does arise from an oligopolistic structure, and that weak organization and poor functioning of the market has adversely affected price formation. But this has been the crucial factor only in retailing, where monopolistic organizations have had ample scope for raising prices — a power exercised more in the case of food products than of manufactures, and more in small localities than in large. In other branches, the organizational structure of the market has been less important than the intervention of administrative bodies in certain areas. Such intervention has been tolerated on the view that the laws of the market in any case play a minor role in planned economies with social ownership of the means of production, and in which production and distribution are intended to correspond to the needs of the socialist community. Price policies have hence been considered as an instrument of planned economic development, although constrained by a market. It would have been more appropriate to see price policies as means to co-ordinate the plan and the market.

It would, even so, have been difficult to achieve equilibrium within a particular sector, let alone the general equilibrium of the economy, in the postwar economic conditions of Yugoslavia. These were distinguished by rapid, but unbalanced, growth : extra-economic factors, erratic harvests, and continuous difficulties in the balance of payments unstabilized the basic material flows and seriously disturbed the market, and price levels and relatives. The aggregate value of consumption grew both by inflation and in real terms, as Table 2 shows.

To implement its plans, and particularly to secure the imple-

TABLE 2

INDEX NUMBERS OF OUTPUT AND CONSUMPTION

1955 = 100

	1956	1957	1958	1959	1960	1961	1962
Social product (physical indicators)	100	122	117	143	160	169	178
Overall consumption (at current prices)	104	128	127	158	190	223	243
Index of retail prices	104	105	109	110	118	129	137

Source : *Statistički godišnjak S.F.R.J., 1963*, Belgrade, 1964.

mentation of the key tasks of development, the State had recourse to various controls over the agents of production and over other economic activities. The measures taken can be grouped as distribution instruments (*i.e.* to relate personal incomes derived from the enterprise to labour productivity and management efficiency), monetary policies, and direct price regulation. Price stabilization was sought not only through economic measures but also through direct State intervention.

Two forms of price control are operated over manufactures : price ceilings are set by the Federal Executive Council for the most important raw materials and semi-manufactures, while, for the major industrial consumers' goods and certain other raw materials, enterprises are obliged to inform the authorities of their intention to raise prices. Price ceilings are normally the highest permissible prices at which producers may sell, but in the case of wool and hides they are the highest prices at which goods may be bought ; fixed retail prices are imposed for some consumers' goods. The Federal Price Control Office has to ratify price increases for products for which the 'early warning system' is in force. About 70 per cent of manufactures are subject to these two forms of price control.

In agriculture, State intervention has had a somewhat different character, to set minimum prices for the most important farm products. Price control in trade is not a federal matter, but is effected by the administrative authorities of the republic or locality. The trade enterprise is required to give notice of an intention to raise charges, viz. the margin between its purchase and its selling prices. Price controls over services are varied. The federal authorities prescribe railway freight, air, postal and telecommunication tariffs, and set regulations for the determination of rents for dwellings. The republican authorities fix the tariffs for freight by other means of transport. Some sectors, such as catering and building, are subject to no price controls whatever.

Present efforts — within the framework of a new long-term plan of economic and social development — are directed towards stabilizing the material flows which should stabilize prices, and towards reforming those instruments of the economic system which obstruct rational price formation. Measures are being introduced to enhance the role of the price mechanism in trade. These changes are part of a broad reform of the Yugoslav economic system, in which pricing should be simpler and more efficient, and, in general, reality should be brought closer to the aspirations of the Yugoslav model.

Chapter 17

THE ROLE OF PRICES IN A
SOCIALIST ECONOMY

BY

O. KYN

Charles University, Prague

THE PLACE OF PRICING THEORY

UNTIL recently pricing was considered a secondary problem in a socialist economy. This was the result both of practices which had become established in the past, and of a set of generally-accepted theoretical postulates. Very little attention was paid to the theory of prices, the deficiency of which profoundly marked recent economic practice.

This neglect of pricing was justified by the assumption that the central problem of the socialist economy was the assurance of planned proportions derived primarily from material balances and their disaggregation as directives for production enjoined upon individual plants. The role of prices was hence no more than as a subsidiary form of cost accounting; to make it independent and related to the market was in fact considered irreconcilable with the system of planning and central management. The retention of prices and of Marx's category of commodity production was ascribed to the remnants of obsolete economic relations, which, however, were doomed as a result of a further development of the economy. This opinion held that socialism left a product exchanged within the state sector with no more than a formal character as a commodity, because the role of the market had been replaced by the central management. A slightly larger role was attributed to the prices of articles sold to households and to and by co-operatives, but, even in this respect, the function of price was to redistribute national income in accordance with planned living standards; it was not envisaged that a price mechanism would provide for a direct feedback between the producer and the consumer.

More recent opinions, however, have favoured some rehabilitation of the classical concept of price, and a more intensive employment of the automatically-operating market within the mechanism of a socialist economy. These new ideas arose after economists in the countries concerned had overcome a limited and one-sided interpretation of Marxist theory, and in response to a number of practical problems in socialist planning. The change of view was to a great extent brought about by the rapid infiltration of mathematics into Marxist economics during the past five years, and by the realization that cybernetics could be applied to the processes of economic management.

It followed that price problems were basic to socialism and could not be brushed aside as secondary. Price theory, formerly devoted primarily to price calculation in individual branches, became inseparably linked with problems of planning, above all in formulating optimization criteria for output and for the use of scarce resources ; it had, furthermore, to be integrated with management techniques, economic information, incentives, conflict of interest, distribution and redistribution of the national income, etc. The old forms of organization were criticized not only for failing to make a positive use of prices throughout the economy, but even for suppressing their role.

Today, by contrast, the socialist countries have at their disposal a substantial theoretical literature on prices and their function in the economic mechanism,[1] and, gradually, changes are being introduced in practical price policy. The theoretical views which have emerged are by no means uniform and the future use of prices could considerably differ from country to country.

This diversity precludes in the present study an analysis of the current price system in all socialist countries and of the criticism to which it has been subjected over recent (and in Yugoslavia many) years. This report hence attempts no more than a sketch of the existing price system, and its shortcomings, a brief review of new theoretical work, and, in conclusion, a personal interpretation of Czechoslovak experience and discussions on the scope for associating the price mechanism with planned management.

The constraint of space requires the omission of a detailed history of the price system by country, but an essay is made to identify their common features. All exhibit the same socialist economic relations,

---

[1] See Čestmír Kožušník, *Problémy teorie hodnoty a ceny za socializmu* (Problems of the theory of value and price under socialism), Prague, 1964 ; Bohumil Komenda, *Ekonomická funkce a působení velkoobchodních cen* (The economic function and effect of wholesale prices), Prague, 1964 ; and Ota Šik, *K problematice socialistických zbožních vztahů* (On the problem of socialist commodity relations), Prague, 1964.

under which state ownership prevails in industry and co-operative ownership in agriculture, engendering four types of transaction, with corresponding forms of price :

(*a*) transactions between state enterprises (predominantly in the supply of raw materials, machinery and equipment, and producers' goods generally) at wholesale prices ;

(*b*) sales by state agencies of consumers' goods to households at retail prices ;

(*c*) sales of farm produce by co-operatives to state agencies at procurement prices ;

(*d*) sales by agricultural co-operatives to households at the so-called prices of the co-operative market.

This characterization oversimplifies : a more precise classification would distinguish co-operative enterprises in industry, state enterprises in agriculture, and numerous other exceptions, and would discuss the problem of traders' margins. But it is hoped that the present approximation will serve.

PRICE FORMATION IN THE ESTABLISHED SYSTEM

Pricing policy in the socialist countries has hitherto been characteristic in five major respects : prices have been centrally fixed, have been constant for long periods, have been formed into two sets, wholesale and retail, with the latter subject to systematic reduction, and a special regime has operated for agricultural prices.

In common with all other economic phenomena, prices have been centrally managed under socialism. If we may distinguish between central determination and central control, we may characterize the majority of prices as directly determined by a central agency, while others — farm produce sold by co-operatives or certain 'local' goods — are determined by district bodies. The term 'central control', which implies absence of such direct instruction, is discussed below.

A second feature of price policy has been stability ; prices once determined are not changed for a long time, the main exception being farm prices on the co-operative market, which vary with market conditions. Stability means that price neither reflects the current relation between demand and supply, nor — save at long intervals and at the discretion of central agencies — responds to a change in costs. The original practice, no longer followed, was annually to reduce selected retail prices and once every five years generally to adjust wholesale prices. This characteristic is not inseparable from the principle of central management, although, in the past, they were thought of as related and presented as the contrast to flexible market prices, considered to be a symptom of competitive anarchy. It is of course perfectly feasible for prices to be both centrally regulated and flexible, or market-determined and stable. The central agency can adjust prices according to the conditions of supply and demand without infringing, in our opinion, the principle of planning ; indeed, planning can be inconsistent with stable prices. Some countries (*e.g.* Poland) have already rejected strict stability of prices and frequently adjust prices in accordance with market conditions ; during 1963 certain steps were taken in this direction in Czechoslovakia, although prices continue to remain stable for the majority of consumers' goods. Price stability is undoubtedly desirable, but only if it does not cloak a violation of economic equilibrium. As long as the economic system is kept in equilibrium, by means of planning and central management, prices can be stabilized without resort to directive fixing.

The price system here described is formed at two levels. Retail prices are determined so as to clear the market of planned household expenditure, itself dependent on the volume of income ; this procedure does not require that the price of any individual product correspond to Marxian value, although the average of all assures equality with $c + v + m$. The level of wholesale prices, on the other hand, does not include the entirety of surplus value (m), and, in practice, wholesale prices are computed by adding a very small profit (three per cent would be a usual rate) to the costs of production ; wholesale prices for a number of producers' goods have been fixed even below production cost, requiring state subsidies.

With some exceptions, retail prices are used only for final products sold to consumers, while almost all intermediate products are transferred at wholesale prices, this gap being bridged by the turnover tax. Historically, the turnover tax evolved from an indirect tax of the kind its name implies, but it has now lost all connexion with a fixed impost per unit of turnover ; on the contrary, it is a differential tax, the amount of which is determined as a difference between the calculated wholesale price and retail price. The rates of turnover tax differ widely from item to item even within a single commodity group : rates range from a few per cent to thirty, fifty per cent and more. Because the state owns the taxable enterprises, there seems to be little difference between profit and tax, since all accrue to the state, which represents society, and economists in these countries used to declare that there was hence no element of taxation in the turnover tax, but merely an alternative channel to the appropriation of profit by the state. Such an approach could be justified only from the point of view of the ownership, not of the functioning, of the economic system.

A fourth rule, less absolute than the three just listed and inoperative since about 1960, was that the only possible movement of retail prices was downward. The extreme theoretical formulation of this policy excluded the possibility of raising prices even in exceptional cases. On a given day of the year, a massive reduction of retail prices of selected goods was decreed. Since about 1960 price adjustments have taken place in both directions throughout the socialist countries : while the practice of synchronized bulk actions has weakened, its principle is woven into the logic of that form of price policy.

The final element in pricing practice common to the countries concerned, farm prices, evolved through two stages. During the first period low procurement prices (in some cases even less than the cost of production) were applied to obligatory deliveries to the state by co-operative farms, and state purchase prices — higher, but generally failing to represent the whole Marxian surplus product — were accorded to supplementary deliveries, although co-operatives, after having fulfilled their compulsory deliveries, were allowed to sell some produce at free prices on the co-operative market. The state procurement prices used to be considered as a tool by means of which part of the surplus product created in agriculture was withdrawn into the centralized funds ; part was returned to agriculture in the form of government subsidies, loans, etc. During a second period, this system of dual prices was abolished and all deliveries to the state by the co-operatives were paid for at uniform prices, the level of which ranged somewhere between each of the former prices. Transfers were maintained of a certain part of surplus product to the state, by means of lower prices, with direct taxation playing a considerably less significant role. Problems of differentiating prices according to production conditions may be mentioned, but are not here discussed.

THEORETICAL AND HISTORICAL ORIGINS OF THE PRICE SYSTEM

In turning to the theoretical aspects and to the historical circumstances which helped to create this price system, it may be observed that, while there always existed some relationship between the practical organization of the price system and its underpinning theory, the situation resulted, in some cases, from a set of *a priori* theories, and, in others, from certain historical conditions which endowed the practice with a concrete form before it was interpreted in theory. There is perhaps no need to stress that the theoretical conclusions criticized in this connexion are to be considered as a product of a dogmatic misrepresentation of Marxism in the past and not of Marxism as such.

The incompatibility of planned development based on central management with the automatic functioning of a market mechanism was part of a theory, particularly prevalent during the cult of Stalin, that socialist economic relations were a simple negation of the corresponding feature of capitalism. The so-called 'law of planned proportionate development' was supposed to be valid under socialism, and a similar 'law of competition and anarchy in production' precluded planning and proportionate development under capitalism. An automatic (spontaneous) functioning of the market was considered a source of anarchy, and the existence of commodities and prices was regarded as nothing but a temporary phenomenon, which would be liquidated during the transition towards communism. Under socialism prices had merely an accounting function and could affect decisions only on consumption and never on production. Such views looked to an ideal economic organization which rested on central balancing of production in kind (including labour in numbers of hours worked), and a direct and centrally-organized distribution of consumers' goods without recourse to a market. As just described, the idea of planning was erroneously presented as inseparable from the administrative determination of targets and of prices. In fact, there was no planning of prices, for they remained constant until glaringly proved incompatible with evolving economic conditions : sets of such prices were more random in their relative values than those formed on the market, for they were a compound of errors in computations, false appraisals of the situation, and lack of information and subjective criteria on the part of decision-makers. It seems entirely justified therefore to use 'central determination' rather than 'planning' of prices. It may be noted that such determination was in line with the view, then common, that the utmost centralization was to be imposed on decision-making in subordinate units, as the only way to co-ordinate development towards ends most beneficial to society. It was also thought that an increase in any retail price would negate the aim of raising the level of living under socialism ; retail prices were regarded solely in the framework of the cost of living.

Indeed, a systematic deflation was seen as essential, because the Marxist labour theory of value implied that, during economic growth, a rise in labour productivity reduced the value of commodities : obviously, the reduction of the labour value of a commodity is inconsistent neither with stable prices nor with inflation. The same sort of over-simplification — in this case on the role of ownership in economic relations — made the planners indifferent on whether surplus product be realized on intermediate or on final products. It accrued to the state at either level and ease of administration favoured a levy on final goods. With all this went an unreasoning repudiation of anything evolved by bourgeois economic theories — such as market equilibrium, the theory of consumer's behaviour and the concepts of marginal utility and of the elasticity of demand. The incomprehensible rejection of mathematical methods, which, as can be seen today, are eminently applicable to pricing, had the same unfortunate results.

False theorizing was not the only factor in creating that price system : certain historical circumstances engendered other features of pricing, which were theoretically supported *ex post* and sometimes incompetently generalized and transferred to other countries.

The fact that in the U.S.S.R. and the other socialist countries the economic system had arisen in conditions of wartime disruption induced readier acceptance of rationing at centrally-fixed prices. But, as consumer-good shortages were overcome, the gap between the actual and the appropriate price relationships widened, and a sudden unfreezing of prices would have caused substantial movements of prices and shifts in demand and consequential planning difficulties. The gradual development of supplies thus induced specific features, which were originally unintended. The dual price level was established in similar fashion. Pressure on wages could not be successfully resisted and raised purchasing power above the value of consumer-good availabilities, and the planners' concern was hence concentrated on turnover-tax revenue to absorb the widening margin between wholesale and retail prices. This attention was given added stress by the necessity to centralize accumulation for industrialization, with agriculture participating through the system of state procurement prices. The policy was defined long before the war as 'primitive socialist accumulation'.

An excessive centralization rendered a flexible price policy impracticable, for frequent adjustments of prices would have required a vast increase in the quantity of information processed at the centre. Had the data been available, it would necessarily have enlarged inordinately the administrative apparatus. But information on changes of demand was not available and, given the priority allotted to industrialization, adjustments of the production pattern would not have been feasible. In this way a long-term disequilibrium on the market arose, a justification of which was sought in the theory that consumption demand had necessarily to exceed production under socialism.

Nationalization and administrative methods of management engendered or enhanced monopoly conditions in a number of branches, under which the market mechanism could never successfully operate ; the directive to keep prices stable thus appeared to be the only instrument against monopolistic price increases.

ADVERSE CONSEQUENCES OF ADMINISTRATIVE PRICE-FIXING

Among the results of the price system must first be counted disequilibrium on the market both in volume and structure of the supply and demand for consumers' goods. The producer is interested above all in the fulfilment of planned indicators and not directly in the production of commodities demanded by the consumer : on the one hand, the demand for certain types of goods continues to be unsatisfied for a long time, while on the other hand unsaleable goods accumulate. Thus the economy suffers heavy losses — materially in the unsold goods and in the time spent in queues ; there is discontent on the part of the consumer who cannot find the goods he requires ; and surplus purchasing power endangers economic stability (as in the case of recurrent spending sprees).

A similar situation arises for producers' goods ; market relations were replaced in transactions between state enterprises by a quota system ('material and technical supply'). The producer has no direct interest in satisfying the needs of the consumer, and supply does not match demand. In consequence, overall economic efficiency is low, technical progress is slow and large funds are sterilized in stockpiling and unfinished construction. An administrative price determination, by severing the link between the producer and the consumer, tended to lower the quality of goods and services and weaken incentives for innovation.

The constancy of prices and the elimination of competition fostered monopoly conditions. The divorce of prices from socially-necessary costs vitiated the criteria for investment efficiency, for the exploitation of scarce resources, for choice of technique, and for foreign trade. Macroeconomic ratios for planning were distorted by a wrong reflexion of costs and by the dual scale of prices, which undervalued material costs in relation to wage costs.

Distorted price relations in retail trade induced an irrational structure of consumption : an excessively low price may waste raw material and labour — in extreme cases it has been known for a consumer to buy a finished product solely to extract its raw material. An excessively high price for goods with high elasticity may, by restricting consumption, result in an unemployment of productive capacity, and the purchasing power which could have been absorbed on that good will intensify market disequilibrium by being directed to deficitary items. Far from solving conflicts of interests, the price system intensified them.

Excessive centralism overloaded the administrative apparatus and created favourable conditions for the growth of bureaucratic tendencies.

CRITIQUES WITHIN THE SOCIALIST COUNTRIES

The price system described in the framework of administrative economic management became the subject of general criticism, which may be roughly divided into two groups. One criticized incorrect price relations (including the dual price level) and led to the call for a uniform basis. Discussions continue on the type or formula of uniform pricing, *e.g.* value, average value, production price, etc. The other criticized the centralized and administrative methods of price regulation, and resulted in pleas for the rehabilitation of the market mechanism throughout the socialist economic system. Two problems remain in debate : how to organize the system of planned management so that the functioning of the market mechanism does not conflict with planning, and the manner of transition to a new system while the old disproportions and disequilibria persist.

The problem of a uniform price system has been most intensively discussed in the Soviet Union, and chiefly connected with the application of the mathematical methods (structural analysis and linear programming) to compute such prices ; the names of Kantorovich,

Novozhilov, Nemchinov, and Belkin were particularly prominent.[1]

Initially, Soviet views (and those in Hungary) concentrated on the correction of price relatives, without impugning the method of central price-fixing. The mathematical procedures suggested were to improve the decision-making of central agencies. Recently, attention has been focused even in the U.S.S.R. on the necessity of restoring the role of the market mechanism: it is of interest that such a conclusion was made by none other than the advocates of mathematical methods (Nemchinov, Novozhilov, etc.), because they adopted the cybernetic view of automated economic regulation. In this connexion also the mathematical problems of market analysis (demand elasticity), long neglected in the U.S.S.R., started to be taken up.

In some other socialist countries, however, theoretical and practical concern was first concentrated more on the role of the market than on the formula of price. This was undoubtedly true in Yugoslavia where not only a theoretical criticism, but also a practical introduction, of the market mechanism had taken place. It was also the case in Poland, as the work of Brus testifies,[2] and in Czechoslovakia, where the theoretical analyses were made by Sik, Kozusnik, and Komenda,[3] and where — at present — intensive preparations are under way for a new system of economic management, based on a broad employment of the market. Many Czechoslovak economists consider the restoration of the market much more important than the problem of a price formula, even though it is essential to the successful functioning of a market and could play an important part in resolving the conflict of group interests. This order of priorities is supported by the work of Novozhilov,[4] who shows that dual prices

[1] L. V. Kantorovich, *Ekonomichesky raschet nailuchshego ispolzovaniya resursov*, Moscow, 1959 (for English translation see footnote, page 81); V. V. Novozhilov, 'On the Discussion of the Principles of Planned Price-formation', *Primenenie matematiki v ekonomike*, vol. 1, Leningrad, 1963; V. S. Nemchinov, 'Basic Outlines of a Model of Planned Price Formation', *Voprosy ekonomiki*, no. 12, 1963, pp. 105–121; V. D. Belkin, *Tseny edinogo urovnya i ekonomicheskie izmereniya na ikh osnovy* (Unified-level prices and economic measurements thereon), Moscow, 1963.

[2] Włodzimierz Brus, *Ogólne problemy funkcjonowania gospodarki socjalistycznej* (General Problems of the Functioning of a Socialist Economy), Warsaw, 2nd ed., 1964.

[3] B. Komenda, Č. Kožušnik, 'Basic Questions of Improving Socialist Economic Management', *Politická ekonomie*, no. 3, 1964; O. Šik, 'Problems of the New System of Planned Management', *Nová Mysl*, no. 10, 1964, and O. Šik (ed.), *K problematice soustavy plánoriteha řiženi ekonomiky ČSSR* (On the Problem of the System of Planned Management of the Czechoslovak Economy), Prague, 1964.

[4] V. V. Novozhilov, 'Problems of Developing Democratic Centralism in the Management of the Socialist Economy', *Trudy Leningradskogo inzhenerno-ekonomicheskogo instituta — 24*, Leningrad, 1958.

may be used without risk under decentralized decision-making, because they ensure that an optimal plan for an enterprise, prepared by decentralized decisions, conforms to a social optimum. Other prices would, however, result in an irrational utilization of resources.

THEORIES OF PRICE

Theoretical work on the price formula in eastern Europe started around 1958–60. Previously, economic texts had often asserted that under socialism the planning of prices should derive from commodity-value, but these were general and impractical proclamations, because such value (in labour terms) could not be quantified. Indeed, nobody believed that a feasible way could even be found for such a calculation. However immature, there were nevertheless valuable and long-standing fundamental concepts of the transformation problem, originating in the works of Marx (in the history of which the essay by Bortkiewicz [1] is of particular significance), and of the structural model, evolving from Walras through Leontief. Both these approaches were combined in one of the most significant of contemporary works, namely in the article by Morishima and Seton,[2] which presents an exact formula of value on the Leontief structural model.

The first formula of value dates from 1904 in the development by the Russian economist and mathematician V. K. Dmitriev [3] of Walras' model of general equilibrium. He demonstrated that labour value — in present terminology cumulative labour — can be computed as an iterative solution of an equation, relating cumulative labour costs with technical coefficients and direct labour costs.[4] It is sometimes described as a Dmitriev–Leontief equation, because an identical set of equations may be derived for cumulative labour costs from Leontief's structural model, which, however, usually envisages not an iterative solution but an inversion of a matrix. The development of the theory of linear programming, resulting in dual (shadow)

[1] L. Bortkiewicz, 'Wertrechnung und Preisrechnung im marxischen System', *Archiv für Sozialwissenschaft und Sozialpolitik*, Band XXIII, 1906, and Band XXV, 1907.

[2] M. Morishima and F. Seton, 'Aggregation in Leontief Matrices and the Labour Theory of Value', *Econometrica*, April, 1961, pp. 203–220.

[3] V. K. Dmitriev, *Ekonomicheskie ocherki: Opyt organicheskogo sinteza trudovoi teorii tsennosti i teorii predelnoi poleznosti* (Economic Essays : an Attempt to Integrate the Theories of Labour Value and Marginal Utility), Moscow, 1904.

[4] The various formulae, set out in the original paper, are not reproduced here, since they are shown in Mateev (pp. 73–80).

prices, is also relevant, and it is in this connexion that the work of Kantorovich and Novozhilov [1] is important.

Prices in terms of labour value may be computed either directly in labour units using the Dmitriev equation (thence converted into monetary units), or directly in monetary units as long as wage costs are calculated instead of direct labour costs. In the first case the problem arises of aggregating labour of different intricacy and intensity, while in the second the problem is to determine the rate of surplus product, which appears in n equations as the $(n+1)$ variable.

The term 'average value' is usually understood in socialist countries as material and wage costs plus a profit at a uniform *ad valorem* rate. The 'production price' formula relates the uniform rate of profit to the value of productive assets. The so-called 'multi-channel' prices, applied in Hungary,[2] represent a combination of the formulae of value and of the production price in such a way that part of the surplus product is distributed according to wages and part according to productive assets. The shadow price formula, the 'objectively-conditioned valuation' of Kantorovich, is not discussed here, because it follows from the theory of linear programming; it is a technique of pricing scarce resources to regulate decentralized decision-makers towards a socially-optimal use of such resources. Novozhilov, finally, takes labour value as his basis and — as shown by the dual — deviates according to the degree of relative scarcity.[3]

CZECHOSLOVAK PROPOSALS FOR REFORM

The group of Czechoslovak economists of whom the author is one postulates the need for reform firstly by rejecting the assumption that planning is incompatible with the price mechanism, and that socialism permits the central regulation of production without recourse to the market mechanism. This leads them to contend that central management is self-defeating, since the information needed to eliminate all uncertainty in decision-making becomes too costly

[1] L. V. Kantorovich, *Matematicheskie metody organizatsii i planirovaniya proizvodstva* (Mathematical methods of organizing and planning production), Leningrad, 1939; V. V. Novozhilov, 'The Measurement of Outlays and of their Results in a Socialist Economy', in *Primenenie matematiki v ekonomicheskikh issledovaniyakh — I* (The Application of Mathematics to Economic Research), Moscow, 1959.

[2] B. Csikos-Nagy, S. Ganczer, L. Rácz, 'The First Price Model Based on a Product System', *Közgazdasági Szemle*, no. 1, 1964, pp. 17–35.

[3] V. V. Novozhilov, *Obshchaya formula tsenoobrazovaniya* (A General Formula of Price Formation), Leningrad, 1963.

and unwieldy. Any restriction of the amount of information transmitted to the centre increases the uncertainty of the decision-making and hence the risk of adopting wrong decisions ; the absorption of a considerable part of the labour force in administrative services decreases overall efficiency. They therefore suggest that a market mechanism automates in a co-ordinated manner a large part of these decisions ; in addition, the producer is stimulated to satisfy the demands of the consumer. A market is thus *prima facie* desirable for the functioning of a socialist economic system. This, however, assumes that prices be freely formed on the market and not set up by fiat.

It is nevertheless evident that the market mechanism cannot by itself ensure the smooth and undisturbed operation of the economy and cannot bring about the achievement of the sort of target which a socialist society endeavours to attain. The function of planning and central management should therefore supplement this mechanism in those spheres where it cannot operate satisfactorily — to implement social priorities and fully to utilize capacity. If this is to be done, planning must be seen in an entirely new light : the plan cannot be a fetter constraining reactions to economic change, but a co-ordinator of the development process from the standpoint of society and with an optimal level in view. But prices cannot fluctuate spontaneously. Some stability is undoubtedly desirable, but it should be achieved not by administrative determination, but by the assurance in the plan that productive capacity would correspond to the demand arising on the basis of planned incomes and planned prices. A situation would then be approached in which the planned price would be a market-equilibrium price. As long as capital investment is centrally allocated, and certain other central instruments of management are retained, such equilibrium prices can only develop as automatic expressions of the law of value and of the economic and social policy of a socialist country.

Chapter 18

SUMMARY RECORD OF THE DISCUSSION —SESSION V

PRICE SYSTEMS

(In the Chair : PROFESSOR RACHMUTH)

Professor Fauvel found five principles of price formation in the system described by Dr. Kyn. The first was that prices were fixed by a central agency (as occasionally in the West during periods of scarcity), and secondly were stable for several years. The third feature was the dual level of prices, viz. those of production (determined by labour value) and retail prices. Fourthly, it had been the practice to deflate retail prices gradually. Finally, the system of prices in agriculture differed significantly from that in the rest of the economy, but for reasons that seemed of expediency rather than deliberation. Generally, price changes tended to be *ex post* adjustments rather than *ex ante* decisions to influence economic activity. Dr. Kyn believed that price formation on the basis of labour value inherently induced a waste of capital and proposed a unitary price system in which, first, an *ad valorem* tax on wages would create the accumulation fund and, secondly, prices would be adjusted to the conditions of demand as well as to those of supply. Professor Fauvel could not accept that this was the only solution because a labour-content price could serve as guide to the general interest in decentralized decision-making, as the Dmitriev and Morishima–Seton formulae had demonstrated.[1]

The paper by Professors Maksimovic and Pjanic had the same objective as Dr. Kyn in seeking a 'normative price', and both concentrated their attention on the concept of 'net income' — that is, total revenue less outlays on materials, depreciation, payment for capital, and taxes. It embraced both labour remuneration and profits ; not all was distributed as a dividend to labour and it could be controlled by the state in the same way that profits were influenced in a capitalist economy. It seemed to him that this practice did not guarantee in Yugoslavia the operation of a market economy, for 70 per cent of prices were still controlled. Nor did

[1] On V. K. Dmitriev, see A. Nove and A. Zauberman, 'A Resurrected Russian Economist of 1900', *Soviet Studies*, July, 1961, pp. 96–101 and A. Zauberman, 'A Few Remarks on a Discovery in Soviet Economics', *Bulletin of the Oxford University Institute of Statistics*, November, 1962, pp. 437–445 (reprinted in A. Zauberman, *Aspects of Planometrics*, London, 1967, pp. 47–55) ; M. Morishima and F. Seton, *op. cit.*

the technique of profit-sharing ensure that the benefit of low rates of interest to stimulate certain branches was not dissipated in labour remuneration. He hoped that, in the discussion, economists from the socialist countries would indicate the extent to which the unique basis of labour value was still tenable ; whether a unitary price system to replace the present dual levels was compatible with the implementation of social desiderata ; and whether a socialist market economy might emerge along different lines (*e.g.* using the Swedish system of 'price listing' to exhibit enterprises which were overcharging).

Dr. Ophir found himself in a large measure of agreement with the two papers under discussion and that by Mr. Laszlo. They all considered prices not in terms of some theoretical-ideological basis, but from the pragmatic viewpoint of their effects on the performance of the economy. The functions and problems of the price system in a socialist economy were analogous to those of intra-company pricing in a large Western corporation, upon which his own interest was centred.[1] A number of theoretical works were available on pricing in a socialist economy, notably Lange's classical work and Lerner's *Economics of Control*.[2] He had found the comparison with intra-company pricing in an article by Nove.[3] In a centrally-planned economy, prices were not strictly necessary, for they were only the dual to the chosen allocation of resources to derive the desired bill of goods, as Professor Mateev's system of equations demonstrated. If, however, decision-making was not completely centralized, prices became necessary. As lucidly argued by Dr. Kyn (pp. 201 and 207–208), the costs of a highly-centralized decision process were prohibitive ; the more decentralized the system, the more important became prices, and hence the problem of price formation. He found Professor Domar's principle of marginal-cost pricing generally unworkable — because the quantity produced had to be known in order to ascertain marginal cost — but valid under certain conditions. Marginal cost could be approximated by average variable cost when surplus capacity existed, but might be many times average cost when capacity was deficient. When fixed capital could not be rapidly expanded, price should serve to ration the limited stock to its most productive uses. A socialist economy could price by negotiation, but this was open to abuse by the exertion of monopoly power. Professors Maksimovic and Pjanic had touched — unfortunately only briefly — on the problem of monopoly control under socialism. The relation of prices to the world market had also to be considered : the domestic price of an imported commodity should be the world price plus transport costs ; similarly, the domestic price of an export good should be the export price minus transport costs. Commodities which were not traded need not

[1] *Intracompany Pricing in the Decentralized Firm*, unpublished Ph.D. thesis, Massachusetts Institute of Technology, 1960.

[2] Lange, *op. cit.* ; A. Lerner, *The Economics of Control*, London, 1946.

[3] A. Nove, 'The Problem of "Success Indicators" in Soviet Industry', *Economica*, February, 1958, pp. 1–13.

Summary Record of the Discussion

be priced in any exact relation to the world price, but would be valued within the ranges set by the above prices, viz. its opportunity cost should be no lower than the export price but no higher than the import price. These relationships would, of course, have to be appropriately modified if the volume of trade in any commodity so priced by the socialist country concerned was large enough to affect the world market price.

Sir Roy Harrod said that he had been greatly stimulated by both papers but found the multiplicity of proposals bewildering. Although it might be paradoxical for a capitalist economist, he had to declare some unease at the claims for greater freedom and flexibility in the price mechanism.

He wanted to stress that he greatly valued the function of price, in a market mechanism, of equating supply to demand. Queues of consumers waiting, when supply fell short of demand at given price, or the inability of producers to procure needed components or materials without delay, entailed a shocking waste. It would be a great gain to remedy those evils. Moreover, if an enterprise produced variants of a certain type of article, it might be expedient for it to be able to test out consumer preferences by some freedom of price manœuvre. Subject to that, he had two points to make.

He was convinced that in a socialist system an official, or 'normative', price was necessary. Adam Smith distinguished the market price from the 'natural' price, the first being that which actually obtained, the second that to which the market price tended under competitive capitalism. The 'natural' price could not be identified and might never be realized, owing to a change of intervening circumstances, but it epitomized the action of capitalists striving to maximize private profit. No such force operated under socialism, and it was for this reason that it was necessary for a 'natural' or 'normative' price to be calculated and promulgated. Without it there would be no guideline for that allocation of productive resources which best satisfied consumer needs. Adam Smith's 'natural' price did not differ substantially from the price based on cost in Marx's *Kapital*, vol. iii. Professor Mateev's paper was a development of Marx and he concluded that price Type II was that which correctly embodied the principle of socially-necessary cost; of the two variants that with capital at replacement cost (p. 78) was the better. If enterprises were allowed to deviate from Marxian prices, in order to prevent market shortages (or surplus stocks), they should be instructed to restore normal prices as quickly as possible by changing their level of output. Information that this had been done, and why, would be conveyed to the planning agencies.

Sir Roy Harrod was also disquieted by the idea that too much laxity in the matter of prices might lead to inflation, specifically to spiralling inflation. It might be that socialist economies had a perfectly firm grip on the wage situation, but feared for the efficacy of such control if prices broke loose. Spiralling inflation had often little to do with the type of inflation that resulted from a lack of balance (or excess of demand) in the

Price Systems

economy, *e.g.* that due to an excess of capital accumulation in relation to the provision of funds for that purpose. The United Kingdom had experienced the excess-demand type of inflation during and after the War ; more recently there had been little excess demand, but spiralling inflation persisted. The British Government had set up an agency to review prices, and many hoped that its function was not to be mere window-dressing : its task would be made far easier if there was already in existence a set of official prices, such as the socialist countries had. Sir Roy Harrod's fears of a serious wage-price spiral led him to enjoin caution upon socialist countries in decontrolling prices : the prevention of inflation was more difficult than its cure.

Professor Dupriez observed that the numerous different concepts of price proposed by socialist economists all represented moves away from price formation by political decision and in global terms to rational 'norms of production' under which individual price relationships would be established. This objective had much in common with the long-term equilibrium price of the market economy. In Western terms, the general principles of the socialist system of prices seemed to be the following. Salaries and prices were planned, although it was not clear upon what criteria. The ideological basis of price was Marx's labour theory of value, as opposed to a system of value determined by the marginal productivity of the factors employed. The socialist economy set a value for labour according to a scale of wages — with only slight variations by location and type of activity — such that the aggregate remuneration equalled the value of the planned production of wage goods. That part of the national product which was not to be consumed by the workers approximated to Marxian surplus value and depreciation ; prices were established to generate the appropriate surplus value and depreciation.

This surplus value comprised government consumption, funds for investment, and amortization as remuneration for the factors owned by the state (rent, interest, and the gross profit of enterprises). Socialist countries seemed always to have determined this surplus value crudely, in the light of government revenue needs and without reference to any norms. The use of capital charges in Eastern Europe reintroduced one of the norms familiar to Western economies. It seemed to him that the global technique of calculating surplus value had tended to cause the level of accumulation to exceed that indicated by the marginal productivity of capital, and that the share of surplus value was hence larger in relation to the wage fund in socialist than in market economies.

Academician Ostrovityanov observed that some Western economists attributed the present discussion of price-formation in all the socialist countries to a crisis in methods of centralized planning ; they perceived a movement towards capitalist methods of the free market and the pursuit of profits. There were even some socialist economists inclined to view as mistaken the entire history of socialist price-formation. Professor

Robinson and others had characterized the pricing techniques of socialist countries as purely administrative. It was alleged that fixed prices, constraint of market relations, and the two-level price system were inherently wrong. Professor Fauvel had pointed out that capitalist economies had recourse to rationing in war-time. Historically, price control and consumer rationing during the Civil War and the Second World War were two of the most important economic conditions for victory. The same was true of the two levels of prices, which had been essential to implement the policy of the development of heavy industry in preference to agriculture and those branches of industry producing consumers' goods : prices ruling for producers' goods were lower than those for consumers' goods. This dichotomy could be relaxed now that the Soviet Union and the other socialist countries had entered a new stage permitting as rapid development for consumers' goods as for heavy industry. This was not to say that there had not been mistakes in the past : excessive centralization, the incorrect substitution of administrative decisions for economic methods, and the inadequate utilization of commodity-money instruments. Such defects were still far from eliminated ; the answer was not the rejection of central planning, but its optimal combination with the wide initiative of local organs, firms, enterprises, and workers' collectives. This meant the restriction of central planning to a determination of the basic lines of development and the granting of much greater managerial and operating independence to the enterprises. A fundamental improvement in the system of price formation would play an important role in this transformation.

Dr. Kyn had frequently reiterated a belief in the value of an automatic market mechanism, but had failed to describe his ideal. Did he reject the planning of prices and of the equilibrium between personal income and expenditure ? Would he abandon the guarantee of income by commodities to the spontaneous forces of a free market ? Should not reliance rather be placed on an awareness and utilization of economic laws, and the elevation of planning to a higher level by taking advantage of modern mathematical methods and computer techniques ? The second choice was the correct one, making the best use of the mechanism of commodity production and distribution — which had centuries of practice behind it — but eliminating those negative features of spontaneity which wasted productive resources and induced cyclic fluctuation. The Scientific Council on Price Formation in the U.S.S.R. was working on the assumption that prices had to be based on the Marxist theory of labour value and, in particular, on the category of socially-necessary labour outlays. The determination of value by socially-necessary labour expenditure stimulated technical progress, because those enterprises introducing advanced technology reduced their labour outlay below that socially necessary, and, selling their commodities at industry-wide prices, received supplementary profits. Those enterprises where costs were higher than socially necessary gained less than average profits or even made a loss at industry-wide prices, and were forced to improve their technology and organization of production. On the other hand, prices set in accordance with relative utility slowed technical progress, because they assured a normal profit to backward industries and increased profits to all other enterprises by artificially inflating the industry-wide price above the value of the socially-necessary expenditure of labour. The cost of production and the average rate of profit had also played important roles in the history of commodity economies : intra-industrial competition had induced a systematic deviation of prices from value and created an incentive for a transfer of capital to those branches of industry where there was a high concentration of living labour and a higher rate of profit.

The essence of the problem was to derive prices which corresponded most closely to value, that is, to the cumulative costs of live and embodied labour. For this it was necessary to elaborate a practical method of determining such costs, the very substance of value, and in the conditions of a planned economy it could be based on the mathematical approach and on modern computing technology. The two implicit problems of mensuration were of skilled labour in terms of unskilled labour, and of the socially-necessary labour costs of any good in the main and ancillary industries contributing to its production. The first problem could be solved by applying a scale of wage relationships used to remunerate workers of different skills ; the second involved the construction of an intersectoral balance. The final cumulation could be made in units of money or in hours of work ; either would be a reasonably exact measure of value as production costs.

Professor Gatovsky had listed a number of factors which require prices to deviate from this value, among them quality differences or other elements of use-value, novelty, supply and demand, and natural conditions. The advantage of determining value, as socially-necessary labour costs, was to permit society to decide consciously and precisely where prices should diverge from value on economic grounds and where they should be more closely correlated with socially-necessary expenditures. The need to reform pricing in such terms had been appreciated in the U.S.S.R., but the manner of change was not yet decided : there would be a gradual approximation of wholesale prices to socially-necessary outlay on criteria which still had to be precisely determined. Dr. Kyn had spoken of using the market mechanism in this connexion, but did not make clear precisely what he had in mind. The Soviet price reform presented many serious problems and could not be accomplished at a single stroke.

In conclusion, Academician Ostrovityanov reproached Dr. Kyn for his scepticism on the definition of value. While criticizing those who said value was unknowable, Dr. Kyn condemned as Stalinist the idea (accepted by Professor Notkin) of eventually calculating value under full communism in work-time. The concept, however, was not originated by Stalin but by Marx and Engels. Until now Marxists had had to accept value on faith since there were no tools to compute it : today, the techniques of mathematical economics could be used to quantify value.

Professor Oelssner felt that it was significant that the subject of prices had come up at every session. In all socialist countries, price-formation was not only the most important and urgent of problems but also the most complicated. In all of them, discussions were taking place which would not be concluded for a long time.

In the G.D.R. a reform of prices on the industrial level became necessary before the theoretical discussions could be completed and the problem satisfactorily solved. The prices for coal and electricity and railway tariffs ruling until April, 1964, were inadequate reflections of cost and had indubitably to be increased. The problem, of course, was by how much. As an interim solution the Commission of the Ministry of Finance, of which Professor Oelssner was a member, had authorized the addition to labour costs of a rate of profit which would assure that each industrial branch was able to self-finance its planned investment. This solution was not ideal, but was the most expedient under the circumstances.

Professor Oelssner recalled that he had already mentioned the working group of the Academy of Sciences of the G.D.R., which was trying to establish work-time expenditures per unit of production. It had raised the question of delineating that part of labour which contributed to value. Marx had observed that one did not have to work oneself to be part of the total work-force. The problem of definition arose, for example, in classifying work on research and development. For the price reform in the G.D.R. it was decided that such outlays should be counted in cost if carried out at the enterprise or in the enterprise-group. But the definition of labour was only part of the problem : the main difficulty was to decide what part of surplus value had to be added to cost. Several proposals had been made, among them basing value on the actual price of production (*Produktionspreis*). Professor Oelssner personally advocated market value as defined by Marx in Chapter 10 of Volume III of *Kapital*, viz. the addition to Marx's cost of production (*Kostpreis*) of a profit rate differentiated by industrial branch. However, whatever variables were chosen, prices had to be dynamic, since productivity was constantly changing. Market value would, furthermore, express such objective factors as worth to the user, and the interaction of supply and demand ; it would hence deviate from normative prices (*Normativpreisen*).

It was because price in a socialist planned economy was not only the money expression of the value of a certain commodity, but also an instrument of planning structural change, that Professor Oelssner disagreed with Dr. Kyn (p. 208) on the automaticity of the market mechanism : price control could only be abandoned if central planning were to be dismantled. In the context of the G.D.R., the current economic reforms would delegate price-fixing to enterprise associations once the substantive price reform had been completed. Since, by that time, profit would have become the main criterion for enterprise operation, it would be necessary to perpetuate central price control.

Dr. Kyn agreed with Academician Ostrovityanov that it was necessary to bear in mind the specific situation of the Soviet Union in the twenties and thirties, when the price system under discussion came into existence. But he felt (as did Professors Maksimovic and Pjanic) that it was wrong to generalize those experiences — the result of concrete conditions in a particular country in a certain period — as the only correct way for all countries at all times.

He strongly denied the contention of some at the Conference that his paper advocated doing away with planning and returning to a pure market mechanism of the sort that operated in the nineteenth century. He assured Sir Roy Harrod that the danger of inflation was fully appreciated in Czechoslovakia, and that means to combat it were being sought. He pointed out that the cause of inflation was nevertheless not price flexibility as such but the state of the economy. If the economy was in disequilibrium, inflationary tendencies could arise independently of the procedure of price-formation.

Dr. Ophir had implied that one of Professor Mateev's price formulae supported a dual price-system. Certainly Professor Mateev seemed to favour prices heavily differentiated by turnover tax, and in this he would be supported by a number of Czechoslovak economists. Dr. Kyn himself felt that the situation in his own country showed that the dual price-system retarded, rather than fostered, growth. Of the three price models which had been programmed on the 1962 input-output table, the two-level price-system was demonstrated to have been the least suited to decentralized (*i.e.* enterprise) decision-making. It had seemed to be Professor Oelssner's view that planning could not operate in a market economy : the proposals for a new system of planning and management in Czechoslovakia were based on the belief that a combination was possible, and its feasibility had already been demonstrated in Yugoslavia. Academician Ostrovityanov had been right in finding him sceptical of work-time valuation under full communism, but there were so many pressing problems facing contemporary socialism that the point could be left for the rather more distant future.

SESSION VI

MATERIAL INCENTIVES AND COST ACCOUNTING

Chapter 19

SOME PROBLEMS OF THE USE OF MATERIAL INCENTIVES IN INDUSTRIAL ENTERPRISES

BY

L. M. GATOVSKY

Institute of Economics, Moscow

I. INTRODUCTION

THIS study is concerned with the use of incentives to guide the work of an industrial enterprise as a whole ; it hence does not deal with problems related to individual remuneration or to the wage structure in industry nor with the specific features of agricultural enterprises. It begins from the standpoint that one of the most important conditions determining the efficiency of national economic planning is the consistency of planning targets with economic incentives : the central plan should formulate the targets which are optimal in the national context, but which can be realized by means materially satisfactory for the enterprises and the staff who implement the plan. The one link is necessarily connected with the other. A plan without fulfilment incentive is less than efficient, and the incentives unrelated to a plan target are not purposive. Abandoning the old notion that the plan is nothing but commands based on economic accounts, we are squarely faced with the need to ensure that the planned economy operates on the principle that : 'that which is most useful for society must benefit the enterprise and its workers'.

Although socialism creates the potential for an efficient combination of the interests of society with those of the enterprise and its workers (under the decisive role of the national interest), such a combination will not develop by itself. To achieve this potential, the indicators by which the enterprise is planned and its performance assessed must be properly connected with its incentives, and use should be made of such economic instruments as cost accounting, prices, profits, enterprise stimulation funds, bonuses, premia, and credits.

This complex of indicators and economic instruments is the transmission gear from the single state plan to the autonomously-financed enterprise, operating the direct production process. Correctly used, such a mechanism is far from passive : it acts to ensure the most effective realization of the plan, and, in the reverse direction, influences the plan in the direction of greater flexibility, concordance with current conditions, and insulation from random variations. An incentive system can demonstrate from below the quality and practicability of the plan, reveal additional resources, and contribute to the elimination of bureaucratic or unrealistic propositions.

Three features of such planning seem to be essential. The first is that economic instruments exerting an influence upon enterprises should direct and guide them in the way most beneficial for the nation. The second is that, without destroying the decisive position of centralized planning, incentives should become powerful enough positively to influence the work of the enterprise. Thirdly, centralized planning should be restricted to key components of the programme, and hence allow enterprises and their associations sufficient economic freedom and the independence appropriate to an operational business efficiently to allocate their resources, i.e. to maximize output with the minimum expenditure in accordance with the national interests.

The three conditions set out cannot be separated : when all are present, remuneration (on the socialist principles of distribution according to work) depends on the efficiency with which resources are disposed to satisfy national demand ; when any is absent, the national interests and those of the enterprise may not only diverge but conflict.

Such contradictions may be eliminated by a two-way flow of planning and cost accounting. In the one direction the work of the enterprise is harmonized with national criteria, as shown by normative standards ; in the other, the inconsistencies of the criteria are revealed. Since both criteria and conditions change, such an economic mechanism must always be rapidly flexible.

II. PLANNING AND MATERIAL INCENTIVES

The interdependent functions of plan indicators in establishing
*   incentives*

To ensure that the interests of the enterprise conform to those of the nation, strict consistency is essential between the quantitative ratios ('indicators') for which the plan is intended, by which achievement is judged and on which staff are rewarded. Appropriate relationships must be established between those incentive-criteria classed as 'main' and those counted as 'secondary' and between such incentives and the funds for paying bonuses, *e.g.* profit.

There is ample experience to prove that planning one indicator in disregard to another causes conflict in plan implementation and leads to the divergence of national interest and the concern of the enterprise to maximize incentives (profit, the stimulation fund, bonuses, etc.). Enterprises may in such cases be actually operating inefficiently but be considered to be outstandingly good and gain substantial premia, while an efficient plant may be counted as backward and get no bonuses at all. Indicators of the quantity of production cannot, for example, be planned independently of those of quality as expressed in the utility to the consumer, *e.g.* efficiency, reliability, durability, period of guarantee, or ease of maintenance. If the life of automobile tyres is lengthened, or the metal content of ore is raised, the real volume of production is increased. Furthermore, a unit of production (including quality characteristics) should be related to input and the per-unit content of fixed assets, of all capital funds, of materials, and of manpower should be thereby determined.

Another relevant question has been that of planning production volume in terms of the value of global output : its use can lead the enterprise to increase such value by using more expensive materials, or by producing a higher-priced assortment which reduces total sales. Enterprises which fulfil, and even overfulfil, the plan in these terms do so at the expense of properly-conducted enterprises and are in effect 'playing' with the profitable product-mix. In this case a 'pseudo-commercial' aspect is fostered to the detriment of that of production. In a number of branches the problems are how to dispense with the effects of material cost in estimating production volume, and how to account for changes in product-mix. Such adjustments would not require the abandonment of the value of 'global' or 'commodity' output as the 'summarized' or 'through' index of a particular branch or of industry as a whole. The issue is to distinguish between a summary index of production and the volume indicator employed by the enterprise in the context of its contribution to national production.

The major fault has been to separate the volume of production from that of disposals, with a consequence of serious shortcomings in production programming and marketing. Nothing is gained if the plan indicator for disposals is purely fictitious and is not based actually on consumer demand. The accurate reflection of purchasers' requirements is one of the most important conditions of the economic validity of the plan and one of the main features of the system of planning from below.

Indices of cost and profit

It is often the case that improving the working efficiency of a machine yields to its purchasers much more profit than the manufacturer's outlay in higher costs of production. If the planned cost of production rises, the producing enterprise will overspend and lose its right to a bonus ; if the selling price is unchanged, profit falls and accordingly the stimulation fund, which is dependent on profits, is reduced. As a result the enterprise appears to have no economic incentives for the improvement of quality, irrespective of the national interest. To rectify this, cost should be planned in the light of the quality of output and be reflected in price (and consequently in profit). The procedure whereby rebates and mark-ups are allowed on the fixed price in accordance with product quality is to be recommended.

When price and profit are ill-planned, when prices go unrevised for long periods, and when the margin between price and cost is widening, all sorts of 'profits' emerge : this variety depends little on the quality of production but rather on the spurious 'advantage' or 'disadvantage' of the product-mix. It should be added that the profit on obsolete products is often much higher than for up-to-date products, particularly where special rules are applied for the pricing of new products.

The random nature of prices often causes enterprises to show increasing profits and declining average costs, while in fact producing less output or using more inputs — simply by processing materials which are groundlessly cheap or producing items which are by sheer chance dear. Neither the individual consumer nor the economy as a whole gains anything from such manipulation by a manufacturer. Such a growth of profitability has nothing to do with the merits of the enterprise. Its work has deteriorated, however much its finances have improved, and the material incentives it thereby obtains encourage nothing but backwardness.

The prevention of such abuse requires not only a thorough

revision of price-formation but also the correlation — for determining material incentives — of the profit index with that of the volume of sales, under the requirement that the product-mix contracted with wholesale agencies is rigorously met. If prices are set so that those goods in greater demand in relation to their scarcity are more highly priced, incentives to earn the profit thereon will contribute to the co-ordination of production plans with demand, to the expansion of output of scarce commodities, and to the discontinuation of poor-selling lines. Similarly, the planned indicators of profitability, costs, production volume, and labour productivity must foster the introduction of new equipment or technology and the production of more efficient goods. Only under such conditions will material incentives work for the interests of society in accelerating technical progress. It should not be the case that during the running-in period of a new installation or product the temporary increase in total enterprise outlay should be accounted as current costs and hence cause the cost target to be overspent. Rather, such outlays should be met from earmarked funds, and allowance should be made in other plan targets for temporary deteriorations which are not the fault of management. Indeed, price and profit policy must be positively beneficial to the installation of new techniques and the production of new goods. These and many other related questions have been the subject of economic discussion in the U.S.S.R. : a number of them have reached the stage of definitive recommendation and implementation ; on others, recommendations have been made and are being experimentally tested or prepared for practical use ; research is being undertaken into others, but many problems await a solution.

Planned indicators as stimuli

It is obvious from practical experience that a coherent set of indicators should satisfy four conditions : first, that they represent the national interest to the enterprise ; second, that they distinguish between factors internal and external to the enterprise ; third, that they allow for the degree of capacity utilization ; and fourth, that they are capable of differentiation for the priorities laid down for specific industries or plants. The number selected as governing the payment of bonuses must, however, be strictly limited.

The first condition, the representation of the national interest, is frequently referred to as 'the achievement of the maximum economic effect with minimum expenditure'. 'The maximum economic effect' has been expressed by such indices as the volume of production (by value and in physical units), the assortment of output (distinguishing the various qualities of the goods desired by users), and by profitability. 'The minimum expenditure' in its most general form has been represented by indicators of capital investment, and of current costs (materials, etc.). Recent contributions by Soviet economists seem to have been concerned mainly with indicators in money terms : this is not because physical indices are being rejected, but to redress the balance in favour of the social interest in the quality of goods rather than in their quantity — to emphasize, that is, the value of a product to the consumer, the aspect which hitherto has been the most neglected.

Among such plan indices in value terms, profit has clear advantages over the cost indicator used hitherto, because it not only reflects more elements on the cost side, but summarizes the actual results of production. Profit is due in the long run to replace cost in the set of plan indicators used to assess the work of the enterprise, but when that substitution takes place depends on price improvement and on the elimination from profit of factors outside the control of the enterprise : the point of profit as an indicator is that it should demonstrate the marketing ability of the enterprise and be responsive to changes in product-mix, etc. The ideas of Polish economists in this field are of particular interest, while Soviet authors are exploring new complements to profit in the form of indicators characterizing the consumer properties of products, that is, their qualities from the point of view of satisfying demand not only directly but, so far as concerns producers' goods, indirectly (viz. to maximize their efficiency as inputs). Some of the proposals put forward by Soviet economists have already been put into practice, while the implementation of others can be expected later. The value indicators concerned solely with quantities (*e.g.* global output) and targets in physical units are thus being replaced or supplemented by qualitative indices, which will promote the expansion of goods which are in high demand, or are the most modern and efficient in productive use, and the withdrawal of little-needed or obsolete commodities.

Soviet practice hitherto has interpreted the principle of minimum outlay mainly in terms of human labour, to the virtual exclusion of concern with the saving of capital, *i.e.* to the efficient allocation of investments and productive assets. It is now more important than ever that attention be paid to outlays other than those directly on labour : technical progress has already assured them a majority share of current inputs. Indicators are hence essential to measure capacity utilization, in addition to those already used for labour productivity and the use of labour capacity. It is worthy of notice that such an indicator is already obligatory in a new system of managerial incentives worked out by Soviet economists and on trial during 1964 at eighty enterprises.

The second condition that an indicator should satisfy is that it serve to separate, so far as possible, factors which the enterprise does not have under its control, while evaluating the efficiency of the measures which it takes independently. External events of this nature include requirements by superior authority or by customers involving a sudden change in production, a shift to a new type of good, and special orders. In particular, it should reveal the extent to which the economic results of a given enterprise are dependent on the work of other enterprises or on the prices of raw materials used in production. Experiments are being conducted on indicators which substantially eliminate the effect of those prices on the value of production, *i.e.* to demonstrate what part thereof is value added by the workers of the enterprise. In these experiments the indicator 'global' value of product has been replaced by standardized cost of processing, skill-standardized employment, or relative net product.

The third condition is directly connected with the second, viz. that indicators for planning and for evaluating the activity of an enterprise should differentiate between plants according to their degree of capital utilization. It is patently more difficult for an enterprise using almost 100 per cent of its productive capacity to increase its production by 5 per cent than for a new enterprise with little of its capacity yet in use to increase its output by 30 per cent. To ensure that planning targets, their evaluation and the authorization of premia based upon their fulfilment take account of variant production potential, enterprises must be classified into groups based, for example, on the quantity, composition, level of embodied technology, and degree of wear-and-tear of equipment, and its ratio to employment, the scale and diversity of production, on the period elapsed since a new line was introduced, the availability of raw materials and manpower and, in some cases, on natural conditions such as geographical situation. Classification in a particular group should be made for each specific enterprise — not for entire branches of production — and frequently reviewed. The practice of stereotyped planning of indicators, which disregards the specific features and possibilities of each enterprise, can be disastrous. It has all too often been the case that enterprise plans have been dictated as the same percentage increment on the current level for every one of them. A differential approach to the enterprise must be expressed not only in appropriate planned norms but also, if plan assignments are the same, in suitably adjusted scales of incentive. The employment of 'accounting prices' tends in the same direction, at least in manufacturing industry, *i.e.* a uniform selling price for a branch which is the mean of different prices paid, through an equalization account, to each producing plant. The same may be said of similarly differentiated taxes on profits, turnover, or capital assets.

The fourth characteristic required of a plan indicator follows from the second and the third, namely that it take account of the priorities laid down for each branch or enterprise. The planning agencies may, for example, lay particular stress at a given moment on accelerating the growth of production ; in another case, while holding down per-unit inputs of materials or components, the improvement of quality is most important ; in yet a third case, special attention may be called for in developing new kinds of production or new processes ; or, again, new enterprises may be required to bring capacity into use as soon as possible. The characteristics of such primordial indicators as profit and efficiency of productive assets in this connexion have been discussed in the relevant literature.

Indicators satisfying these four conditions should be interrelated. Any one indicator taken alone involves at some point a contradiction to some task of the national economy : a set of not more than two or three indicators (differentiated for branches and groups of enterprises) is needed. Similar considerations apply to the use of indicators for assessing and rewarding the work of sub-divisions of an enterprise (shops, teams, or production areas) ; strict differentiation should ensure that account is taken of specific features and concrete tasks, the definition of which is at the discretion of the enterprise itself.

The inverse dependence of plan targets on material incentives

For a plan to be effective, it must be based on a full and realistic statement of its production potential, which can only be made by the enterprise concerned. Its willingness to furnish information to the plan-setting agency is conditioned by its expectation of the effect of its report on its next plan targets. An enterprise will submit a report understating its potential in any of three circumstances, viz. if incentives will not depend on a plan target related to its possibilities ; if overfulfilment is proportionately more highly rewarded than fulfilment ; or if the premium attached to any improvement of activity is unavailable in the ensuing plan period because the better results achieved by the enterprise are embodied in that plan.

Such conditions generate numerous abuses — an enterprise would under-estimate its productive potential, would strive to have a plan issued to it which is easy to fulfil, or would keep its annual overfulfilment down to a margin which would not lead the planning authorities to realize its possibilities for the following year's plan. An enterprise which had worked hard and used all its internal reserves would on the other hand be issued with a target incorporating an increment, and, by underfulfilling this (or not overfulfilling), its premia would be reduced, because only the degree of fulfilment, not the increment over the previous year, would be counted. The procedure is detrimental to the dynamic, and advantageous to the backward, enterprises. Incentives should be arranged so that rewards vary with the extent to which the enterprise implements possibilities foreseen in the plan, and so that workers and managers are anxious to have big increments for their enterprise plan and make efforts to achieve it.

Three bases may be proposed for plan figures conforming to this requirement : namely, as an increment over the previous period (whether it be, for example, production, profitability, or cost) ; some normative ; or the results achieved by the best enterprises. The premia attached to plans formed in this manner should ensure that the reward is greater for each per cent of the planned increment than for each per cent of the plan overfulfilment. This principle is in fact already on trial at eighty enterprises.

It is more advantageous in a planned economy for an enterprise to fulfil a high plan which accurately states its potential than to overfulfil an understated plan. In the first case, the allocation of resources can be better, all the components of the plan are considered and, because discrepancies and disproportions between branches and enterprises have been eliminated in advance, difficulties are reduced in the relations of suppliers and purchasers.

Incentives should also relate to indicators, the dynamics of which are planned for the long run — two, three, or even more years. The increments planned should diminish with time, since the changes of economic conditions would otherwise be unaccounted for. The level of the previous year should have a significant, but not an exclusive, influence on the incentive-geared indicators for the current year and in certain cases some — but still less — effect on those for the following year.

Some general requirements of good management

Any system of economic incentives must clearly delineate the powers which are devolved upon the enterprise, and superintending administrations should refrain from petty encroachments thereon. The enterprise, on the other hand, cannot assume authority to judge the national interest in production and investment : mere profitability is no sufficient guide. However precise their economic accountancy, the enterprises would not severally secure the national optimum. Optimality cannot arise spontaneously from the operational results of a hundred thousand enterprises ; it is not the mechanical outcome of a multiplicity of enterprises each making the choice best for themselves. The most telling evidence on this score is the incapacity of the enterprise to exercise time-preference — to judge the nationally-appropriate rate of saving and to select the technological pattern of investment. Decisions on capital formation and on technical progress must in the last resort be made by central agencies, in the light of domestic and foreign considerations. To dismantle the central planning of investment — continuously mobilizing capital resources on a large scale — would appear to abjure an unquestionable advantage of the socialist system and to permit the structure of capital formation to fall short of maximum efficiency for socialist production.

The problem is to limit this centralized direction to those elements crucial to determining the main proportions and relationships of the economy : it should be combined with the effective independence of enterprises and of their associations. The principle of the devolution of initiative to the enterprise has already been accepted in the U.S.S.R., and Soviet economists are elaborating measures for its implementation.

These prospective measures fall into six groups. The first extends the practice of 'planning from below' — devolving detailed decisions on production, development, sales, and marketing to the enterprise. The second selectively diminishes the number of indicators used by central agencies for assessing the work of enterprises and authorizing the payment of incentives. The third accords further rights to enterprises to contract for supplies and purchases within the framework of the general directives given by superior authorities. The fourth group of measures grants enterprises control over the number and skill-composition pattern of their employees and discretion over the wage system, provided only that certain standards are respected. The fifth offers more funds (from profits, premia, depreciation charges, working capital, credits, etc.) to enterprises for the development of production and modernization of equipment, for incentives, and for cultural and residential amenities, and makes more of such money available as of right and not as a budget grant. The final group permits enterprises to sell off surplus equipment and material and to apply the proceeds for the development of their own production.

The further suggestion has been made that economic associations ('firms') — which are already functioning well in some branches of Soviet industry — could be developed into a network of specialized entities either on the scale of large economic regions or Union-republics or nation-wide. They would improve management by making it more flexible and more closely related to enterprise cost accounting. Their creation would relieve planning and other central agencies of attention to detail and at the same time bring planners nearer to the actual needs and specific problems of enterprises. The firms would be of real assistance to enterprises in developing and improving production, in solving problems of supply and sales, in obtaining finance and credit, in pursuing an efficient and progressive technical policy, and in fostering enterprise specialization.

III. STRENGTHENING THE INSTRUMENTS OF ECONOMIC MANAGEMENT

Price, profit, incentive funds, and credit

Extending the incentives in Soviet enterprises and their associations demands a more efficient system of price formation and a more sensitive application of profit, incentive funds, and credit to the economic life of the enterprise. The system of incentives at the level of the enterprise cannot be efficient without price reform, which, in the U.S.S.R. today, is being pursued along two main lines.

If profits are to be used correctly to evaluate the quality and the economic results of the enterprise, prices must more closely reflect outlays in the national economy as a whole, relating the expenditure of individual enterprises (current cost and capital intensity, etc.) to the average expenditure of a branch or group of enterprises. Prices should assure adequate profitability for an efficiently-operated enterprise and encourage the less efficient to reduce their costs.

In the second place, the rational deviation of prices from cost could enhance the incentive role of price : for this, they must change with the conditions of demand (national requirements) and supply (cost accounting).

It follows from these two functions of price, which together implement the law of value, that reform must account for capital employed (differentiated by branches), quality and consumer properties (*i.e.* the national utility of the good), the time element in supply (whether it uses a new technique or new materials, whether, as a consumer good, it conforms to fashion), the balance of supply with demand (*i.e.* scarcity or glut), and a rent for natural resources.

Nevertheless, however price formation is adapted to socially-necessary expenditure, some deviation from such expenditure is inevitable, because, as well as its accounting function, price always has an incentive and distributive role. This justifies the use of operational prices as well as accounting estimates : for the latter various procedures, including input-output, are available.

To fulfil these functions efficiently, prices should be periodically revised to maintain alignment with cost and the standard profit. Where production plans are set up on a basis of orders for consumer enterprises, firms should be allowed to settle prices by agreement with the purchasers (although within defined limits and under a supervision that verifies whether the price demanded is appropriate to the qualities and types supplied) ; this practice is now on trial in the Soviet Union. It is further necessary that 'accounting prices' for individual plants be set in addition to the average branch price ; and that ex-factory prices should vary with the degree of obsolescence of the product. Applied to an obsolescent producers' good, the latter practice would not cheapen price to the customer — for this could give a new good an inordinate advantage — but would affect only the manufacturer's revenue : an annually-increasing tax would be imposed on obsolescent products to encourage new output. A reform of Soviet wholesale prices — of both producers' and consumers' goods — is now in preparation ; it is hoped to apply them from the beginning of 1966. By aligning prices more closely to costs, a rationally-operated enterprise should be profitable, should be able to invest at an appropriate level of technology, and should deliver products in the qualities and types demanded; this last criterion requires prices to reflect equilibrium of demand and supply. Applied to consumers' goods, the practice should — as at present — allow a temporarily higher price to be charged for new products, with the tax margin (if any) unchanged: this would encourage enterprises to broaden their product-mix and improve the quality of production.

It has already been emphasized that profit is coming to play a more active role in evaluating the work of the enterprise: the volume of profit, and its ratios to cost and to assets employed (total or productive assets alone) are now computed. Some proposals go further — to allow, for example, an enterprise systematically to increase the share of profits it retains, by corresponding cuts in the profit surrendered to budget. In the long run, profit should become the only source for the payment of incentives and bonuses, and recent discussion in the U.S.S.R. has brought forward numerous proposals in this field.

One of these suggests that the 'Enterprise Fund' (from which bonuses and discretional investment are financed) should vary not only with the profit-retention percentage but should also be subject to a gradual increase in the levy on capital assets (*i.e.* a rate of interest on all installed assets and working funds). Another suggestion is that payment into the Enterprise Fund be a function of both total profit and the wage-bill, to eliminate the advantage gained by some enterprises under the present regulations, which provide only a relationship to profit: it might pay the same levy on its capital but have a quite different return on its assets. The idea has also been put forward that the levy on capital (rate of interest) be reduced while an enterprise is mastering a new technique or increasing the share of new products in the volume of output. Other schemes are directed towards encouraging successful enterprises to increased self-financing of capital formation: various artificial obstacles should be eliminated and allowance made for the limiting factors uncontrolled by the enterprise. A final group of proposals recommend the division of the Enterprise Fund in two, one part to be assigned for productive development and the other for collective incentives. They differ substantially from each other in character, sources, and objectives; thus proper use of depreciation charges affects the production process, but the value of equipment affects only the 'Development Fund', not the incentive fund. A formal division would, moreover, help to stamp out the practice now prevailing of using one part to cover outlays of the other. In these connexions not only Soviet suggestions must be analysed in detail, but also the experience of those socialist countries already using profit as the source of collective incentives.

Soviet economists have recommended that the bonus be made a larger share of the remuneration of managers, engineering staff, office employees, and workers, and that bigger premia should be paid for the mastering of new techniques and of new kinds of products ; schemes are similarly being developed for granting premia on the basis of the quality of production. Profit should be made the unique source of all the collective incentives and personal managerial premia, but, as an interim measure, independent bonus funds should be established as an integral component of the current and long-term plans of each enterprise. It is essential to give the enterprise which works well the security of its incentive payments, unaffected by casual factors, but the importance of the rational use of capital requires that such incentives depend upon the proper allotment of productive assets and the prompt utilization of new capacities (all assets, of course, being subject to a tax-charge whether they are in use or not).

The charge on assets should be deducted from profit in such a way that the part retained can be related to an evaluation of the activity of the enterprise and to an incentive scheme ; the rate of charge should be differentiated by industrial branch and by group of enterprises (in relation, for example, to capital quantity, quality, and profitability) ; the rates should be high enough to serve as incentives but not so high as to absorb an excessive share of profit ; and should be levied not only on fixed assets but also on inventories of materials and uncompleted production, any surplus thereof thus reducing the amount of profit. The problem of capital charges to be paid by the unprofitable or low-profit enterprises requires special investigation : in such cases material incentives should foster the optimal allocation of their equipment.

The sphere of credit relations and the share of loans in capital investment is now being extended in the Soviet Union ; the existing arrangements for granting credits for the development of new techniques are also being enlarged. Soviet economists see the problems of credit in the following ways : long-term credits for capital investment should to a large extent replace budget financing ; the function of the banking system in furnishing funds for working capital and for temporary difficulties should increase ; the rate of interest on credits should be differentiated in the light of the profitability of the enterprise ; and, finally, credit should be available whenever properly arranged materials and equipment are delivered.

Material incentives for technical progress

A number of measures have been introduced, or are in prospect, to furnish incentives for mastering new techniques and producing new products. Firstly, enterprises classified in this category can retain proportionately more of their profit for incentive funds. Secondly, special funds have been formed in many branches of industry to recompense such enterprises for their planned expenditures on design and experimentation. Thirdly, price formation and norms of profitability are to be significantly altered to yield a greatly increased margin on new products ; prices are nevertheless being planned with account taken of the technical and economic efficiency of the product in the hands of the user. Wholesale prices on some machinery and other goods of which the product-mix changes rapidly will be revised without waiting for a general price revision. Fourthly, the norms of labour input on new products are to be increased during the running-in period, so as to permit enterprises to devote adequate manpower to assure proper reliability, durability, and other qualities. Finally, individual workers associated with the introduction of new equipment or products are to receive special bonuses, minima and maxima for which will be determined by the annual saving to be achieved by the use of new products.

The relationship of supply to demand

Great significance must be attached to the experiment now being conducted in the consumer-manufactures industry whereby industrial enterprises (or associations, *i.e.* 'firms') plan their production on the basis of orders placed by marketing outlets. Firms in the garment-making industry themselves determine the volume of their production, their sales, their purchase of materials requirement, and their wage bill on the base of such orders. They are required to achieve only two plan indices for a given period, viz. the volume of orders executed and a planned rate of profitability. Thus the managers of the firms and of the shops settle by negotiation the quantity and quality, the supply terms, and the design, pattern, and colour of clothes to be delivered. Contracts embodying the decisions so reached must be signed at least six months before the beginning of the year during which delivery is to be made. Sanctions are envisaged for non-fulfilment of contract, which can only be varied under specified conditions. Some latitude is allowed firms making such contracts to increase the price above that of the state-controlled list to account for the extra work necessary to meet qualitative improvement and to set retail prices of new clothing items before they appear on the price list, but such prices must be based on local norms for the quantity of fabric and other material used, manufacturing costs, commercial expenses, input prices, etc.

This experiment, which is systematically affecting more and more enterprises, will eventually base production plans for consumer-manufacturers on negotiation terms, *i.e.* on orders from trade firms which operate to satisfy consumers' demand. It is being copied for producers' goods, allowing output plans to be set up in direct negotiation between suppliers and purchasers. As has already been observed, these changes will not dismantle centralized planning so far as concerns the general guidance of the economy.

Material incentives will act most efficiently when monetary encouragement is given for good work and sanctions are levied for the material damage caused by a given enterprise or by workers. Enterprises should be granted firm rights to change, dismiss or rearrange their manpower resources in the light of experience. They should seek to create a reputable image for their products and compete with others to improve quality and to lower cost. Success in such competition should be rewarded both morally and materially, and in all ways material and moral incentives should be directed to the national interest.

Chapter 20

THE ROLE OF ECONOMIC INDICATORS IN THE CONTROL OF INDUSTRIAL ENTERPRISES

BY

A. HEGEDUS

Sociology Unit, Hungarian Academy of Sciences

CENTRALIZED control of production and its purposive co-ordination with social needs are becoming increasingly accepted elements in national policies. Economists must therefore devote deepening attention to the clarification of the economic aspects of the control system, and must elaborate methods to establish a management practice conducive to optimal results. The development of a specific branch of economic science to deal with this question has become a social necessity.

Under these circumstances economists cannot be satisfied with investigating objective interconnexions or, more exactly, with determining the methods for arriving at the most favourable solution in a particular case. They must also deal with the analysis of the social conditions (*e.g.* the regulations for the flow of materials, goods, inputs, and outputs, and for finance, planning methods, the pattern of material incentives, etc.) which are determined primarily by the control system and which are necessary for scientific decision-making.[1]

The economics of the control system are still virtually ignored; even the rapidly developing theory of decision-making (praxeology) is largely restricted to the aspects mentioned above. This backwardness is at least partly due to 'voluntarist' ideas, which have often influenced practice, and have caused the failure to see the economic control system as an objectively existing social phenomenon follow-

[1] In a socialist economy, state-owned industrial enterprises are self-contained economic units drawing up a separate balance sheet and headed by a director acting under the principle of 'one-man responsibility'. They are obliged to operate according to plans worked out by themselves and approved by the supervising authority. In this paper, 'economic control' means the guidance, instruction and supervision of these units by the authorities.

ing intrinsic laws ; the system has been assumed to be a perfectly flexible medium, either strictly executing the orders of economic policy, or acting in conformity with the postulates of common sense (in recent times often clothed in mathematical formulae).

One of the problems of perfecting the control system is the degree of quantification of the different aspects of economic activity, and how far such quantified information can be utilized in economic control — that is, in formulating instructions (as in the plan directives), in deciding on economic development (*e.g.* evaluating investment projects), in appraising the activity of enterprises, and, in this connexion, in the application of material and moral incentives. There is little doubt that the manifold possibilities of applying quantified information for the purposes of economic management do not depend simply on subjective considerations. They have definite limits, constraints, and practical technical aspects that can be calculated. The foundation for this kind of research has been laid by the recent work of a number of economists and enhanced through international co-operation. We now possess a rich variety of methods of measuring economic phenomena by the application of mathematics. However, valuable as is the research in many countries on quantitative economics, only sporadic knowledge has been accumulated on economic control, and even this is being applied all too slowly in practice. This may be due, among other causes, to the fact that the elaboration of various techniques for quantifying economic information has not been followed by reasearch into their use in the control systems extant in individual countries.

Hungarian experience and the author's personal opinion lead to the conclusion that two important aspects are missing, viz. analysis of mutual interdependence between data of different character, *i.e.* lack of a theoretical system into which the results found could be integrated ; and examination of the measure of usefulness of the different types of quantified information, and the functions they could fulfil in economic control under particular conditions.

In 1962, a research group was established at the Institute of Economics of the Hungarian Academy of Sciences, to investigate the economic interconnexions of the industrial control system. In the belief that neither models nor methods of the control system can be investigated until the problem of quantified information has been elucidated, the research group has tried to solve this task as the first stage of its work.

The present paper seeks briefly to summarize the results of recent research and those hypotheses which, while requiring further verification, have played an important role in the enquiries.

ECONOMIC INDICATORS AS SPECIFIC TYPES OF QUANTIFIED INFORMATION

The immense volume of quantitative information available on the activity of industrial enterprises can be classified in many ways, but division into two groups is adequate, viz. numerical data on the number of, or ratios between, objects and activities, whether or not identified by specific quality criteria (division of products by quality groups); and numerical data on the quantifiable properties of different objects (prices of products). The distinction between the two groups as made by Yule and Kendall in their now classic work [1] plays an essential role in the present analysis, though, as will be seen later, in both groups there arises the problem of accuracy in reflecting the economic fact to be characterized. From among the highly diverse set of quantified information the group selected those particularly important items which have, or should have, a function in the control system : these data it termed 'economic indicators'.

It is easy to see that much of the information contained in statistical and accounting returns on the activity of enterprises cannot play an independent role in the control of the enterprise, and may serve merely as a starting basis for constructing indicators. Other data are necessary only for the operation of the different sub-units of the enterprise, and others again represent a typical product of bureaucracy, as they do not have even an indirect function in management and are, strictly speaking, useless. On the basis of current or potential utility, three major types of economic indicator can be distinguished to define enterprise activity. First, there is that which reflects with sufficient accuracy some important economic activity and is hence properly employed in management ; second, that which is used in management, but either fails to reflect any important economic activity or is of dubious accuracy and usefulness ; and, third, that which reflects some important economic activity with due accuracy (and thus should be employed in the control system), but which, however, has not yet been implemented ; such types of information are generally created by recent advances in economics. It is clear

[1] G. U. Yule and M. G. Kendall, *An Introduction to the Theory of Statistics*, London, 1950.

that the investigation could not be confined to the first two types ; all three had to be independently examined.

Systematic reflection upon the type into which any economic indicator should be classed is necessary to ensure that the evolution of the control system does not lag behind new theoretical developments. The control system is as much defective if it applies indicators inadequate for economic evaluation as if it neglects new methods for the quantification of economic activities.

ECONOMIC INDICATORS AS STATISTICAL FACTS, AND THEIR CONNEXION WITH ECONOMIC ACTIVITIES

The most important criterion of the applicability of economic indicators to the control system is the extent to which (and within what limits of error) they can reflect individual economic activities.

Referring to Lenin, the Soviet Academician Nemchinov was right in defining indicators as 'statistical facts' as distinct from the 'social facts' which they are expected to reflect. This logical distinction plays an important role from two aspects. First, it helps to correct the erroneous identification of quantified information with economic facts, often occurring in public opinion — the increment in productivity is, for example, commonly identified with that in *per-capita* global product. Secondly, it emphasizes the difference which must be made between the quantified information and the economic facts if mathematically-derived results are to be correctly used. There is a risk that, as a consequence of mathematical abstraction, the quantified information may become detached from its economic content, and in practical application may achieve a certain independence, irrespective of the limits of error within which it is capable of reflecting economic reality. Mathematical models established on such a basis hence cannot be used in practice, however refined may be the solutions they embrace.

The divergence between the economic activities and observations may take different forms and have a great variety of causes. Without being able at present to suggest a comprehensive typology, one might enumerate the more significant modes whereby a divergence between economic and statistical facts is manifested. One typical instance is the reflection in the quantified information not only of the activity to be measured but also of other elements (*e.g.* the *per-capita* global product mentioned above is not solely influenced by changes in productivity). Another is the basing of the quantified information, as a statistical magnitude of some quality criterion, on an uncertain classification (*e.g.* the classification of products may be such that a change in the material incentives for the operating personnel can have a significant effect). Finally, the quantified information may be ambiguously defined (*e.g.* the prices of industrial products expressed in terms of money units are not unambiguous equivalents of social inputs).

An examination of the history of the industrial control system seems to show that two extreme positions frequently co-exist : while some make a fetish of economic indicators and treat them as economic facts, others form economic judgements entirely without the support of quantified information. In a poorly-organized control system, the appearance of both is almost inevitable.

Avoidance of these extremes depends not only on the development of economic theory, but also on the extent to which the control system can adapt and use the results of such development. The interdependence between basic and applied research and practical application is well known in technological development, and may also be distinguished here. But this process can be hindered, and the one-sided fetishism of the economic indicator can be promoted by the paralysis of the investigation of the economic content of quantified information which can be termed the 'statistical approach' to economics.

At the opposite pole is the renunciation of almost all the quantitative information available for the purpose of industrial control. In the course of establishing central planning, far-reaching economic illusions have from time to time been attached to some indicator or group of indicators. Imagining that the trend in a single indicator correctly reflected the interests of society as a whole, policy-makers endowed it with inordinate importance. In Hungary, as in other socialist countries, a high value was thus long placed on the indicator of the growth of the volume of production. This was done many times so one-sidedly that other aspects seemed to be ignored. The career of the production-volume indicator was promoted by the view that the efficiency of the economic system could be measured almost exclusively by the quantity of global output, to the disregard of opportunity cost and of the character of the product — whether it was of acceptable quality and available in adequate variety. This in fact is usual during certain periods of tension such as in times of war, but such an attitude is harmful when it is no longer justified by circumstances of stress. Clearly an increase in the volume of production is not the unique (nor often even the primary) aim of industrial development. Furthermore, the volume indicators generally used are valued in producers' prices, and influenced by the many distortions implicit in those prices. It would be a digression to analyse producers' prices in this context ; all that should be indicated here is that those in general use are incapable of guarding against ambiguity in the indicator, *e.g.* in distinguishing growth from change in the product-mix, both in aggregate and at price level.

Criticisms of this nature have led to the replacement of such indicators by others of productivity, on the (fundamentally correct) view that the efficiency of production manifests itself primarily in an increase of labour productivity. Even so, an erroneous identification of economic and statistical facts has resulted in its measurement by production per head or per working hour, a method which involves all the distortions mentioned above in connexion with production indicators. Indeed, the use of labour productivity in such a form has helped to maintain the preponderance of the production index in the industrial control system, preserving it, although apparently dethroned, as a clandestine guide for centrally-planned economies.

Even apart from the problem of aggregation, labour productivity — contrary to the supposition of many economists — cannot be considered as resuming and characterizing all important aspects of the activity of an enterprise. It accurately reflects neither change in the magnitude of social inputs (because the divisor is limited to current labour at a certain stage of production), nor the results of technical progress. The use of this indicator is especially unsatisfactory in Hungary, because, due to the inadequacy of raw materials, a change in production structure towards the more labour-intensive and less material-intensive branches is desirable. Thus, it can occur that, from the point of view of the national economy as a whole, the activity of some enterprises where labour productivity has not developed favourably may be much more advantageous than that of others which achieved formally better results when judged by this indicator.

At length aware of these readily-verifiable shortcomings, control agencies have advanced various indicators of profitability (particularly those of enterprise profit and cost) to a place of growing importance as industrial management in almost every country with a centrally-planned economy. Some economists believe that an improved indicator of profit could reflect in a single figure every major aspect of the activity of the enterprise.

Given an efficient price system, the interests of the national economy as a whole may be better expressed by the postulate that the net revenue of enterprises should grow, and their mean costs should fall, than by the growth of the volume of production in sum or *per capita*. For the present, however, the effective use of any of the available measures of profitability as a single indicator is, at least at the present level of knowledge, an illusion. Under existing economic conditions, the activity of an enterprise can be reflected only by a system of indicators, each set selected with the function of the enterprise in view and intended to give both a general picture and a detailed analysis of activity. In such a system, indicators which combine a variety of measurements will be valuable, but must be seen as a function with many variables rather than as indicators embodying many aspects in a single figure.

A SYSTEM OF ECONOMIC INDICATORS AND PROBLEMS OF INDUSTRIAL BRANCHES

In developing the system of indicators, the features of the individual industrial branch must be carefully considered. In Hungarian industry there are branches where the modernization of the product is given first priority (*e.g.* telecommunications and machine-tool production). In other industries the optimal exploitation of existing capital capacity and the restriction of the current inputs are crucial; in these industries development cannot be assured from internal resources (*e.g.* chemical fertilizers and textiles). There are still other industries where demand is rapidly changing and imperatively requires the adaptation of production.

The increase of production in any industry is desirable only in so far as it responds to demand, for otherwise assets are immobilized and the national economy is disrupted. This problem, however, presents itself differently in various industries. In some, production must fluctuate in accordance with demand (*e.g.* the clothing industry); in others a maximum of production is aimed at through the optimal exploitation of capital capacity, and the aims of technical development and decreased costs are pushed into the background (in Hungary, the production of bauxite, aluminium hydrate, and aluminium). In view of this, it does not seem reasonable to establish a system of indicators for industry as a whole, or to assert that the same set of indicators can be used in the control system of every industry.

Material Incentives and Cost Accounting

THE USE OF ECONOMIC INDICATORS IN PLANNING

Socialist experience in planning and plan implementation has shown one of the greatest difficulties to be the extremely wide scale of obligatory plan targets, the rigidity of which restricts the initiative of enterprises, while giving no real guarantee that the requirements of efficiency will be actually observed. The cause of such wide-spread transformation of 'overplanning' into 'planlessness' is the erroneous assumption that purposive development can only be enforced by the prescription of obligatory plan indicators for as many economic activities as possible. This way of thinking neglects such important mechanisms as material incentives, and the economic relations between producers and consumers.

If the aim is both to give the enterprise a free hand in decision-making and to ensure that its decision will be optimal from the point of view of the economy as a whole, obligatory targets must be chosen with the greatest care, as was that of the 'average wage' in Hungary, which has figured in almost every type of plan since 1956. Although, for reasons which can be studied in other works, wage inflation (money increasing faster than wages) was not successfully checked, the prescription of an 'average wage' has facilitated the near-autonomy of directors of enterprises and trade unions in almost every important wage question, and has helped to create far-reaching possibilities for the deliberate structuring of industrial, occupational, and enterprise earnings.[1]

Economic problems are raised not only by the selection of economic indicators that can be used successfully as obligatory plan indicators, but also by the changes in the control system which arise when an activity is translated to the status of obligatory indicator. The use of economic indicators in planning, especially if material sanctions are attached to their non-fulfilment, can evoke consider-able slack between plans and real resources, to counter which several Hungarian industries have applied 'incentives for exact planning'. This method evaluates the activity of enterprises by the degree, not of overfulfilment of the plan, but of the accuracy with which the activity had been forecast. Although this method was proved satis-factory, it does not provide a complete solution, first, because even then enterprises, if not leaving the slack of the earlier practice, still

[1] See the present author, *A munkábérezés rendszere iparunkban* (The Wage System Applied in our Industry), Budapest, 1960.

242

tended to leave themselves a safety margin, the curbing effect of which may result in the exploitation of productive capacities at less than the desired level. For similar reasons, the programme for technical change should not be an obligatory plan target.

On the basis of such considerations, the Hungarian government over recent years has considerably reduced the number of obligatory plan indicators. In many industries not even those indicators which served as the most important criteria for evaluating the activity of the enterprise some years ago are now compulsorily prescribed in planning. In many branches global production value no longer figures (*e.g.* in the obligatory plans of the cotton industry), but supervising authorities have sometimes offset this by requiring adherence to so-called 'plan guide-lines' which, though not considered as obligatory plan indicators, remain significant factors in the control of enterprises and often play no less a role than the obligatory plan indicators themselves.

ECONOMIC INDICATORS AND MATERIAL INCENTIVES

In industrial control, economic indicators owe their influence to the fact that their fulfilment affects the bonuses paid to management, viz. the premia of the director, chief engineer, chief bookkeeper, and technical and administrative staff under the system of profit-sharing (which may reach a maximum of one month's earnings),[1] and in some industries to the workers generally (by determining the permitted average wage-level). Changes in the indicators to which managerial premia are attached reflect the developments that have taken place in economic attitudes and priorities. Today, in most of the socialist countries the director's bonus frequently (though not exclusively) is related to the decrease in costs compared with the previous plan period and the fulfilment of the export plan. It is not, however, always reasonable to set up an automatic relationship between one or two specific indicators and personal premia. Only very rarely do they truly reflect either the activity of the enterprise or the national requirements it should fulfil. Some have hence suggested — at least in some industries — that premia should be paid retrospectively, thus allowing the evaluation from many aspects of the activity of enterprises in view of long-term, as well as short-term, results.

[1] See Laszlo Ozswald, *A müszakiak premizáldsa* (Bonus Payments to Technical Workers), Budapest, 1962.

Opinion today is still guided by a schematic view which prefers the linking of premia with indicators to subsequent awards based on a thorough analysis of economic results. There can be little doubt that such a view is based on erroneous theory, and in practice would be detrimental. It would seem more expedient to adjust not only premia but also salaries to actual results on the basis of a more differentiated and more thorough economic analysis.

In most socialist countries, as in Hungary, the indicators are largely instrumental in determining collective premia : this seems to have had no distorting effect because the transmission is indirect. Even so, the dependence of premia on indicators is not always the best solution.

In Hungary there is an increasing tendency to formulate a part of the premium fund according to the demands of current tasks, rather than to the results of the previous year. This is especially important in enterprises where large-scale technical development is taking place ; here, the premia serving as incentives for technical progress cannot by their nature be related to past performance : indeed, use of the preceding year's technical development could give a reverse image of current operation.[1] Unfortunately, such indicators as may serve for the direct measurement of technical progress are still largely undeveloped, and unsuitable for linking with any considerable material incentives. It may be doubted whether indicators of technology could ever be sufficiently improved, despite the search for appropriate measures in all countries with centrally-planned economies. The technical development tasks to be undertaken by each enterprise should be determined first, and only then should the premium to promote their successful solution be set up.

It has often been suggested that the permitted average wage should be related to the labour-productivity indicator. In theory, this requirement seems to be justifiable, because higher effort should be compensated by a better wage, but in practice it would seem difficult to find a reliable measure of labour productivity, and to ensure that any increase in labour productivity does not take place at the expense of the quality or variety of products or of technical progress.

A new type of material incentive introduced in Hungary since 1956 is profit-sharing, depending on the net revenue of the enterprise. In the first form of this method, the net revenue of the previous year served as the basis of payment and thus gave only a

---

[1] See the present author, *Müszaki fejlesztés a szocializmusban* (Technical Development under Socialism), Budapest, 1962.

short-term incentive, even acting in some degree against technical progress. In 1962, a major change was made, fixing the basis of the computation of the sum to be paid out at the same level for three years. Even this solution, however, cannot be considered as final.

This, of course, by no means precludes the consideration of profit-sharing as a successful form of incentive. According to Hungarian experience, this method plays a significant role in the consolidation of the workers' relationship with the enterprise, giving them a sense of ownership. Nevertheless, the search for a better solution and for better co-ordination between the interests of the individual worker, the enterprise, and society as a whole, demands further thorough analysis of the role of indicators in economic management.

Chapter 21

COLLECTIVE ECONOMIC INCENTIVES IN A SOCIALIST ECONOMY

BY

BRONISLAW BLASS

Polish National Bank and Higher School of Planning and Statistics, Warsaw

DEFINITION OF INCENTIVE PAYMENTS

THE operation of economic incentives in socialism is bound up with the nature of its characteristic productive relations, which in the first phase of development require — by reason of the limitation of consumption in the interests of growth — that the distribution of personal income (and hence of incentives) be effected only in accordance with the quantity and quality of labour rendered.[1]

The use of incentives may be defined as 'a situation which urges men to the realization of the particular aim of their economic activity'; [2] they may be applied personally or collectively. Individual incentives, paid in accordance with personal qualifications and services, play a decisive role in the fulfilment by enterprises of their economic tasks. The major part of a worker's income derives from individual remuneration, a practice which has the advantage of stabilizing his income, since a wage received in this form is not subject to substantial change over short periods.

Individual incentives cannot, however, ensure the fulfilment of all the tasks upon which an enterprise is engaged, and collective incentives must hence be used in addition. Since these are by definition paid in relation to the achievement of the whole collective or other defined group of workers, they cannot, as a rule, be disaggregated to measure the contribution of the individual workers.[3]

[1] Lenin observed in 1921, in his 'Fourth Anniversary of the October Revolution', that socialism should be built, 'not directly relying on enthusiasm, but aided by the enthusiasm engendered by the great revolution, and on the basis of personal interest, on personal incentives and business principles' (*Works*, vol. 33, Fourth edn., English trans., Moscow, 1966, p. 58).
[2] O. Lange, *Ekonomia polityczna*, vol. 1, Warsaw, 1959, p. 59.
[3] The present writer does not believe, as some Polish economists do, that socialist productive relations are properly reflected when profit-sharing is justified.

COLLECTIVE INCENTIVES

The benefits distributed as collective incentives may be enjoyed either individually or collectively : the former is more attractive to the worker — and hence more inducive of effort in relation to reward — but, despite this, more benefit is in practice made over collectively, partly in order to maintain the stability of personal remuneration, and partly because such channels are more subject to central budgetary control.

The magnitude of benefits in certain systems of collective incentives depends upon the fulfilment of 'basic' tasks by the enterprise, but actual payment is only authorised upon completion of 'secondary' tasks : complete (or partial) non-fulfilment of the 'secondary' tasks results in loss (or reduction) of benefits.

All systems of collective incentives in current use in Poland are based upon some overall indicator of the work of the enterprise : this has its advantages and its shortcomings, and efforts are being directed to promoting the former and limiting the latter.

Quantitative or value indicators of the work of an enterprise, upon which incentives are evaluated, may be classified as 'simple', 'compound', or 'synthetic', depending on whether they reflect one, several, or all the tasks undertaken by the enterprise. From another point of view these indicators may be divided into 'directive', 'plan', and 'dynamic', depending on whether the work of the enterprise is evaluated on the basis of the fulfilment of the tasks set by a superior organization in accordance with the directives of the national economic plan, on the basis of planned tasks decided on by the enterprise itself, or on the basis of the progress made by the enterprise in relation to a previous period (*i.e.* without taking into account the fulfilment of any plan). As stated above, indicators are considered as either 'basic' or 'secondary', but basic indicators may act directly (remuneration being paid *pro rata* thereto) or indirectly (*i.e.* in conjunction with other indicators of the work of the enterprise).

'Simple' indicators reflect only one aspect of the work of an enterprise, *e.g.* the volume, or cost, of output or the use of a particular input ; they may be employed either as the 'basic' or 'secondary'

by virtue of workers' ownership of the means of production, rather than as a return to labour (Z. Mikołajczik, 'Problems of profit-sharing', *Życie gospodarcze*, no. 46, 1957), or by the function of the collective as entrepreneur in partnership with the state (C. Krzyżanowski and L. Martan, *ibid.*, no. 42, 1957, and no. 8, 1958), or as a right (S. Bulczowski, *ibid.*, no. 14, 1958).

release of incentive payments. A variety of input-related indicators are in use (consumption of raw material, semifabricates, fuel, or power, in absolute terms or proportionately to an established norm), but the most widely used is the global volume of production, sometimes employed with indicators of product-mix and quality.

The question of using global output is one of the most hotly debated on the subject of material incentives. It has the disadvantage that an enterprise, the operation of which is measured in this manner, often produces the more expensive goods, irrespective of the direction of demand, or more capital-intensive goods, irrespective of economic efficiency. At the same time one should emphasize that this indicator played an important part in the initial period of socialist industrialization, and even now, in a number of countries, has an important function as the numerator in calculating the productivity of labour whence the authorised wage fund and the bonuses of the engineering and technical staff are determined.

'Compound' indicators are exemplified by production cost: it falls short of the 'synthetic' indicator because it does not reflect every aspect of the enterprise's work. In particular, it does not necessarily move in sufficiently close relationship to the growth of output, for, although costs tend to decline with growth, only 'comparable output' (*i.e.* goods produced both in the current and base year, and connected with the aggregate volume of output tenuously, or not at all) are taken into account. Apart from this, an index of cost-reduction for comparable output has a number of shortcomings as a criterion for collective incentives. It is difficult, and sometimes impossible, to define any significant range of goods for comparison when the variety of products is broad and unstable ; changes in the indicator tend to be exaggerated by variation in the composition of sub-groups ; and the improvement of quality is discouraged, since the outlay needed raises cost, whereas the equivalent increase in sales price does not affect the indicator.[1] If the restriction to comparable items is ignored, some of the difficulties can be avoided, but in effect this allows the indicator to be affected by changes in the product-mix : should there be large and varying differences between cost and sales price for individual products, the objective of the indicator is frustrated.

The 'synthetic' indicator of the work of an enterprise is the

---

[1] The Soviet economist, E. Liberman, has drawn attention to the adverse effects on quality of the use of the cost-reduction indicator ('An answer to critics', *Ekonomicheskaya gazeta*, no. 36, 1962).

financial result of its activity. At first sight, it appears to reflect without exception all the achievements and miscalculations of the work of the enterprise : the magnitude of these results is influenced by the size of production, the variety and quality of output, and the amount of capital and labour expended ; the efforts of the enterprise and the workers' collective towards improving the financial results of their work tend to maximize production with a minimum input of labour. But the use of this indicator is open to criticism on closer examination : the financial objectives of the enterprise, the workers, and the state are contradictory. The enterprise seeks to increase its financial returns, the workers seek to increase their wages, which are a component of enterprise cost, and the state is concerned with the increase of net national income. The expediency of using financial results as an enterprise indicator may also be criticized on the grounds that the effect of separate factors on the efficiency of the enterprise is obscured. Finally, society is not indifferent to the methods and sources used by the enterprise to achieve its financial results.

INCENTIVES AND THE CONDITIONS OF PLAN FULFILMENT

While the financial results of an enterprise concentrate all aspects of its activity and the work of virtually all of the collective, it does not follow that the maximization of financial results should be considered as the aim of its activity. The socialist enterprise must seek to satisfy to the maximum the requirements of society by furnishing buyers with the goods they need in a variety corresponding to those needs, and of the most appropriate quality. Financial results are one of the indications that this task is being fulfilled and at what cost, but they depend only partly on subjective factors such as the initiative and work of the collective ; there are also objective factors which, in a socialist state, are outside its control.

Two basic groups may be distinguished among these objective factors. The first consists of changes in price, piece-rates, wage-scales, etc. They are in practice excluded for the technical purpose of calculating material incentives on the basis of financial results : exclusion is not too difficult when comparison is between the actual and the planned results for a given year, but difficulties are considerable when it is with the previous year, and still greater when reducing to comparability financial results over several years. But the problem is more than a technical one. Price and wage-rate changes are made to affect the use of certain means of production and of certain services by other enterprises : the exclusion of such changes limits the full achievement of the substitution thereby intended. The practical experience of socialist countries has not yet solved the problem.

The second group of factors comprises those whose effect on the financial results of the work of an enterprise cannot be excluded. These concern the environment of, and regulations governing, enterprises in the framework of national planning. Enterprises are set planned production tasks and the means for their realization. These tasks, set in more or less detail, are mostly directive. For their fulfilment the state provides the enterprises with finance and such equipment and materials as are subject to regulated distribution. The state fixes both the purpose and the amount of capital investment, sets limits to the wage fund, and so on. Moreover, to a certain extent the possibility of enterprises finding a market for their goods depends on the policies of the state, which affect the size and direction of demand. All decisions in this field affect the economic activity of an enterprise, and the financial results of its work depend largely thereon.

In these conditions, the direct dependence of the material benefits obtained by a collective on the financial results of its enterprise (or on their improvement from year to year) could lead to a substantial difference in the material position of the workers of different enterprises. These benefits would be partly determined by the objective conditions of the activity of the enterprise, that is, independently of the work of the collective. For this reason, in almost all systems of collective incentives, financial results are evaluated by comparison with plan goals, on the assumption that both planned outputs and planned inputs adequately reflect the objective and subjective possibilities of the enterprise. But because the enterprise is rewarded in relation to those plans, it seeks — contrary to the intentions of the central organs — to establish planned financial results at a level easier to fulfil and overfulfil ; this encourages a concealment of potential for the growth of production and of labour productivity.

This criticism is bound up with that of the regulation of enterprises by over-detailed directives, which limit the power of enterprises to decide production problems on the criterion of profit or loss, and to adapt themselves to changing conditions for plan fulfilment. As a consequence, both the initiative of the enterprise and its responsibility for its results are constrained : the incentives should be organized in such a way that the enterprise constructs the optimum plan and efficiently fulfils it.

One solution is that of the Soviet economist Liberman, who suggested [1] that the list of directive instructions be limited to the quantity and variety of output within a fixed time-schedule. All other directives implied in the national plan would be passed down no further than the enterprise's administering authority. Communication to the enterprise would not be necessary, since the system of incentives proposed by Liberman would encourage them to fulfil these plans in the best possible manner. To achieve this, Liberman envisaged that the bonuses due to workers be determined by a scale of incentives which would lead the enterprise to produce goods fully corresponding to the needs of buyers, and to lower costs (by technical and organizational means and by the most efficient possible use of fixed assets and working capital). This scale must have effect for the whole period of a five-year plan. The advisability of establishing long-term norms for incentives of material interestedness is undeniable. But the possibility of so establishing them depends on the stability of the economic environment of the enterprise. The conditions for such a stability are being analysed in all socialist countries, and we may assume that it will be promoted by the further economic development of the socialist countries, and co-operation between them — by co-ordinating economic plans and production specialization. But such stable conditions for enterprises have not yet been created ; as witness to this, one has only to consider Czechoslovakia, where the long-term norms of profit incentives established in 1958 were subsequently abolished.

Liberman's proposal to abolish the central determination of the volume of work capital, the wage fund, the cost of production, etc., is necessary for the abandonment of the link between incentives and directives, and envisaged identical incentive scales for groups of enterprises having more or less similar technical equipment. To retain directives would require the enterprise to be twice assessed on its potential to achieve a certain financial result — once when establishing the plan, and again when establishing the scale of incentives. Thus, one may reduce the problem to the question whether the conditions exist for substantially limiting the list of directive targets passed on to the enterprise.

There is a school of thought which holds that rapid growth in

[1] *Pravda*, 9 September, 1962.

socialist countries has led to the establishment and realization of plans without the creation of sufficient reserves to guarantee balanced growth, inducing a sellers' market in producers' goods. It hence became necessary to employ direct methods of control over the economy, including a fairly extensive schedule of directive targets. It is now, however, becoming possible — in Poland, for example — to build up enough inventories and foreign-exchange reserves to ease this pressure, and consequently to extend the indirect methods by which enterprises can influence the process of planning.

While this is a prerequisite for improving the incentive system, there are some changes in practice which could attenuate the short-comings in the relation between collective incentives and fulfilment of the financial plan. One cannot, in present conditions, envisage straightforward profit-sharing, viz. relating the incentives to the absolute or incremental earnings of the enterprise, because, given the great influence of objective factors on these results, a considerable and unwarranted differentiation among enterprises of worker rewards would ensue. But incentives could be geared to constructing an accurate financial plan — for a given actual increment over the previous year, a higher bonus would be paid if the increment corresponded to that planned than if it were an overfulfilment of plan. Similarly, a degressive scale could be applied to transfer the rate of over-plan profits to the incentive fund.

This paper has been limited to the basic problems of an incentive system, and their implications for macroeconomic policy and management. But one must not forget that economic incentives are only part of the motivation towards economic development in the socialist countries : political and moral stimuli have helped them to overcome their great backwardness and rapidly to take their place among the economically-developed countries of the world. Theoretical and practical research is being intensified in all the socialist countries on ways to improve incentives, and, in particular, economic experiments have been started on a broad scale to test a wide variety of new proposals.

Chapter 22

SUMMARY RECORD OF THE DISCUSSION — SESSION VI

MATERIAL INCENTIVES AND COST ACCOUNTING

(In the Chair : PROFESSOR JEANNENEY)

Professor Grossman introduced the discussion with the observation that the three papers were of great significance in their concern with the problem of re-designing the basic model of the Soviet-type economy and of finding more effective forms of control. But their focus was the short-run (and their dynamism was at most on a year-to-year basis) : they therefore passed over questions of the rate and direction of investment, or of income distribution. They all had in common a link with the problem of pricing (and hence to the observations made the day before by Academician Ostrovityanov and Professor Oelssner). None of the papers undertook any optimization in the Western sense, but, rather, sought ways of avoiding obvious waste and of subordinating particular actions to social goals. Although the title of the Session, 'Material Incentives and Cost Accounting', might seem restrictive, it correctly reflected the area with which the papers dealt. He would interpret 'material incentives' as the link between a particular action and a social goal, while 'cost accounting' (the Russian *khozraschet*) should be seen in terms of 'businesslike management', although recently it had been used by Soviet authors [1] as a virtual synonym of enterprise autonomy. He found Professor Gatovsky's paper particularly significant in providing an up-to-date review of Soviet thinking on the fundamental problems of the economy and in foreshadowing changes which were imminent. Although it was in concrete terms (unlike the more formal presentation by Dr. Blass), it did not always distinguish clearly between measures which had already been put into effect ; those which were on the point of promulgation, on the basis of a government decision on the principle of reform ; proposals which were based on a consensus ; and ideas which were propounded by a minority. Where proposals were at issue, Professor Gatovsky avoided attribution to any author. Western economists might find rather inelegant Professor Gatovsky's emphatic rejection of a single 'success indicator' for the enterprise and his preference for systems of indicators differentiated by

[1] *E.g.* V. Nemchinov, 'Socialist Economic Management and the Planning of Production', *Kommunist*, no. 5, 1964, pp. 74–87.

branches. More importantly, a multiplicity of indicators involved the possibility that one — and not necessarily the 'correct one' — might come to predominate. If the indicators yielded an equal incentive, then the problem of marginal trade-offs between them became serious. The question was whether such trade-offs would be rational and uniform among enterprises. Or, would they cause disequilibria to persist and exacerbate a maldistribution of resources ? If so, the result might be a further proliferation of indicators and a gradual re-centralization, in the manner suggested by Dr. Hegedus.

Professor Gatovsky's treatment of prices seemed to be unenlightening : either his value-based relationships would not be equilibrium prices or — because he hinted at balancing demand and supply — the need to keep prices at equilibrium would result in divergence from conformity to value requirements. Prices were crucial to the greater enterprise autonomy which he seemed to advocate : autonomy functioned best under equilibrium prices whereas rational resource allocation required efficiency prices. Any thoroughgoing decentralization (which was not necessarily proposed in Professor Gatovsky's paper) would entail much more than the devolution of authority to the enterprises and an appropriate price system. In common with other Soviet proponents of reform, *e.g.* Academician Nemchinov and Professor Liberman, he was vague on the principles of price formation, and did not declare how much decentralization was needed : as Czechoslovak experience in 1958–59 showed, half-way decentralization could be worse than useless. Decentralization would also entail a reform of the system of generating and processing information to support managerial decision-making ; the formation of more subsidiary institutions for trade and finance, etc. ; and a redefinition of the relationship between the enterprise and extra-economic organs such as the Government, the Party, trade unions, and the various control agencies.

The paper by Dr. Hegedus supported Professor Gatovsky's opposition to a single plan indicator for an enterprise, while pointing at the same time to the dangers of multiplicity of instructions. Overplanning, as he rightly stated, amounted to planlessness. Dr. Hegedus's contribution was useful also in setting out the various incentive and profit-sharing schemes introduced in Hungary since 1956. Dr. Blass's paper covered something of the same ground, although concerned more with the taxonomy of payments to a collective group (workers and management). The high level of abstraction at which Dr. Blass operated obscured the practical advantages of the 'indirect indicators' which he advocated.

Dr. Hegedus stressed the importance of profit as an indicator of the operation of an enterprise and hence of price reform. His own concept of price formation was the same as Academician Ostrovityanov's : price had to reflect social outlays, and to serve as a medium of incentives. The conflict which could arise between these functions was exemplified in Hungary by the problem of technological choice. The domestic price set for inputs differed significantly from that ruling on the world market : a production process, which appeared technically efficient in home prices, might not appear so at import prices and vice versa.

Professor Domar, on reading Professor Gatovsky's paper, had been struck by the difference in the Western and Soviet approach to the formulation of economic problems. The former sought an objective function to be maximized or minimized, subject to certain constraints. The solution — perhaps only approximate — could be expected to yield the indicators to be used in economic planning. The Soviet approach, as typified by Professor Gatovsky, adopted a large number of indicators as equivalent to the objective function. Thus, a branch of a capitalist firm would be expected to maximize profits, subject to certain restrictions regarding budget, risk, long-run considerations, etc. ; in the event of unsatisfactory profit, the head office would examine a number of indicators (perhaps even more than Professor Gatovsky set out), but as possible explanations of the deficiency and not as surrogates for final objectives. There was no problem when the set of indicators, described by Professor Gatovsky, such as profit, productivity of labour and capital, and unit cost, moved in the same direction (allowing for difference in algebraic sign). It only arose when the indicators moved in opposite directions : was it worthwhile to increase output when unit costs were rising, or should the productivity of labour be increased at the cost of a fall in the productivity of capital or of a raw material ? These fundamental questions on the purpose of economic activity had to be resolved before incentives could be discussed. The directors of enterprises might otherwise be stimulated 'correctly' to do the wrong thing.

Mr. Nikiforov pointed out that the aim of production was not necessarily profit. First, profit might grow while the income of the contributors to production fell : an increase in production should generate higher incomes for the staff. Second, profits might grow rapidly, while output stagnated. Third, the rate of profit might incorrectly reflect relative utilities.

Professor Sorokin observed that the reform of Soviet wholesale prices planned for January 1966 would ensure that profits covered funds for investment and material incentives. The majority of economists in the U.S.S.R. opposed the use of a single indicator in the form of profit, because the amount of profit did not always depend on the efforts of the enterprise. The price system did not assure the correspondence of profits to socially-necessary labour. Proposals to decentralize the price system would be against the public interest if producers raised prices to maximize oligopoly profit : it could not be expected that they would set prices to the advantage of consumers.

255

Material Incentives and Cost Accounting

Dr. Ophir asked the previous speakers, and in particular Mr. Nikiforov, for a clarification of their criticism of the profit indicator. Profit was no more than the difference between the value of outputs and the value of inputs; provided that prices correctly measured each, profit constituted the appropriate composite indicator for the success of an enterprise. For example, an increase in output without a corresponding increase in costs, or a reduction in costs with constant output, would show up as an improvement in the profit indicator. He was also surprised by Professor Sorokin's aversion to profits, for he could see no divergence between profits and the interest of the state when profits accrued to the state. Concern should only arise if a state enterprise operating in imperfect competition was able to set a price for its products which induced an allocation of resources diverging from the flows envisaged by the state.

Mr. Kaser hoped that one of the Czechoslovak participants would elaborate more fully on the reasons for the failure of the 1958 reforms in Czechoslovakia; as Professor Grossman had observed, the chief factor seemed to have been that they were not sufficiently comprehensive.

Professor Lipinski rejoined that attempted reform had also failed in Poland by being only a half-measure — chiefly because global production was retained as an indicator from the old system. Enterprises were not properly constrained by a profit bar from recruiting more workers, and inflation resulted. He felt that the discussion on the difference of profits under socialism and under capitalism had misinterpreted the function of the market. This united the aim of socialism, viz. the satisfaction of the needs of the population, with that of capitalism, viz. profit maximization. No individual entrepreneur could realize a profit if consumers would not buy their profit-yielding output. Under imperfect competition some entrepreneur would exploit the consumer, but some consumer would have to undertake the transaction if the monopolistic profit were to accrue. The socialist economy also operated a market on which goods and services were realized for the satisfaction of needs. The aim of production was not to fulfil a plan (although some firms in fact produced goods for unmarketable stocks, *i.e.* not aimed at the satisfaction of the market). The concept of market was not abstract, for it implied the existence of a consumer either as individual or enterprise. Nor should the market be abolished by the production of goods free of charge, for this would destroy cost accounting, which had been rightly accepted as a principle of socialism. For the same reason, the cost accountancy of capital should not be nullified by failing to charge for its employment.

The difference between capitalism and socialism did not hence lie in the phrase 'market', for both must produce to sell. If demand-prices and supply-costs were correctly reflected in the transactions, the test of production would be profit. Profit should be generated when an enterprise produced goods which could be sold to the community. He understood

Professor Sorokin's reservations, but felt that profit was the only valid indicator which should guide the output of producers' and consumers' goods. Output should be raised if profits were excessive, and reduced if profits were too low. This feedback function was the signal of good management. This did not mean that other indicators could not be applied in assessing the operation of an enterprise, whether socialist or capitalist, but profit was the most important to promote dynamism and rationality in an economy.

Professor Robinson commented on Professor Domar's remarks on profit as an indicator in American corporations. It might be true that profit was the dominant indicator, but, certainly, in other capitalist countries in Europe, profit was seldom, if ever, the sole indicator, and very few large corporations with numerous plants used short-term profit as an indicator, for example, of the desirability of investment. The problem of the plant manager was largely that of minimizing costs. Various indicators measuring costs per unit of output (in general and for particular inputs) were normally used. This was particularly relevant for industries where final prices (or those of materials) varied with business conditions; in such cases, profit might not always be a good indicator of performance and might be misleading as a policy indicator. Profits in capitalist countries were at the same time a test for efficiency; a test of success in minimizing costs and in finding markets which required supplies —and a source and form of income. Economists in capitalist countries were very seldom capitalists themselves; they traditionally identified themselves with consumers rather than with industrialists. Many of them were in whole-hearted agreement with Professor Lipinski regarding the practical value of profit as a test of efficiency, and as an indicator of success in planning production, but they were cautious in approving economies where profit formed an excessive share of income. They did not hesitate to advocate profit taxes and increasingly regarded profit as desirable only to the extent that it was needed as a source of accumulation.

Professor Maksimovic noted Professor Domar's stress on the crucial position of the maximization problem, which occupied far too small a place in socialist economics. Maximization was the proper course and the process could be much facilitated by mathematical and computer techniques, but the question remained what was to be maximized. Professor Lipinski had pointed out that socialist theory made social needs the objective function, but the exact nature of such needs had been little discussed and, in practice, left to the decision of central planning or political bodies. Marx had limited his criticism of profit as a sole indicator to the conditions of private property; profit under socialism was different. The profit motive was not the sole objective, but under the control of state preferences. It might perhaps be useful to distinguish different types of profit under socialism, as different types of market existed. Profit arose in one form from the interplay of supply and demand, but was justified under socialism only under full factor-cost pricing and the free competition of microeconomic units. Such conditions would permit the use of profits as a unique indicator, but, needless to say, they did not currently obtain. Another type of profit was that generated to make enterprises responsible for their own investment. The Soviet introduction of profits as a source of self-finance was significant, but had to be accompanied by changes in the price system and institutional structure. In Yugoslavia, profits had never been used as the sole indicator; other interventions were necessary until it was decided who should make the final investment decision. The trend of Yugoslav policy was to devolve more responsibility to the enterprise and limit central planning bodies to the control of the rate of growth and the assurance of the appropriate accumulation.

He agreed with Professor Sorokin that some contradictions existed between micro- and macro-economic interests. If microeconomic units controlled the rate of growth, profits could be a unique indicator, but, if resources were to be socially allocated, the behaviour of microeconomic units had to be correspondingly adapted.

Sir Roy Harrod said that some economists, including those from socialist countries, had suggested that realized profit was a sure and sufficient indicator of the contribution of an enterprise to the public good. It followed then that realized profit could be used as the sole indicator for incentive bonuses, etc. He suggested that there were at least three cases in which there might be a divergence between realized profit and contribution to the public good. First, advocacy of the profit criterion had been accompanied by the recommendation that enterprises should, generally, be allowed to fix their own prices. In some instances, viz. when there was a shortage in the market, raising the price might be of good service, but the resultant profit might be excessive in relation to the service provided. Prices, moreover, could also be raised when the market required no change. Under capitalist perfect competition, a rise in price was held to be impossible unless justified by market conditions. But, in the majority of cases, there was imperfect competition, monopolistic competition, or a strong monopoly: in such cases, it was perfectly feasible and profitable to raise prices unjustifiably. This was a defect which defenders of capitalism usually admitted. Yet socialist enterprises would surely not be operating under perfect competition, and making profit the main indicator would accordingly give an incentive to enterprises to raise prices under conditions in which this was anti-social.

Secondly, official prices were likely to be somewhat out of date for most of the time (until computers began producing weekly data at the national, regional, and enterprise levels). If, in the interval between price adjustments, material and labour costs changed, individual enterprises would be differently affected: the profits of some would be depressed and those of others raised. Profit could be a false criterion if a change in the profit of an enterprise in such cases was held to indicate a variation in its contribution to the public good.

Thirdly, unless the authorities had means of continuously checking quality, the profit indicator might be an incentive to reduce quality. If such control was inadequate, bonuses would in effect be granted for anti-social action.

Doubts had been expressed about the use of a multiplicity of indicators, and it was feared that one (perhaps not the most desirable) would dominate. Sir Roy Harrod suggested that they might be ranked in an 'If, then' form. Some might be expressed as targets which must be fulfilled if any bonuses were to be payable at all; subject to this, bonuses would be in proportion to overfulfilment of the other targets.

Professor Oelssner accepted the parallels which had been made between the subsidiaries of capitalist corporations and managers of socialist enterprises. Corporations had a central organization and management, which issued planning directions in the manner of a 'central administrative economy' in socialist conditions. Just as the general manager of the board of directors of a corporation ran the whole business, the socialist state had to manage the economic affairs of the country in the name of society. But the similarity was strictly institutional because the objectives of management differed under the capitalist and socialist ownership of the means of production, as Mr. Nikiforov had already stressed. When surplus product was appropriated by society as a whole — and not by a group of private organizations — profit was not an ultimate aim but only a means to assure the complete satisfaction of the material and cultural needs of the community. The management of a national economy was of course more complicated than that of even a giant corporation, but socialist countries were prepared to learn from the capitalists. It was no secret that the G.D.R. had studied the structures of large corporations in the United States and Western Germany (*e.g.* Krupps) before working out its present reforms. He believed that useful lessons had been drawn.

Professor Sorokin's paper had accepted that contradictions existed between society and the enterprise in socialist countries. There was also a non-antagonistic, but objective, contradiction between the enterprise and the worker, who was primarily concerned with getting as much money as possible. The aim of socialist economic policy was an agreement between the interests of society, the enterprise, and the individual worker.

Professor Domar had invited comments from socialist economists on the operation of plan indicators assigned to state enterprises. The new economic system in the G.D.R. tried to reduce the use of such indicators, other than profit: profit on the sale of marketed goods was decisive, because production was seen as culminating in the final sale. The new economic system placed the responsibility of marketing on the association of state enterprises. Professor Sorokin and Sir Roy Harrod had here drawn attention to ways in which the profit motive might adversely affect production ; they were difficult to counter as long as utility (value in use) was not measured in price. He agreed with Dr. Hegedus that specific indicators might be needed for different branches of industry, but their use should be limited as much as possible.

The three papers dealt mostly with collective incentives, but seemed to devote insufficient attention to material incentives for the individual. In practice, great dissatisfaction could arise in the distribution of bonuses : one worker would be discontented because he did not know why he had received less than another, and a third was still more unhappy because he had received nothing. Research into this field was random and should be undertaken more systematically. He hoped that Dr. Hegedus would elaborate on his statement that for some time workers in Hungary had been sharing profits : any experience along these lines would be valuable.

Professor Dupriez felt that Mr. Nikiforov had exaggerated the difference between the role of profit under capitalism and the concept of profit which socialist economists were trying to evolve. In Marxist terms, capitalist profit was the goal of the entrepreneur only under 'expanded reproduction', *i.e.* when the economy was growing ; it was absent in a stationary economy, that is, under 'simple reproduction'. It was the instrument of qualitative and quantitative progress, for it demanded that the entrepreneur select the production process ; the maintenance of a positive margin of profit was a condition for survival in a dynamic society. Conversely, the objective of the economy was to assure economic growth to the benefit of all owners of factors of production. It was fair to point out that capitalist profit, net of interest payments, was only a small share of national income ; its share did not rise with income growth. It was in fact clear that, since 1950 in Western Europe, the remuneration of labour had grown faster than the increase in labour productivity, and had led to the reduction of the ratio of profits to total income. A moral justification could be made for profit when it attracted capital to the most efficient uses. Profits would not automatically conduce to this end if prices were regulated by the state. Many examples could be cited of the maldistribution of resources arising from such controls, and he readily appreciated the crucial nature of profit in a managed economy.

Academician Ostrovityanov regretted Professor Lipinski's excessive diplomacy in formulating trivial dialectical differences between markets under socialism and capitalism to obscure his contention that profits were the same under socialism and capitalism. For Academician Ostrovityanov they were two different things.

He turned, first, to the concept of profit. Professor Domar had frankly declared that the goal and motivation of corporations was profit maximization. From this point of view, profits were seen as desirable regardless of how they were obtained, be it by ruining one's competitor, by speculative operations, by lowering the quality of output or by the exploitation of labour (particularly in the underdeveloped countries, as had emerged in discussions of colonial and Latin American income distribution at the Palermo Conference.[1]   Both the substance and role of profit differed in socialist countries : the motivating force behind socialist production was the maximum possible satisfaction of the growing demands of the people at any given level of productive forces. It was implemented by systematically adjusting the flow of production to the changing pattern and volume of demand. Profits were not an end, but a means to stimulate production accordingly ; they were also signals of the efficiency of production and a source of socialist accumulation. A socialist economy did not foster profits indiscriminately, but only those which had been achieved as a result of satisfactory operation by the enterprise.

Professors Grossman and Domar had expressed surprise at the apparent absence of a principle of optimization in Professor Gatovsky's paper. Although the word 'optimization' did not figure there, it was embodied in the socialist principle : 'that which is most useful for society is economically advantageous for the enterprise and its staff'. Each enterprise and each individual worker was rewarded in accordance with his labour for society ; from this, it followed that profits gained as a result of conditions independent of the enterprise were not considered in evaluating the operation of the enterprise and were not encouraged.

In many of the papers and comments at this Conference, frequent reference had been made to the law of supply and demand and to the market mechanism. Academician Ostrovityanov declared that a socialist society did not subsume those concepts in the same manner as under capitalism ; it planned its supply both by taking account of and at the same time influencing, demand. This was the essence of the 'balance of income and expenditure of the population', which determined the wage-fund and other income of the population at the same time as it assured the equivalent quantity of wage-goods. This was not to say that deficiencies in consumer supply did not persist, nor that, for a variety of reasons including inadequate attention to quality and marketing, stocks were accumulated of unsaleable goods. To correct these faults, experiments were being conducted in composing plans for the production of consumers' goods on the basis of orders from retail agencies, thereby permitting greater precision in assessing the growing demands and changing tastes of consumers. Even more attention was being given, during the elaboration of long-term plans, to the problem of studying the needs of the entire population with regard to consumer articles. The same principle was being applied to the planning of producer-good flows between socialist enterprises. Within certain limits, it was proposed that enterprises and enterprise-associations ('firms') entering into agreements with producers and consumers would be allowed to negotiate the prices

[1] J. Marchal and B. Ducros (eds.), *The Distribution of National Income*, Proceedings of a Conference of the International Economic Association, London, 1967.

of their goods : the system of price determination should make prices both more flexible and more stable.

Dr. Kyn replied to Mr. Kaser's request for details on the system of management used in Czechoslovakia since 1958 and on the reforms in preparation. The main reason for the failure of the 1958 system, apart from the material difficulties already mentioned, was inconsistency of the system. It introduced only partial decentralization, retaining the basic centralized and directive character of management. Economic incentives did not form a relationship between production and consumption, but, presupposing a perfect plan, sought only the fulfilment of that plan. Furthermore, even the changes drafted were not fully implemented, and it was relevant to say that the problem was recurring in connexion with the present proposals. Part of the trouble lay in the fact that the new system would be put into effect by those same people who had become used to planning and management under the old order. The difference between the new system and that dating from 1958 might well be illustrated from the present discussions. The papers presented by Professor Gatovsky and Dr. Hegedus discussed the problem of the number and type of indicators to be used in planning and management. Dr. Kyn discounted this approach, for the central question concerned not the indicators themselves but their function : the new system would not abandon the use of indicators, but it would reject their directive nature. Neither profit nor gross product should be understood as 'indicators' in the old sense of the word. Rather, they should demonstrate the desired results of production. Such production would have as its aim the market, not the plan, and the market hence had to provide a feedback connecting production with the consumer. The plan should give information and co-ordinate decentralized decision-making to ensure that the needs of society be met under the constraint of economic development. Fulfilling the plan in itself should never be the aim of production, for a planning official could hardly know better what the consumer wanted than the consumer himself.

SESSION VII

AGRICULTURAL PRICES

Chapter 23

SOME PROBLEMS OF AGRICULTURAL PRICE POLICY

BY

J. LASZLO
Institute of Economics, Budapest

PRICE RELATIVES AND THE GENERAL PRICE-LEVEL

Two problems are fundamental to decisions on pricing farm produce, viz., those of the relationship of agricultural prices as a group to the general level, and of price relatives within agriculture. The present paper deals with the second aspect, and investigates mainly the requirements to be met in respect of the income to be derived from the various products.

The determination of the agricultural price-level allows the state both to assure incentives for production and to set the ratio of farm income to wages and salaries. The agricultural price-level expresses the gross income of farmers, and, if prices of other goods and taxes remain constant, determines their purchasing power. Thus, it is a significant factor in the distribution of national income and the relations between agriculture and the economy as a whole. The concept of the agricultural price-level is, however, confined to these grand proportions; the connexion of agriculture with the rest of the economy through the exchange of products is expressed not by the average, but by relative, prices. The interconnexion of the conditions of agricultural supply and of national demand requires that a planned economy determine such relative prices : the material incentives for producers must be measured by the state in respect of each product, if control over the development of agricultural production is to be maintained. A farmer can derive his income from various products ; he examines the income offered by each, with a view to deciding what pattern of production will yield the most favourable result within the limits of his potential expenditure on inputs. Since the producer takes this attitude, the state should set the prices of different products to stimulate production of those goods of which output must be increased and to decelerate the production

265

of others for which expansion is less desirable. Thus, price policy can, and should, be used to influence the pattern of production.

It is demonstrable from experience that a change of relative prices alters the pattern of production. Even in those sectors of a planned economy where the producing unit is subject to obligatory output targets, unfavourable changes in relative prices often react on production patterns ; still more so if — as in agriculture — there is no such compulsion. The determination of the prices at which government agencies are obliged to buy all that is offered (*i.e.* state procurement prices) must hence take into consideration the fact that any change in relative procurement prices involves some change in relative procurement structure : in most cases a significant change in the price of one or two products influences the whole of agricultural production, and a change in the supply of many products will occur even if the price of only a single product is changed.

ADHERENCE TO THE PRINCIPLE OF RELATIVE PROFIT

The mere correlation of relative prices and of product outputs cannot reveal the mechanism through which agricultural production is affected by prices. Until the mechanism is understood, it is impossible to optimize prices so as to reconcile the interests both of the economy as a whole and of the producers. Moreover, because it is the income derived from sales at such prices which affects production, the determination of relative prices must be made in the light of the incomes necessary to ensure the planned transformation of the production pattern. This problem is of basic importance in agricultural price-formation, and its solution has been sought in both theoretical and applied economics. It is generally agreed that prices should satisfy the requirements of relative profit, but opinions differ upon the criteria to be used.

It must first be made clear why the principle of relative profit should be even more carefully observed in agriculture than elsewhere. The production conditions of a great part of farm products are similar with respect to soil and other requirements : where wheat is grown, for example, there may also be produced maize, barley, lucerne, and various industrial crops. In this, farms differ from industrial units, the production possibilities of which are limited to certain products by their equipment, etc. In agriculture this essentially holds only for permanent plantations, and farms are free (within certain endogenous constraints) to choose their own pattern of production.

Observance of the principle of relative profit in price formation is not primarily advocated on behalf of the farmers. It is in the first place in the interest of the state that farmers should produce in such variety and quantity that the demands of the economy are met. It can virtually be said that farmers are indifferent between crops, and are concerned only with the income yielded by the product-mix : appropriate prices will result in over-production of some goods and scarcity of others in relation to demand.

It is to avoid such disparity between demand and supply that a planned economy seeks to adhere to the law of proportionate development. Such proportionality requires — in agriculture as in any branch — a division of labour which assures the equilibrium of demand and supply. The allocation of means of production and of manpower according to the requirements of the law of proportionate development is achieved by the state through various measures regulating production. Conformity to this allocation may be implemented by the state either by plan-instructions or by material incentives ; the latter predominate in the co-operative sector of agriculture. Thus, the relationship of incomes is a manifestation of proportionality and must be achieved by setting price relatives. Other material incentives also affect the profitability of an operation, but it is here assumed that their action is in the same direction as that of prices. The requirement of relative profitability can be met at any given time by determining price relations, but this is far from implying that it can always be satisfied by the same pattern of price relatives.

RELATIVE PRICES IN THE CONTEXT OF CO-OPERATIVE FARMING

Income is the main material incentive operating on co-operative farms. While this is generally agreed among Hungarian economists, some erroneously concentrate attention on the margin between production cost and price. Co-operatives, however, seek to maximize annual gross receipts per member. Both land area and the number of members are given, and receipts per product are hence subordinate to annual gross receipts per head. The various products will compete with each other for the limited land area and will be ranked according to their contribution to gross annual receipts per co-operative member under local conditions.

Agricultural Prices

Hungarian economists have tended to neglect this characteristic of co-operative farms, or to attribute to them features which they do not possess. Many contend, for instance, that co-operative farms maximize net income per unit of work for individual products. They propose, therefore, that prices should be fixed by the state so as to secure equal incomes in relation to each unit of manpower. There are also those who advocate prices proportionate to total inputs. It follows from the specific nature of co-operative operations and ownership that members have a common interest that the farm maximize its gross receipts, both to increase personal income and to enlarge the productive assets held in common. But the alternative uses of income do not appear as separate criteria for determining the pattern of production, and co-operatives do not even decide the distribution in advance. The volume of labour applied by a farm member is both the determinant and the consequence of the receipts of the co-operative. Labour is not separately costed (since it is remunerated by dividend on the basis of standardized labour-days), and net receipts cannot be measured.

The maximization of annual gross receipts per head follows not only from the practice of division, but also from the objective of fully employing the available labour. Whereas stock-breeding ensures year-round employment, a cadastral yoke [1] under a fodder crop requires between 20 and 150 labour-days and under grain only 8 to 12 labour-days. If the state fixed prices in direct relation to labour input, the receipts from one cadastral yoke under sugar-beet would be nearly eight times, and from tobacco more than twenty-five times, that of wheat (see Table 1).

It is hardly necessary to prove that, with the above income proportions, producers would prefer the production of such commodities as entail a bigger income per unit of land to that of products yielding a smaller income (unless these are demanded by some intra-farming input — a factor in any case inessential to the present argument). Relative prices must hence secure a correct proportion between incomes per labour-day and per unit of area : the requirement of fixing prices so as to ensure relative profitability must be approached from each aspect.

To stimulate the production of crops which are less labour-intensive, prices should counter-balance the relatively more advantageous position of those more labour-intensive per unit of area. Clearly, it cannot be expected that each crop should bring an equal

[1] 0·575 hectare or 1·067 acres.

268

TABLE 1

NOTIONAL RECEIPTS PER UNIT OF LAND IF PRICE VARIED
DIRECTLY WITH LABOUR INPUT

Crop	Input of Labour-days per Cadastral Yoke	Notional Receipts per Cadastral Yoke *	
		Forints	Index (Wheat=100)
Wheat	7·08	424	100
Autumn barley	7·01	423	99
Rice	32·06	1,924	450
Potatoes	37·52	2,251	530
Sugar-beet	55·31	3,319	781
Onions	61·58	3,695	870
Tobacco	179·48	10,789	2,535

* Valuing a labour-day at 60 forints ; in practice the labour input per labour-day varies slightly by crop, but data on the differentials were not available.

Source : Sample survey of 100 co-operatives by the Agricultural Management Institute of the Hungarian Academy of Sciences.

income per unit of area irrespective of its labour intensity. Not only is this idea indefensible in itself, but it would imply disadvantageous results for labour-intensive products to the point of eliminating them from the farms. The proposed practice is not, of course, of this extreme case; it is rather that the disparity in income per unit of land should be reduced between crops of differing labour intensities.

This may be demonstrated by the example of wheat and sugar-beet, the gross incomes from which are respectively 424 forints and 3,319 forints per cadastral yoke. In pursuance of a policy to encourage the production of wheat or to restrict the significantly more advantageous position of sugar-beet, prices might be adjusted so that income from wheat is raised by 600 forints and that from sugar-beet cut by the same amount ; by producing wheat, the farm would obtain 1,024 forints, and by producing sugar-beet, 2,719 forints per cadastral yoke. The gross income per labour-day, formerly 60 forints from each product, would be 144 forints per labour-day from wheat and 49 forints from sugar-beet. This example is not, of course, intended to furnish any general conclusions on relative prices, let alone indicate the actual price changes desirable : it merely shows how the contradiction between products with differing labour intensity can be solved.

The method employed contrasts two fundamental aspects of

producer's incentives. In our example, the income differential per unit of area was reduced and that per labour-day was increased. If prices were fixed in such a manner that the income per labour-day were highest for the least labour-intensive product and lowest for the most labour-intensive, and, further, that the income per unit of area were lowest from the former and highest from the latter, producers would be obliged to examine the income to be earned from individual products both per unit of area and per labour-day.

No production pattern satisfying the needs of the economy could be achieved through fixing incomes involved in the prices proportionately to current labour inputs. This would affect farms unevenly, even those where the ratio of land to manpower is high. Manpower differences between co-operatives must also be taken into account: on farms where the land area per worker is large, those products ensuring higher incomes per labour-day are preferred, whereas farms with high manpower density favour produce carrying a bigger income per unit of area.

RELATIVE PROFITABILITY BY PRODUCT AND PRESENT-DAY PRICES

Pricing must satisfy the requirement of relative profitability by products even if agricultural production is controlled. This is even more necessary when there are no (or few and indirect) controls on the pattern of production or sales. The trend of prices in Hungary is to stimulate the production of less-labour-intensive products by causing the income earned per labour-day significantly to exceed that for more-labour-intensive goods. As may be seen from Table 2, this criterion had not been properly applied when the survey was taken. Thus, although sunflower is more labour-intensive than wheat, the income from its cultivation was lower than for wheat, not only per labour-day but also per unit of area. Clearly, the price of sunflower had been fixed unreasonably low, as indeed was demonstrated by the unfavourable development of its production. The price of sunflower has since been raised, and its profitability enhanced. Sugar-beet, on the other hand, was very profitable both in co-operatives surveyed and on the national average,[1] and its price has been reduced.[2]

[1] The average yield of sugar-beet in the 100 co-operatives surveyed was 16·4 tons per cadastral yoke in 1960, while the national co-operative average was 14·2 tons.
[2] By 8 per cent since the sample was taken.

TABLE 2

INPUTS AND RELATIVE PRICES AND INCOMES IN
HUNGARIAN AGRICULTURE

Crop	Price paid by State Agencies		Current Costs		Labour Input	Gross Income (before Tax and other Levies)	
	Forints per Metric Ton	Index Wheat =100	Forints per Metric Ton	Index Wheat =100	Labour-days per Cadastral Yoke	Per Labour-day	Per Cadastral Yoke
Wheat	2,331	100·0	1,068	100·0	7·08	276	1,950
Autumn barley	2,000	85·8	1,109	103·8	7·01	279	1,956
Spring barley	2,000	85·8	1,054	98·7	6·93	291	2,020
Maize	1,782	76·5	1,200	112·4	18·84	82	1,549
Sugar-beet	483	20·7	278	8·0	55·31	109	6,039
Potatoes	910	39·0	805	75·4	37·52	63	2,350
Sunflower	2,998	128·6	205	191·9	14·85	90	1,336
Tobacco	13,454	577·2	12,032	1,129·6	179·48	56	9,968
Hemp-fibre	1,186	50·9	266	79·0	9·70	93	1,389

Source : As for Table 1.

The income data on fodder crops and maize must be assessed in the light of the profitability of animal husbandry, not covered by the Table. Maize production, for example, was thereby profitable, even though the relative income from it was unfavourable both per labour-day and per unit of area. Nevertheless, despite yielding an exceptionally high income per labour-day, the sown area of wheat decreased between 1957 and 1963 ; the sown area of fodder crops is increasing year by year, as is that of maize and sugar-beet, though the latter yield lower income per labour-day than does wheat.

The combined income per labour-day from animal husbandry and fodder-crops may be estimated (within limits of a certain variation) only between one-third and one-fifth of that from wheat growing. Yet producers still consider the profitability of these branches as more favourable, because they offer higher employment and personal earnings. As a result, in recent years the sale to the state of slaughter animals and animal products has increased annually. If the incomes included in prices had been determined either according to manpower inputs or according to current costs, the pattern of production would have differed fundamentally from that demanded by the needs of the economy. Even with prices as they are, more favourable growth has been noted for those products the prices of which yield a lower income per unit of prime costs and per unit of manpower input.

PRODUCTION INPUTS AND SELLING PRICES

In recent years, despite difficulties, agricultural production has developed in the direction of intensive farming. This would be inexplicable on the basis of current cost, for a number of official estimates [1] have shown that prices are below cost for numerous commodities. The most labour-intensive crops, and nearly all branches of animal husbandry, appeared to be deficitary while their production was increasing. In contrast, the production of some branches yielding a high net income according to such computations developed unfavourably. This seems to indicate that current costs computed on present methods are unsuitable for fixing agricultural prices.

It should not be inferred from this conclusion that current-cost accounting is not of importance in other connexions. The computation of both current and capital inputs is as significant in co-operative farming as in other sectors. A record of such inputs is needed both for planning production by commodity, and for the retrospective declaration of income earned by individual branch, used by the central authorities for statistical as well as for price-fixing purposes.

No special problem arises with those inputs which are monetary outlays (*e.g.* purchase of fuel or insecticides, and charges by machine-tractor stations). The crucial difficulty — and one which faces co-operative, but not state, farms — is that of valuing current labour. In the state sector, workers are paid a fixed wage : thus, all items of production inputs arise as outlays and production shows a net profit (or loss) as sales receipts exceed (or fall short of) outlays.

The average production cost on state farms is 460 forints for a ton of sugar-beet and 1,200 forints for wheat ; the procurement prices are respectively 450 and 2,200 forints. The procurement price thus falls short of production cost by 10 forints per ton for sugar-beet and exceeds it by 1,000 forints for the same quantity of wheat. Clearly

[1] Including that of the Agricultural Management Institute of the Hungarian Academy of Sciences.

sugar-growing means a loss on state farms and wheat a profit : if co-operatives were to pay their members wages at state farm rates, they too would have the same net revenue experience.

In reality, however, the situation is different. In co-operatives, production and efficiency are not, and cannot be, analysed in the same way as is done in the state sector, because the crucial parameter is gross income per unit of land earned by current-labour inputs.

To examine co-operative practice, we must separate capital from current costs (*i.e.* embodied from live labour) : we take 700 forints per ton to be the capital element in wheat costs and 200 forints that in sugar-beet costs ; current labour costs are 500 and 260 forints respectively. On an average yield per cadastral yoke of 12 tons for beet and 1 ton for wheat, a farm's gross income per yoke (at the prices just cited) is 2,200 forints from wheat and 5,400 forints from sugar-beet. The deduction of capital inputs leaves 1,500 forints to compensate current labour inputs per cadastral yoke under wheat and 3,000 forints for that under sugar-beet. Whereas the state farm would reject beet growing, co-operatives prefer sugar-beet at 3,000 forints per cadastral yoke in gross income to wheat at 1,500 forints.

In the example given above the current labour inputs of the co-operative sector were priced at the wage-rate on state farms. So far as concerns relative returns, similar results may be obtained by computing current labour inputs at the national average labour-day dividend in co-operatives.[1] For the co-operative sector this is evidently more appropriate, but not even the current costs thus derived permit adequate conclusions to be drawn on the appropriate price proportions. It is indisputable that, until co-operative farms practice cost accounting (particularly for current labour inputs), estimates of cost and profit must be used to determine the prices best suited to influencing their production patterns.

The average price on the planned product-mix must, as stated, also regulate the ratio of incomes of co-operative farmers to wages ; for state-fixed prices, the operative ratio is wages on state farms. It is impracticable to start from the requirement that the income to be earned in co-operatives per labour-day (or other unit of labour cost) should be identical for all products. For some, but not all, products there must necessarily remain a net revenue after deduction

[1] In attributing notional labour on co-operative farms, the Agricultural Management Institute of the Hungarian Academy of Sciences applies the wage paid on state farms ; the Financial Department of the Ministry of Agriculture, however, uses the average dividend per labour-day.

of labour remuneration if suitable income proportions (both as regards workers and products) are to be secured.

This might seem *prima facie* to discourage the growing of products showing a 'deficit' : this would in fact follow if an actual loss were incurred, but — as mentioned above — in the co-operative sector of agriculture, the cropping pattern is not selected on relative net income, but on relative income per unit of area and per labour-day, and on the ratio of these to each other.

Investigation of the profitability of co-operatives shows that the dispersion of gross income per labour-day is due to varying labour intensity. In the 100 co-operatives examined (with a mean gross income per labour-day of 60–65 forints) the gross income per labour-day was 30–35 forints for highly labour-intensive crops, but nearly 300 forints for the least labour-intensive, while the gross income per cadastral yoke was 1,800–2,000 forints for the least labour-intensive products and 6,000–12,000 forints for the most labour-intensive.

The income per labour-day from the most labour-intensive product but the co-operatives considered the production of these goods as advantageous, because they yielded a high income per unit of area.

Several studies have shown that if co-operatives decide on the pattern of production on the basis of gross income, funds available both for distribution and for accumulation may increase. In a co-operative with a total annual dividend per member of, say, 9,000 forints, the value of a labour-day (before tax, etc.) is 45 forints when each member has performed 200 labour-days. If members decide to earn a higher total income the following year, by increasing the mean of labour-days worked per member to 240, they must turn to more labour-intensive crops, because they cannot increase their land area. If, by so increasing the work input, total income increases from 9,000 forints to, say, 10,200, income per labour-day falls from 45 to 42·5 forints, but the marginal dividend (30 forints per labour-day) is still acceptable because distributed income has increased while the amount available for investment is unaffected.

Producers react to state-fixed prices according to their individual conditions, based upon the marginal income per member, while making the best use of available manpower and land area. The production pattern of farms with differing natural conditions will vary accordingly : in co-operatives with high manpower density, the products yielding a high income per area will be preferred, while co-operatives where manpower is scarcer will choose produce ensuring a higher income per labour-day. From Table 3 it may be seen, first, that the relative area of labour-intensive crops is greater where there is less land-area per member. Secondly, the area sown to food grains varies with land per member. Thirdly, the stable proportion of cereal and rough fodders suggests that animal hus-

TABLE 3

PERCENTAGE DISTRIBUTION OF SOWN AREA BY SELECTED CROP-GROUPS ACCORDING TO MANPOWER AND INCOME PER UNIT OF LAND

	Farms with Income per Cadastral Yoke (Forints) of :							
	1,500 and below	1,501– 2,000	2,001– 2,500	2,501– 3,000	3,001– 3,500	3,501– 4,000	4,001– 4,500	4,501– 5,000	Over 5,000
Area (cadastral yokes) held in common per farm member	11·9	10·3	9·0	8·7	8·2	7·5	6·9	6·9	5·8
Maize	10·0	11·6	12·3	12·6	12·3	14·1	13·7	13·5	12·1
Other grains	49·1	50·2	48·4	47·8	48·1	47·1	46·9	46·8	44·3
Fodder crops	16·7	17·0	17·3	16·6	17·1	16·5	15·9	16·2	17·0
Industrial crops	5·8	6·8	7·1	7·7	8·2	8·8	8·5	9·0	9·8
Green fodder (roughage)	20·5	19·5	20·7	20·9	21·0	20·0	20·4	19·4	22·1

Source : Hungarian Central Statistical Office.

bandry is universally considered important, and, since these crops are not very labour-intensive, they are increasingly produced in farms where the land area per member is smaller, so as to release labour for the large-scale production of industrial crops, which are even more labour-intensive than maize. This policy is widespread, because the expansion of animal husbandry is possible without greatly increasing the production of maize. Finally, the Table shows that on farms where manpower density is high, an adequate income can usually be reached only by preferring crops that secure a high income per unit of area, while on farms where the land area per member is considerable, farming is more profitable if less labour-intensive crops are cultivated.

THE EFFECT OF VARIATION IN PRODUCTION INPUTS ON PROFITS

It would be erroneous to take gross income proportions per labour-day and per unit of area as given once and for all. Profit changes with conditions of production and with the needs of the economy. The relationship between production and prices, the development of production conditions, and the needs of the economy itself must be continuously taken into consideration.

To increase production, agriculture applies to an ever-increasing extent new production techniques, the efficiency of which, however, varies so that the rate of development is uneven. It is thus essential that the state should assess the results achieved by different techniques and new materials, etc., in the production of different goods.

Increased mechanization, the use of fertilizers, insecticides, etc., affect not only yields, but also production costs, bringing changes in the efficiency of the current labour applied, and (assuming unchanged agricultural prices) altering the relative incomes from various products.

At the same time, income proportions have a decisive influence on the pattern of agricultural production. It follows that relative prices must be changed whenever the input-output proportions of the various branches fall out of line with targets set by the state. In agriculture, changes in income proportions will indirectly affect many products, even if the change directly affects only one. For example, when a change of technique reduces the input requirements of maize-growing, the cost of stock-breeding (especially of pig fattening) diminishes. The effect of this change on the branches of animal husbandry is not, however, uniform, since fodder requirements vary by type of animal. Furthermore, the cheapening of maize not only stimulates livestock-breeding, but causes the production of sugar-beet, sunflower, etc., to be cut back. In fact, the effect can be felt throughout agriculture. If the state did not change prices, farms would increase maize-growing at the expense of other crops, and raise more pigs, cattle, and poultry for meat, but would diminish the production of milk, beet, and sunflower. Had supply and demand for these products not been in equilibrium at the previous prices, the new product-mix might be appropriate, and all that is necessary would be to adjust the overall level of prices to maintain proper income proportions. If, however, the change induced in the pattern of production is unfavourable to the economy, it would be essential to decrease the profitability of maize-growing and its connected branches.

A knowledge of the composition and trends of inputs of the various products is therefore indispensable for fixing relative prices and for maintaining correct income proportions. In Hungary, this is complicated by the fact that in agriculture there are different forms of ownership. Research must be carried out separately for the different sectors, since the production conditions of state farms and those of co-operatives differ in several broad aspects.

The intention of this paper has been primarily to discuss the major objections raised against differential price formation in the light of their effect on farm income. The ideas put forward can by no means be considered as final ; they are still under lively discussion in Hungary itself. While we can affirm nothing, we are convinced that corresponding questions should be raised for pricing the produce of state farms, and that such an extension of the analysis would contribute to the study of price policy as much in general as particularly in agriculture.

Chapter 24

SUMMARY RECORD OF THE DISCUSSION
—SESSION VII

AGRICULTURAL PRICES
(In the Chair : PROFESSOR RACHMUTH)

Professor Fauvel, who opened the discussion on Mr. Laszlo's paper, found considerable similarities between the Hungarian problems treated and those of Western European governments in seeking to influence agricultural production by price control. He felt that, whatever happened, some fluctuation between over-production and under-production of specific commodities was almost inescapable if reliance were placed entirely upon pricing. Over-production tended to emerge, because technical progress in farming advanced more rapidly than changes could be made in pricing policy. He took as an example the experience of the Third Plan in France : price relations had been changed to discourage wheat-growing and to favour meat, but the product-mix had not changed as intended. For his part, he found two explanations. The first was that the elasticity of supply had been too low for the changes to be effective : the French authorities believed that no change of more than 5 to 10 per cent could be made without the inflation they desired to avoid ; the European Economic Commission in fact believed that even rises of up to 12 per cent would be ineffective on production. The second explanation was that French peasants had different attitudes to different products : the production of milk was seen as a regular, indeed a basic function, and, while the farmer might increase, he would not reduce, production. On the other hand, meat was thought of as a speculative product, and its output was highly responsive to price change.

Professor Fauvel saw something of this attitude in the reactions of Hungarian farmers. Peasants everywhere sought to maximize their gross income, and he had explicitly shown that a crop, deficitary in net terms, might be expanded simply to add to gross income. Mr. Laszlo had convincingly shown that price-fixing could be efficient neither on a basis of labour input nor per hectare used.

Professor Maksimovic believed that Professor Fauvel was mistaken when, in Session V, he had equated the objectives of himself and Professor Pjanic with those of Dr. Kyn. The Yugoslav system, though based on social ownership and not far removed from the other socialist economies

278

of Eastern Europe, radically differed in its institutions. Particular stress should be laid on the divergence represented by workers' self-management. He did not agree, as Professor Fauvel had seemed to imply, with Dr. Kyn's requirement of a unitary price structure. He felt that the dual price system was necessary so long as decisions were divided between those at the macro- and those at the micro-economic level. The correct concept was not that of two sets of price relatives but of two social approaches : investment decisions were not to be left to the microeconomic unit. The present socialist system could achieve unity of pricing only in the future : in Yugoslavia, attempts were being made to bring the two sets of price together, but administrative control over many producers' goods remained in order to ensure the equilibrium of supply and demand. Professor Domar's suggestion of marginal pricing was not particularly relevant to the Yugoslav price system, because it assumed a static theory of prices. If, however, the dual pricing procedure took care of accumulation, marginal techniques could be used separately for producers' and consumers' goods.

Professor Dupriez, and to some extent Academician Ostrovityanov, had posed the problem of the relative share of wages in national income, and of the reasons why surplus value was proportionately larger in socialist than in capitalist countries. This did not have the welfare connotation which might be attributed at first sight, because the surplus product under a socialist system was at the disposal of society as a whole. Nevertheless, it was essential to develop greater worker participation in economic decision-making, on a parallel with political democracy, in order to ensure that this surplus value was distributed in accordance with the desires of the community.

Professor Oelssner accepted Mr. Laszlo's view that, at the present stage, most concern had to be with the valuation of current-labour outlays on co-operative farms (p. 273). This would, however, not always be the case, as new farm technology, particularly in field crops, raised the capital-to-labour ratio. Farms were now beginning to use extremely complex and expensive equipment but, with the difference from industry, that such machinery and plant was used during only two or two-and-a-half months of the year. For the rest of the time, it was idle but still required maintenance. As a result, the recoupment period was about four to six times as long as in industry (and reached at least 25 to 30 years). Naturally, the equipment was obsolete before the capital outlay was recouped, but prices could not be raised to effect this recoupment during the actual life of the machine. This seemed to imply that modern farm techniques required some sector to bear a loss, *e.g.* the co-operatives, the state, or, under capitalism, the farmer. He wondered whether Mr. Laszlo had observed this problem in Hungary, and how this problem was being handled in capitalist countries (particularly the United States, where a wide range of such machinery was employed). Did the pricing of agricultural produce fully reflect the depreciation of plant and equipment ?

Professor Lipinski believed that he should reply to Academician Ostrovityanov's strictures on his view of the difference between socialism and capitalism. His contention had been that the difference lay in the absence of private property under socialism and the explicit declaration of consumer satisfaction as the objective of the economy. There was no difference, however, in the market : under capitalism, the market was exploited to gain maximum profit ; under socialism, the profit yielded on the market was not the purpose of production, but it was nevertheless a test of the productive process. It was common ground with Academician Ostrovityanov that socialism did not produce goods for the sake of production. A market had always existed in the socialist countries for consumers' goods, and the aim of the current economic reforms was to assure a formal market for producers' goods.

He could not believe that any Marxist would require rational price formation to be restricted to labour value. Marx had stated that a law of re-distribution was implicit in the theory of value : exchanges between sectors could only take place if equivalent. Manpower, according to Marx, would move from one sector or resource to another only if the social need justified the transfer : it was perfectly appropriate to interpret the differentials making for such transfer in marginal terms.

Professor Maksimovic was correct in saying that subjective marginal utility was no longer accepted in the West, but this should not be taken to mean that consumer preferences could be ignored. There was the sound criterion of social necessity in Marx, which was better than any complex set of pseudo-Marxist indicators.

Professor Notkin believed that the determination of prices by their cumulative labour cost (reduced to a standardized skill content) was not only impossible and unnecessary, but contradicted the very essence of commodity-money relations. The proper solution was iteration on the basis of value relationships at each stage of production. The essence was of course the procedure whereby surplus value was added to labour cost. The procedure (supported at this Conference by Professor Mateev's paper) was to generate surplus product in direct proportion to labour input. This was scarcely feasible, for it would require so high a proportion of surplus product to be created in the extractive industries as to render their output unsaleable, nor was it properly Marxist, since it ignored the velocity of circulation of capital, to which Marx made specific allusion in Volume III of *Kapital*. Professor Mateev also described the procedure of relating surplus product to an average return on capital, and it was to this alternative that Professor Notkin, after long embracing the former view, was now inclined. He did not see this, however, in the simple form of adding to labour cost an average profit on capital in the way that this seemed to have operated under early capitalism. In the nineteenth century capital intensity was positively correlated with technical progress. It had been appropriate that those sectors — notably the basic industries and engineering — should grow fastest, which had the highest capital-to-labour ratios. The flow of capital to those branches was facilitated by their earning profits *pro rata* to their productive assets. Once, however, heavy industry had been established in its dominating position, the need to maintain an average rate of profit on capital led to the concentration — *i.e.* the monopolization — of industry and the exploitation of foreign markets through colonialism and economic imperialism. It no longer served, as it had done earlier, the interests of technical progress. There was no sense in a return by the socialist countries of today to the system of price formation of the nineteenth century. Because the state set planned prices in the interests of society as a whole, it could stimulate technical progress in a differentiated manner.

Professor Notkin therefore felt that the distribution of surplus product among the various branches of production should be on the basis of a formula related both to the capital-labour ratio (the 'organic composition' in Marxist terms) and to the coefficient of capital efficiency in the particular branch (*i.e.* the turnover rate of productive funds in Marxist terms). It would then be possible to dispense with the dual price level, the operation of which now hindered smooth economic development. Dual pricing had been necessary to channel resources into the priority sectors, but balanced development was now feasible. The branch efficiency coefficients would ensure both centralized accumulation and the use of profits for self-finance within the enterprise, and would thus replace turnover tax. In fact, the ratio between turnover tax and profits had been changing in this direction in recent years, and the gradual transition to such a price system would merely complete the process. The price system could thus be unified without changing the relative levels of prices and wages, that is, without incurring the risk of inflation ; changes in relative wages and relative prices would certainly be necessary in the reform, but the general relationship of the one to the other would not be affected. He hoped that his points contributed to an answer for Sir Roy Harrod.

He had been both surprised and puzzled by the nihilistic attitude of Professor Lipinski, whom he so highly respected, towards a theoretical analysis of the problem of prices. He believed that the construction of a price theory for a socialist economy would aid in solving the practical problem of price formation : if it did not do so, the theory was worthless.

Sir Roy Harrod asked Professor Notkin if he were right in supposing that the dual price system meant that an enterprise received one price ex-factory, while the purchaser paid a higher price. He also wondered whether the margin was used to provide funds for capital accumulation in the economy as a whole (and for other purposes). He was not clear where such funds would be generated under a single price system. Prices

Agricultural Prices

would be distorted if each industry were to provide its own funds for capital accumulation by charging a sufficient margin in selling price. There was no relation whatever between the amount of fresh capital accumulation socially needed for an industry and the value of its annual output or its existing capital. If, under a single price system, each industry had to charge prices sufficient to provide for its own requirements for capital accumulation, the scale of relative prices would be wrong and productive resources consequently misallocated.

Professor Notkin replied that the margin derived from application of the efficiency coefficient would be divided between the state and the branch for reinvestment. Macro-economic proportions would not necessarily be disturbed, but surplus value would equal capital effectiveness.

Dr. Kyn stated that the opinions that he expressed in the previous discussion were not held by all the Czechoslovaks present and were of course his own, and not official, views. The new system of management was still in a preparatory stage and had not been finally approved. Its practical implementation would soon begin, but would not be completed for several years. Neither he nor the Czechoslovak economists who shared his views, were over-optimistic that the new system would solve all the existing problems of the economy. Eliminating disproportions and rebuilding the Czechoslovak economy were long-term tasks, and introducing the new system would itself create a number of new problems.

The new system did not make planning less effective; on the contrary, it sought better and more scientific methods of planning. As Professor Lipinski had rightly stressed, the plan was only a means for specifying the needs of the market, and it was essential to differentiate between the role of the plan as a forecast and as a programme. The function of forecasting had been underestimated until now : many direct techniques of management (*i.e.* the issuance of orders and prohibitions) would have to be replaced by indirect methods of planning (*i.e.* the influencing of economic conditions, on the basis of which decentralized economic decisions were made). Contradictory interests would arise which would have to be taken into account, and he thought it likely that some of these problems, notably in the relations between enterprises, or between enterprises and central agencies, could be solved by games theory.

He did not understand why Mr. Nikiforov opposed the role of profit under socialism. One must distinguish between profits as incentives and profits as a source of income. Marxists could not agree with the proposition that profits were a natural and just income accruing to capitalists, but he saw no objection to the role of incentives in the form of profits in a socialist society. At present in Czechoslovakia, gross income (viz. value-added less depreciation) was to become the incentive fund which it was already in Yugoslavia. In this respect, he pointed out that Professor Maksimovic had not understood one detail quite correctly : income was to be used in the Czechoslovak reforms as an incentive, but not under the system of 'income prices' which was currently emerging in Yugoslavia. Studies were being made in Czechoslovakia on the influence of monopoly in the socialist sector, and he drew attention to an article which proposed a theoretical solution to this problem.[1]

Dr. Ophir expressed surprise that apparently everybody, including Academician Ostrovityanov and Professor Sorokin, agreed with Dr. Kyn's criticism of the existing system of turnover taxes. It seemed to him that this criticism was unjustified. Any tax had undesirable side-effects, but in that respect the turnover tax was no worse, and probably better, than most other taxes, provided, of course, that the tax was levied only at the final stage of sale to consumers and not on intermediate goods (as shown in Professor Mateev's paper). A Western economist would tend to prefer a uniform rate of turnover tax, so that relative prices to consumers would reflect relative production costs, and the production of goods be efficiently governed by consumer preferences. However, there was no reason why a socialist state should not use differential rates whenever it chose to superimpose a social preference on that of the consumer : this was done in Western countries by the taxation, for example, of cigarettes and alcohol.

[1] Z. Kodet, 'Monopoly and Competition in the Socialist Economy', *Politická ekonomie*, no. 8, 1964.

SESSION VIII

THE SOCIALIST ENTERPRISE

Chapter 25

THE THEORY OF THE SOCIALIST ENTERPRISE[1]

BY

EDWARD LIPINSKI

Polish Academy of Sciences

THE FUNCTION OF INFORMATION IN THE ENTERPRISE

THE enterprise constitutes the basic productive unit in the process of social production, of which the dynamic elements are initiative and organization. The degree to which given resources of knowledge, information, materials, and manpower can be mobilized for the production of goods and services depends on the potential initiative and the state of organization. In a centrally-planned socialist economy the initiative for forming new branches of production and new enterprises rests with the chief planning institution, which, on its projections of consumption over a specified period, will decide on the structure of the productive capacity required. Enterprises established by virtue of a planning decision justify their existence as the instruments through which the planned future development of the country is achieved.

Technological advances and the extension of the resources of knowledge and information, as well as changes in consumer needs, force the enterprise to innovate in production technique and range of products. Such changes will tend to alter employment and organization in the enterprise, which may either copy existing technology or products (a 'passive' reaction) or independently develop new methods and products (an 'active' reaction). It is characteristic of contemporary economies that the rate of technical progress and of change in product-mix is accelerating. Developments in science have to a great extent come within the scope of the enterprise as a large and complex production unit. The information made available to it from scientific discovery is most effective when it is intimately related to the production programme.

[1] This paper was not available at the Conference; the discussion was based upon a verbal presentation by Professor Lipinski (Editor's note).

The principle of enterprise autonomy is a natural corollary to its initiating and organizational functions. Information would fail to be transformed into decisions, and initiatives would fail to be implemented if the enterprise were completely deprived of autonomy, especially as regards the scope, differentiation, and fulfilment of tasks, and the degree of co-operation from the employees. These factors are controlled in each enterprise, within the limits of its resources, by a management appointed at its establishment and empowered to make binding decisions aimed at fulfilling a prepared plan.

While the central planning office (itself an innovator) delegates definite targets to the enterprise, it also devolves authority. The general scope of activity is mapped out for each enterprise far in advance, but, in order to be self-supporting and to develop in response to changing environment (of technology and of demand), it has at its disposal an autonomic sphere of decision. This area would not exist if the central plan agency could call upon all sources of information on technology or the range of possible goods, and if transmission of such information were totally efficient. This, however, would require such a vast expansion of the central planning office that the complexity and cost of the operation would defeat its object.

Other factors determining the autonomic sphere of activity of the enterprise are the existence of unexploited productive capacity, initiative, and invention.

Economics has hitherto, in considering economic growth, been mainly concerned with the bill of goods — seeking for it a rational allotment of scarce resources. It appears, without denying the significance of this problem, that its emphasis should less be placed there than on identifying centres of initiative to secure the most effectual use of resources and the greatest adaptability to the changing environment of technology and products. The enterprise has to mobilize both information and initiative in the constant process of change in its environment and interior organization.

It is a principle of socialism that production should be directed towards the satisfaction of demand, not to maximize profit, but technical factors had in any case under capitalism displaced individual ownership of productive assets as the causative factor of development, growth, initiative, and innovation. An enterprise is not motivated by profit maximization : indeed, if it is big enough to be managed by functional teams based on a division of labour, it can work more efficiently than one working for profit. National and local authorities and political organizations are managed by persons who are not motivated by profit and yet work dynamically and effectively. This does not imply that the nationalized enterprise loses its individuality, for it retains its own personality, its focal points of initiative and inventiveness, and it remains a social organization with its own individual life. It is impossible to arrange an enterprise in advance : to set up optimal interpersonal relationships, to ensure correct discharge of duties by management at all levels ; to provide the best conditions for social life, sport and cultural recreation for the labour force ; to secure ideal conditions for manpower and training, etc. The exertion of individual, localized energy and dynamism can create, or may not create, within the enterprise a social system engendering technical inventiveness and the best personal conditions for employees.

The layers of knowledge and information are scattered and cannot be channelled into one single centre. Only a certain amount of knowledge and information reaches the top, whence it can be utilized. Some knowledge cannot be relayed to the central planner, and forms a changing stream not always accessible to all in its path. Of this, innovation is a typical example. Opportunities to innovate at a given state of technology and relationship of demand to supply can occur to anybody, but the practical implementation of any innovation, *e.g.* the marketing of a new product, depends on ability to overcome unforeseeable and accidental obstacles — or, one could call it 'the innovational flexibility' of the enterprise. Decisions connected with local knowledge can be centrally regulated only at a loss to the efficiency of the economic process.

RESEARCH AND THE ENTERPRISE

The enterprise is long-lasting, and its expected time-span exceeds that of an annual or five-year production plan ; because its assets wear out, retirements and renewals must be planned over the long run. Technical progress alters its range of products and a creative enterprise does not merely adapt an outside process but undertakes research on new products and exploits the discoveries of science. It is, moreover, not enough for an enterprise to limit its adaptation to the changing environment : to last, it has to grow, to develop, to change, and to influence the environment.

In a planned economy the enterprise partly receives its tasks from the top — not all tasks, because the central planning office does not always dispose of sufficient information to request the production of a new good or a new method of production. Information in this sphere is more effective when accumulated and mobilized in the same enterprise, because the enterprise itself can best assess available resources. For such conduct to be most effective, the authorities must motivate innovation and the management must possess sufficient initiative : changes will, of course, only be carried out if they are profitable or meet some such need as prestige or recognition.[1]

Inventiveness and a sense of organization are both a function of the degree of industrialization and a condition of its growth. If they are to be instilled deliberately, the conditions must be set up to induce managers and staff so to act. For some radically-new organizational procedure, such as PERT (Programme Evaluation and Review Technique) — a method of planning the order of executing a construction project of thousands of component activities — to emerge, the processes studied must repeat themselves sufficiently often, there must be an adequate supply of technical ability (in this case mathematicians) working on the problem ; and the popular environment must engender centres of suitably-directed interest. There is no doubt that the technological change should be understood as a constant process of cumulative synthesis, resulting from the perception of deficiencies in existing technology and science ; even the most modern technical equipment imported by a country which is technically less advanced than the exporter will be differently effective than in its original surroundings.

For an enterprise to carry out its long-term tasks, its managing personnel must be prepared for innovation and future change. The theory of games is particularly useful for imagining future surroundings. In a competitive economy old-fashioned firms are eliminated ; in a planned economy it is necessary to foresee both the working of the mechanism which enforces progress from the top and the outcome of institutional factors. It is safe to assume that the role of research by the enterprise will increase in importance, and that scientists, management and information specialists, mathematicians and programmers will have a much enhanced function therein.

[1] C. White, 'Multiple Goals in the Theory of the Firm', in K. E. Boulding and W. A. Spivey (eds. *Linear Programming and the Theory of the Firm*, New York, 1960), pp. 181–201.

CONFLICT AND HARMONY OF INTEREST

Even in a socialist economy an enterprise can survive and expand only if it safeguards or expands its consumer market. It must find potential markets and simultaneously create suitable and constant preferences among consumers. Growth and technological progress are impossible without a certain degree of 'monopoly', because a particular monopoly element decreases the risk inherent in innovation.

Many kinds of need exist only potentially. By introducing new products — in new forms, in new ways of satisfying needs which until now were dormant, barely felt, or still buried in the subconscious — the firm fosters growth and prosperity. In the developed socialist economy of the future, in a prosperous economy, competition in prices will have a very limited, or perhaps no, influence, but competition in quality and novelty will be the basis of the system. Adapting to the market must be active, that is, a conscious moulding of certain exterior conditions : the analysis of the market acquires specific significance, for it must underlie the sales strategy and substantiate forecasts by purposively influencing the development of the enterprise.

The enterprise, as the fundamental production unit, is condemned to perpetual adaptation to changing conditions ; its reaction will depend upon the notice that it has of change. If the change is planned, that is by allocating productive resources in advance for the new tasks, the transition generally occurs without loss and waste. If the change is sudden, with the factors of production already tied to previously-planned processes, factors have to be uprooted and reassembled, causing losses from the discontinuation of old plans to carry out new. The second method characterizes a 'strained' economy, wherein the process of adaptation does not occur in an organic manner, where planned tasks are never certain and are not the result of actual observations or effective demand, and where 'wishful thinking' from 'on high' governs without basis of adequate information.

This raises the problem of decentralization as a means of rationalizing decisions and plans, of which the crux is the harmonization of interests, aims, and plans of the economy as a whole with the interests, aims, and plans of local organizations (which can be considered as partial enterprises). Decentralization fails if the price policy of the enterprise aims at extracting monopolistic profit and if there is no mechanism in the enterprise automatically to induce economy of materials, to improve quality, to introduce new goods and processes, to limit staff to the number justified by production, and to rationalize work organization. Not even the highest degree of central control and centralized decision can force the enterprise wholly to conform to general national aims, because one at least of the parties involved would invariably believe that its particular interests had been overruled. It is not possible to achieve full and perfect compatibility between the interests of the public, those of the enterprise, and those of the labour force in the sociological-historical conditions which are known to us. It is more to the point to assess an economic system on its dynamism, human initiative, effectiveness, and flexibility to changing environment and information.

The enterprise is a unit which has been set up to execute certain tasks which represent its 'basic law'. Organization consists of separating functional parts, and giving each person so concerned a specific role to fulfil the primary task. This function may be incorrectly discharged either because the personal aims of the executant deviate from the harmonizing link with the primary task or because management is distorted.

A generalized theory, which commands the writer's acceptance, states that a normal person, seeking his own goals, is inclined to co-operate in the realization of an alien or social goal if he does not feel 'wronged'. It may well be true that such a person tends to co-operate if the personal needs which he himself considers 'important' are satisfied as a result of that endeavour, and if his condition of life does not create hostile and indifferent attitudes during and outside the process of work. He is even inclined to 'engage himself' and accept responsibility above the border-line of commensurate remuneration, if the given task will produce a specific emotional or intellectual response within him. The more work becomes a personal act, the greater is the personal involvement of the 'worker'; the more incommensurable is financial reward in relation to the task, the more willingly will he tackle higher responsibilities for submarginal payment. Such are, nevertheless, inadequate conditions to harmonize the aims of the firm's activity with general goals. In certain favourable conditions the firm could maximize, say, its financial gains, and raise social advantages at the same time. On the other hand, if remuneration is low — or the workers believe it to be low — and a multiplicity of bonuses seek to compensate an incorrect wage structure or attitude towards specific duties, the management and staff attempt to maximize the bonuses by avoiding tasks unconnected with a bonus, and an increase of bonuses generally fails to harmonize the aims of the firm and of society.

It is a real problem of the socialist economy to motivate staff and management to formulate and achieve realistic social goals for their enterprise. The experience of years has proved that this can be achieved neither by directives nor by intensifying central control. If 'self-control' or an automatic interior mechanism, which continually corrects any deviations from the 'balance' with 'social' duties, does not act, then no outside control can do it. Every process of directing composite systems is based on the autonomic, automatic activity of a part towards the maintenance of control ('homeostasis' in cybernetics). Thus detailed control of the wages fund will be ineffective, or even harmful, if there is no mechanism to induce the enterprise to employ people 'rationally'.

Planning techniques now in use can be further developed ; the present system has shown advantages and disadvantages. An important advantage is the possibility of concentrating means for specified goals, and enabling massive goals to be achieved. Concentration of means gives enormous benefits, but also results in bottlenecks, for concentration in one sphere means neglecting another ; neglected parts of the production process develop into factors limiting the exploitation of many other parts. Low consumption permits greater accumulation, but it can adversely influence the worker's output. Carelessness in the house-building industry can not only waste the existing supply of dwellings but generates an alarmingly vast housing problem. A centrally-planned decision to increase output may require an over-ambitious investment plan, which results in a critical balance-of-payments deficit, which in turn cuts back investment projects already started. If mistakes are made in wage policy or if the individuality of enterprises is repressed, resources of human ingenuity, inventiveness, and initiative are thereby restricted. It happens that producers' goods are planned in a manner inconsistent with their envisaged consumption, despite the fact that production serves consumption directly or indirectly. Any output of producers' goods can eventually be used for the production of goods which satisfy the material or cultural needs of people ; but if the plans for such goods are out of harmony with planned consumption, a powerful capacity in metal production and engineering, quite incapable of raising the standard of life, will have been built.

CONCEPTS OF MANAGEMENT AND PROFIT

The legal form of socialist ownership does not in itself bespeak the effectiveness of the production system, the mobilization of human initiative and creativity, the satisfaction of its participants, or even the degree of utilization of material resources of the natural endowment and potential supply of ideas. It may become an effective tool to mobilize human and material resources, but it is not such a tool *sui generis*. 'Social' ownership can exist in a variety of forms determined by a set of aims, which in turn are a product of a defined political-historical situation and of the political system of values acknowledged by the planning and ruling social group. It posits interaction between the planning group and executants and an area of spontaneous action and initiative : it contrasts with a sphere of imposed action, not based on the agreement of the subordinates.

Incentives must secure the most effective decisions by the basic unit — the enterprise. Those decisions cannot always be correct, but they will contain fewer mistakes because they will rest on a wider information basis, will more effectively acknowledge changing environmental conditions and more forcefully originate from interest in shaping the future. To entrust responsibility to an enterprise manager is not just a moral-psychological act : it is an evocation of active adaptation and of independent action to create positive conditions for a better future. Planning, mathematical methods, input-output techniques, and the like are auxiliary means for co-ordinating, or for mapping the general points of, development, but they are not the essence of the economic process.

The postulate of profit as motive of economic activity can be presented as the avoidance of losses, and in such form it functions as a regulator of the socialist economy. If prices more or less correspond to the degree of scarcity of products, it is possible to judge relatively easily which decisions on production or investment are advantageous. Extensive planning does not automatically assure full co-ordination, nor does it guarantee optimal allocation of scarce resources to specific uses, because constant change in technology and demand precludes planning in detail ; its reactions must be erratic, for the many objective and subjective conditions comprise not only some calculable risk but also elements of uncertainty.

Economics in the socialist countries has been slow to deal with the efficiency of the enterprise : at first it was thought that the process of directing production was something simple and uncomplicated, provided there was a 'plan' and incentives to execute it ; more recently it has been hoped that, by many 'directive suggestions', super-enterprises and associations would manage subordinate enterprises, using various types of premia as an encouragement. What is needed is thorough analysis of the socialist enterprise and of its perception of profit.

Investments, which are the basis of development, should pay. If the price structure corresponds to that of the scarce resources applied, the profitability of investments shows that an approximately correct choice of investment was made. Profitability is not a goal, but a measure and test of the degree of correctness in the application of resources to the realization of aims (*i.e.* satisfying social needs).

But the measurement of profit is not applicable to all cases in an equal way. If profit is calculated as the difference between revenue and costs, it is obvious that profits will vary between enterprises and between branches because of their different velocities of turnover on assets. But even equal turnover velocity does not assure equal profit. Enterprises which have a better reputation (*e.g.* from manufacturing goods reputed to be of better quality, etc.) may have higher profits, because sales are higher on a stock of assets the same as that of the others. If profit is not the motive of the enterprise but a criterion of realizing goals, profit acts as a constraint of loss avoidance. It serves as a kind of switching device : the absence of profit is a signal that there is deviation from 'balance', and that regulating mechanisms must be activated.

Profit, as a measure of enterprise efficiency, will fulfil its role only as average profit over many years. Accidental and short-term factors must be left out of account, and permanent factors, including technical progress, only considered. Profit may be a measurement of the past, but embodies a future which became a past during a specified period. By contrast, the choice of profit as goal and main motive of activity contradicts the character of the enterprise as a vehicle for future tasks. Avoidance of loss can, however, be treated as a system of signals to elicit response to deviations from the path leading to plan fulfilment. The concept of losses, of course, must not be treated too narrowly. Preparation of future technology and product range can cause outlays resulting in some losses, but those losses represent an inseparable element of innovation and progress.

The Socialist Enterprise

OVER-ORGANIZATION

The 'over-organization' of an enterprise or of an entire production process, by the proliferation of levels of management, destroys initiative, creates the need for complicated controls and for control over those controls, and limits the true quality and flexibility of the enterprise.

The negative side of so-called scientific organization is its mechanical 'rationality', which stems from the logic of machinery without taking into account the decisive human role of inventiveness, creativity, and continual adaptability to change in the supply of information and in the environment. On the other hand, even the most refined premium system to increase productivity will fail, if organization is inappropriate. The most advanced specialization of activity will not cover up facts such as defective production, excessive output, or grossly mistaken technology. The worker will both be deprived of satisfaction from his work and develop a careless attitude: these will lower productivity and increase absenteeism and the rate of job-changing.

An examination of the developed economies and of current technology suggests that some hitherto accepted principles of economic organization are no longer tenable; and that ideas which seemed utopian a century ago are the commonplaces of today. Thus the advantage of the division of labour still has some validity — it lowers production costs, shortens the time needed for learning a trade, and accelerates the tempo of work. But as specialization increases, personal stimulation to work decreases: there is less inherent interest in the job, a smaller personal satisfaction, and a lower readiness to accept responsibility; excessive specialization stimulates frequent change of employment, decreases quality of output, and increases 'tension' between management and labour force. Experiments have been undertaken in broadening and integrating work-activity in demonstrating the relationship of the job to the end-product, and in increasing the worker's field of decision and raising his sense of participation. Persons employed in highly-specialized occupations, deprived of initiative, or in an uninteresting and meaningless job tend to be irresponsible and apathetic. The management seeks to correct this by increasing supervision, but thereby creates resistance among the workers, who either fail to respond to the control or seek ways of avoiding it.

At times active opposition groups can emerge.[1]

An excess of organization evokes strict and constant control and supervision, which in turn require further controls to secure the appropriate degree of co-ordination between each unit. A simpler type of organization can be co-ordinated in an informal manner since there are fewer barriers, but, even then, co-ordination cannot be achieved spontaneously, for if each unit acts within the border of its system, conflicts result with other units. In fact, co-operation between administratively-separated functions normally requires controls at many hierarchic levels and a specialized staff to implement them.

Once such dissected controls are in operation, the system fails to perceive the overall picture. The whole organization loses its flexibility and adaptability, and — in short — its efficiency. The management becomes more and more centralized despite recognizing the need to delegate authority. The more penetrating the controls, the more rigid will the organization become, and attitudes of fear and anxiety will ruin the effectiveness of management. At the same time, the manager has little chance of displaying initiative. In a simpler organization people are judged according to the results of their work, and are concerned with those results, not with the control system.

The size of any institution, as much as of an enterprise, can be solved only in economic terms, as a question of the most favourable and rational division of functions. An association of enterprises is no different, and one which has a heterogeneous production programme[2] must be decentralized, although common services and the function of co-ordination can be carried out more effectively through the association. The aim of the organization is to release the maximum of initiative, efficiency, and dynamism. Such examples of over-organization as separation of technological planning from production, or of production from sales, will partially paralyse the sources of these virtues and, by engendering superfluous bureaucracy, will substitute 'reporting' for real economic activity.

---

[1] C. Worthy, 'Organizational Structure and Employé Morale', *American Sociological Review*, April 1950, pp. 179-186.

[2] In this connexion it is now time to reconsider the division of industry into 'heavy' (producers' goods) and 'light' (consumers' goods) and, indeed, any other classification which is not based on economic analysis, *e.g.* a common raw material, market of sale, or technology.

Chapter 26

SUMMARY RECORD OF THE DISCUSSION
—SESSION VIII

THE SOCIALIST ENTERPRISE

(In the Chair : PROFESSOR STOJANOVIC)

Mr. Kaser observed that the Conference had so far pointed to a number of concepts common to Eastern and Western economics, even where the words used had differed. The contrary was the case in dealing with the theory of the enterprise. In all three working languages of the Conference, the root of the word 'enterprise', describing the basic decision-making unit, was the same, derived from the 'undertaking' of the classical economists. But there was a fundamental divergence in the form an enterprise took under capitalism and socialism.

In capitalism, an enterprise brought together factors of production to make any good which the entrepreneur (managing director, board, shareholders, partners, or owner) believed profitable : its field of choice was limited only by access to capital. In socialism, the definition of the enterprise was in terms of technological processes, joint supply, or joint demand. Some vertical integration of enterprises had been practised in the Soviet Union before the war and, as Professor Lipinski had said, had emerged recently in Eastern Europe. The motive, however, which fostered such diversification was not the entrepreneurial initiative of competitive capitalism but its opposite, caution, that is to assure supplies for each further stage of processing. Because the Eastern European and Soviet enterprise tended — the assurance of inputs apart — to define its activity technologically, familiarity with the appropriate process was a criterion for management ; there were fewer engineers at the helm of capitalist enterprises, because each undertaking might involve many branches. Only in Yugoslavia could enterprises ramify, and the power had in fact been little used.

From this delineation of productive units arose the problems of price formation, which Sir Roy Harrod had made in questioning Professor Notkin's technique. The price of a good need not necessarily cover new accumulation, for a capitalist enterprise could raise funds from others which had a surplus. The criterion that the profit of a branch should ensure the finance of all capital formation must induce distortions which could only be corrected by administrative direction. Such intervention was at present exercised in Eastern Europe by separating the function of profit-making (operational finance of the enterprise) from profit-taking (investment control by central agencies).

Professor Lipinski implied that this separation could obstruct movement towards a long-run optimum, for dynamic decisions could not be taken by enterprises so constrained, that is, without the entrepreneur seeking the best combination, not only of current, but of capital, resources. It was not enough that the choice of current or future inputs be effected by the shadow prices derived from input-output programming, *i.e.* centralizing decisions and leaving the enterprises (required only to break even) free to react to the shadow prices communicated to them, for the plan authority formulating the programme took its technology from outside the system, as two Polish economists, Wakar and Zielinski, had observed.[1] The attempts made by planning agencies to evaluate technical progress by consultation with research institutions were not of the form which capitalist enterprises used, that is, to project price trends both of outputs and of inputs to select the most profitable technical relationship. Hence, the capitalist enterprise made decentralized evaluations not only of its own technical progress (in its purchase of capital goods) but of that of its suppliers. The interaction of prices and future combinations of inputs was crucial to the incorporation of technical change into the programme. Enquiries among British firms by the Department of Applied Economics of Cambridge University, in setting up its Social Accounting Matrix for the United Kingdom, had demonstrated this approach.

The socialist enterprise was, moreover, limited in its choice of techniques, not only as to capital but also as to current inputs. This limitation had arisen because enterprises were seen as executants of a plan for inputs as well as of a plan for outputs. The pre-arrangement of purchasing and selling targets by central authority in the Soviet Union had reached the point that the director of an enterprise disliked the obligation of output goals without a supporting input plan. This attitude stemmed from the difficulty of obtaining inputs which were not specifically earmarked, and was the root of the present trouble with experimenting enterprises: those allowed freedom to select their product-mix (as under the 'Bolshevichka-Mayak' experiment) remained dependent for their inputs on enterprises whose outputs were still centrally-planned.

Professor Sorokin contended that there were serious contradictions in Professor Lipinski's presentation. On one hand, he had said that the main problems were economic, but, on the other, he alleged that they were moral and political. He agreed with Professor Lipinski that the main function of an enterprise was to organize labour: this did not

[1] A. Wakar and J. Zielinski, 'Socialist Price Systems', *American Economic Review*, March 1963, pp. 109–127, and J. Zielinski, 'Centralization and Decentralization in Decision-making', *Economics of Planning*, December 1963, pp. 196–208.

mean, however, that wages had necessarily to be paid with the sole aim of satisfying the worker. Rather, the wage was an instrument for fostering an increment in productivity and for the better utilization of manpower.

There was no contradiction between economics and politics : his own studies of the French planning system had shown that capitalist planning took serious account of class considerations. In a socialist enterprise, moral and political stimuli had a part to play, and Professor Lipinski had some valid points on the improvement of material incentives, but it was surely more important to be concerned with the 90 per cent of remuneration formed by the basic wage than with the 10 per cent which represented bonus. The introduction of a correct wage system was of primary significance, and he found incomprehensible Professor Lipinski's preoccupation with worker tension and opposition. Even in war-time when patriotic motivation was at its highest, a decisive role was played by wage differentiation.

Since Professor Sorokin had already discussed Professor Lipinski's points, observed *Dr. Hegedus*, he would reply to Mr. Kaser. Mr. Kaser's views on a socialist enterprise were based on a juridical-technical phenomenon, and his conclusions followed therefrom. If the essence of a socialist enterprise were properly seen as the division of production, it could be interpreted in its economic-sociological function. Mr. Kaser seemed to have confused freedom with independence. It was possible, as in the socialist countries, to have formal independence without freedom of decision, which required knowledge of the conditions under which the decision would be executed. The present powers of socialist enterprises should be increased with respect both to independence and to freedom. A small capitalist enterprise, enjoying independence but not knowing market conditions, was not a free enterprise.

In Hungary, after 1956, enterprise independence was enhanced in two regards. Enterprises were given, and still had, the authority to distribute some part of profits among the workers. Profitability appeared to have been stimulated by this measure : on the one hand, the director felt responsible for gaining the profit to remunerate workers, and, on the other, workers sharing in profits more closely identified themselves with the enterprise. The humanization of labour relations with management was an important by-product of the reform. A second change worthy of notice had also been introduced in Hungary since 1956 : enterprise directors were free to determine the wage structure and piece-rate norms in their plant, with merely a minimum and a maximum set by central planning bodies. Even if this measure had not been wholly satisfactory — by inducing over-differentiation of wages — it had helped directors to adapt wages to concrete conditions. It was right that enterprises should operate different wage systems (*e.g.* group systems in some, individual payment in others) when this was justified by different sociological factors.

Summary Record of the Discussion

The essential function of the enterprise was rational current operation, and it should be allowed as much independence as was needed to execute this role. But decisions on investment were no part of this function, and decentralization in this field would be dangerous.

Professor Maksimovic thought that Professor Lipinski was right in emphasizing the need to specialize management decisions, but was too cautious to admit ordinary workers to microeconomic decision-making, as was being done in Yugoslavia. This association with management could develop *pari passu* with the level of education and knowledge of workers, and was not only a question of psychological de-alienation and re-integration of the masses, but also ethically desirable.

Mr. Kaser had been clear and precise on the comparative advantages of the enterprise under capitalism and socialism. But, like all high-level abstractions, it avoided the practical problems of the size of the unit and the political and sociological context of the enterprise. It was true that, under capitalism, microeconomic units operated on profits which did not define a map of production possibilities, on the basis of prices which did not cover accumulation. It was also true that a centrally-planned socialist system used technical units as executants of the plan. But such an exposition was not the whole of reality. Profit-making was not the only end in capitalist decision : the entrepreneur was limited by sociological, political, and external economic factors. Correspondingly, the socialist enterprise took account not only of central indicators, but also of microeconomic factors. Mr. Kaser appeared to treat its desire for 'security' as a vice, or at least as the opposite of a capitalist virtue, but it should be recalled that an enterprise was a unit in a planned mechanism and was obliged to ensure fulfilment of its tasks.

Dr. Ophir suggested that the theory of the socialist enterprise should recognize the factor of uncertainty and the cognate need to disseminate information. It seemed to him that, in this respect, a socialist economic system might have a definite advantage over a capitalist, free-enterprise mechanism. Under capitalism, the dominant characteristic of the process of management was decision-making under uncertainty ; among the causes of uncertainty were commercial secrets, patents (*i.e.* technological secrets), and, above all, uncertainty about future developments in the economy in general and in related economic activities in particular. While uncertainty could not be eliminated, it could be appreciably reduced in a socialist economy by the systematic exchange of information in the above-mentioned areas. This would lead to improved management decisions. He did not, however, favour the reduction of management uncertainty by detailed directives to managers from central planners. On the contrary, he visualized the ideal socialist economy as one in which there was a maximum degree of decentralization and autonomy for managers of enterprises. Signals to the enterprise would be given via the price system, with prices made to reflect the appropriate social values and social priorities. Enterprise profit would then be capable of use as the indication of success.

Professor Hutira described the extent of worker participation in Rumanian management, notably in the form of worker-consultation in the construction of the plan; corrections were made to the plan during such drafting and consultation regularly took place on plan fulfilment. There was substantial promotional mobility through the training of workers and farmers for managerial responsibility. The management of the economy was none the less centralized, because the state made the ultimate allocations and finance. Mr. Kaser had contrasted the centralized consultation of research institutes with exploration by the capitalist enterprise of profitable technical change : in Rumania, the recommendations of the Committee for New Technology served to link economics and technology in planning.

Although, said *Professor Jeanneney*, Mr. Kaser had been juridically correct in describing the freedom of action of a capitalist enterprise, an over-diversified concern — '*une touche-à-tout*' — was destined for bankruptcy. The capitalist enterprises that succeeded were those which specialized in areas closely related by technology or by consumer group. The successful firm maximized the rewards it could draw from specialized production or marketing experience. In France there had been a tendency for some years for diverse enterprises to become more specialized. For example, Saint-Gobin, which was principally a glass-maker, and Péchiney, mainly a producer of aluminium, had each divested themselves of their chemical plant and combined them into a joint chemicals subsidiary, Péchiney–Saint-Gobin. Professor Sorokin would have the Conference believe that the capitalist enterprise was at an end, and that the market was dominated by trusts and banks. Certainly, some giant corporations existed and prospered, but they were far from controlling the entire economy. An essential role was still played by many small and medium-sized enterprises. The most rapidly growing capitalist countries (Germany, Italy, and France) were those where medium-sized enterprises, operating on their own capital or through specialized bank loans, had immense vitality. Individual enterprise in this form was one of the reasons for such rapid growth. Many of the really big concerns — which Professor Sorokin called 'trusts' — were inadequately close to the consumer to respond to the almost daily adaptations he required ; they were burdened by cumbersome administration, and achieved flexibility only at a high sales cost.

Dr. Hegedus had described error and consequent bankruptcy as a constraint on the freedom of a capitalist enterprise. Evidently, medium-sized enterprises bore their own risk — ruin and bankruptcy — of making errors. But this risk was assumed by the individual preference of the entrepreneur. An engineer, having the choice of working for a large corporation or starting his own enterprise, would opt for the latter if he had a taste for risk. From the social point of view, the failure of such enterprises could have serious consequences for their staff in the absence of full employment. This system might seem somewhat irrational to a socialist. Certainly, error and waste occurred, but was socialist planning free from error?

Professor Lipinski declared his surprise at Professor Sorokin's criticism. He had had in mind the historical background to any system of management. The socialist system in Poland had initially borrowed its form from the Soviet Union, but, as it developed, change was necessary. The IV Congress of the Polish United Workers' Party had decided on reform, which he, as a member of that Party, wholeheartedly supported : the previous direction of the Polish enterprise by 30 plan indicators obstructed, rather than encouraged, economic development.

In Poland, general policy was laid down by the Planning Office in accordance with considerations which were social and political, as well as economic. He was no champion of a free economy, but it was demonstrable that economic potential had only partially been used under the old system, and resources employed had been grossly wasted. The new system was intended to foster adaptability and to permit each worker to show intelligence and initiative. To interest him in the results of his work (and hence to raise productivity), the Party programme did not embrace 'free enterprise', but simply made management more effective. It was not easy, however, in the present search for reform, to discover the means of making socialist management efficient : the present intensive discussion would not be taking place if a certain and effective method of management were known.

Much harm had been done to the Polish economy on pseudo-political grounds. The enterprises of small artisans had been destroyed ; among socialist countries, only the G.D.R. had not done the same. Artisans could not obtain materials, and the tax system was prohibitive to such enterprises. Yet, even after such mistakes had been recognized, they were hard to correct.

He thought that Professor Sorokin's remarks on the purpose of wages had been chiefly intended to justify past history. This was the only explanation he could find of Professor Sorokin's implication that wages did not have to be concerned with worker satisfaction. Certainly, it was right to correct mistakes — Nietzsche said that everything could be attacked if only everything were understood — and only by criticism of the past could the present be improved. Professor Lipinski made his remarks on reform in the belief that they were pertinent to all socialist countries, and not just to Poland : the need for change had become obvious in the U.S.S.R. itself. Central planning was essential to the socialist system, and the concept of freedom for the enterprise did not extend to all investment. There were some investments which could best be decided at the plant level, but the establishment of new industries, and even relatively small extensions of existing capacity, must be determined at a higher level ; the former was the sort of choice which had to be made by the central planner, while the latter typified the decision appropriate to the enterprise association. Freedom in the present context was principally the liquidation of curbs on initiative, innovation, and adaptability. Much had been said at an earlier Session about stimuli, but what was more important today were anti-stimuli.

THE APPLICATION OF MATHEMATICS

THE EDUCATION OF MATHEMATIC

Chapter 27

STRUCTURAL MODELS AND THEIR APPLICATION

BY

J. BOUSKA

Econometric Laboratory of the Institute of Economics, Prague

INTENSIVE work has been done recently in Czechoslovakia in the field of constructing structural models at the level of enterprises, of groups of enterprises, of industries, and of the whole national economy. This work is another step forward in the introduction of mathematical methods and modern means of calculation (computers) into practical planning and economic analysis in that country.

In the control and planning of large production units, whose individual operations overlap and are interconnected, the need becomes increasingly apparent for the fullest and most quantitative information about mutual relations and dependencies. Without this information it is impossible to assure the consistency of the individual operations and activities, or to take appropriate decisions on production control and planning.

Present planning methods attempt to ensure the harmonious working of the production unit through a system of plans elaborated for each level of management, and based mainly on balance calculations. Consistency between the individual components of the production system requires very many planning calculations which must be repeated for every change in production or marketing conditions. The volume of work involved inhibits the introduction of such changes. Hence the drawbacks of such planning methods are over-simplification, rigidity, and inadaptability of production control, especially now that production is developing very rapidly and becoming more complex.

Much attention has lately been devoted to working out means of assuring the mutual harmony of individual operations within an economic system, while safeguarding its versatility. It seems from first experience that one useful method is to employ mathematical models depicting different economic and technological relationships within the unit under study. Mathematical models facilitate the application of up-to-date technology to the process of planning and of operational decision-making.

In the following pages attention is concentrated on one type of model much used in planning, and known in Czechoslovakia as the structural model.

CHARACTERISTICS OF THE STRUCTURAL MODEL

Structural models represent schematically the production activity of an economic unit as a process in which purchased raw materials, materials, and semi-manufactures are transmuted, through means of production and manpower, into other semi-manufactures and into final products. The production activity of an economic unit is represented in the structural model not only as a whole, but also at the same time as individual, but interconnected, components (production operations).

The object of structural models is, therefore, the rapid and complex balancing of individual production operations of an economic unit, assuring the compatibility of the output-mix scheduled for clients with the requisite materials, energy, fixed capacity, and labour ; projecting changes in production and in delivery demands into production operations ; and determining the consequences of such changes on the supply of energy, raw materials, and labour and on the parameters of operation.

In calculating plans by means of structural models it is generally essential to use computers. Their use much enhances planning efficiency, since the wide scope of such calculations profits from full co-ordination, and obviates the crude devolution necessitated by subdivision into manually-feasible tasks. The use of structural models and of computers makes calculations in planning substantially more rapid, whether for conventional annual or quarterly plans, or for longer-run plans, and more precise, based on an analysis of the projections of consumption, labour standards, etc. It is also possible to set up several variants of a plan, and then to select the most suitable : this could not be done with the present gradual balancing of individual production operations, inevitably carried out stage by stage because of the bulk of work involved. To select the most suitable variant of a plan, balancing calculations carried out by means of structural models are combined with optimization procedures for which linear programming has hitherto been most frequently used.

There are various types of structural model — the Leontief type, the Pichler type,[1] and models of linear programming. The latter type includes the two others, and permits optimization. Up to now, models of the Leontief type have found the broadest application, being also the simplest and least exacting as far as the amount of fundamental data necessary is concerned : they are also the basis for more exacting models of the Pichler type, and for optimization models.

In a structural model it is assumed that the production activity of the economic unit consists of a large number, n, of partial products, mutually dependent and connected, usually described as 'fields'. Fields exhaust the production activity of the modelled unit fully, without any remainder. Within this constraint of homogeneity, a field is usually formed by a product, or a group of similar products, produced by the system or by one of its organizational components (workshop or plant).

The basis of the model is a system of tables, showing according to individual fields of production the consumption of specific types of semi-manufactures and products made by the system modelled (see layout on page 311, Table I, which corresponds to quadrant I of an input-output table), the consumption of purchased raw materials, energy, materials, and semi-manufactures (Table II), wages (Table III), other production costs and profit (Table IV), labour consumption according to qualification and profession (Table V), and the requisite production equipment by specific types (Table VI). Table VII shows the final production — *i.e.* deliveries of the individual types of products to clients. Since most fields do not correspond strictly to the organizational units (enterprises, plants) which comprise the economy, it becomes necessary to register the requirements of the individual production factors in the same organizational cross-section.

The basis of the structural model is a system of balance equations, which are expressed in the matrix form

---

[1] See Otto Pichler, *Ingenieur-Archiv*, no. 3, 1953, pp. 157–175 ; *Chimische Technik*, no. 6, 1964, pp. 293–300 ; *Zeitschrift für Messen, Steuern, Regeln*, no. 2, 1959, pp. 122–125 ; and in *Bericht über den Internationalen Kolloquium über Probleme der Rechtentechnik*, Dresden, 1955, pp. 5–13.

$$
\begin{bmatrix} x \\ \hline s \\ \hline m \\ \hline u \\ \hline p \\ \hline k \end{bmatrix}
=
\begin{bmatrix} X \\ \hline X_s \\ \hline X_m \\ \hline X_u \\ \hline X_p \\ \hline X_k \end{bmatrix} e +
\begin{bmatrix} y \\ \hline 0 \\ \hline 0 \\ \hline 0 \\ \hline 0 \\ \hline 0 \end{bmatrix}
\qquad (1)
$$

Where x = vector of total production (global turnover)
s = vector of demand for purchased raw materials, materials, and semi-manufactures
m = vector of overall wage costs
u = vector of other costs and profit
p = vector of labour inputs
k = vector of capacity requirements
y = vector of final production
e = summation vector (of column matrix of units).

For notation of matrices, see layout on page 311.
More briefly, it may be expressed as follows :

$$
\begin{bmatrix} x \\ \hline z \end{bmatrix} = \begin{bmatrix} X \\ \hline X_z \end{bmatrix} e + \begin{bmatrix} y \\ \hline 0 \end{bmatrix}
$$

where

$$
z = \begin{bmatrix} s \\ \hline m \\ \hline u \\ \hline p \\ \hline k \end{bmatrix} \quad \text{and} \quad X_z = \begin{bmatrix} X_s \\ \hline X_m \\ \hline X_u \\ \hline X_p \\ \hline X_k \end{bmatrix}
$$

Symbols denoting matrices are in capital, and vectors are in small, letters ; vectors are understood to be column vectors.

Bouska — Structural Models and their Application

In a structural model of the Leontief type it is assumed that the consumption of a production factor i (raw materials, wages, etc.) in the field $j(x_{ij})$ is proportional to the scope of production x_j

$$x_{ij} = a_{ij}x_j.$$

In a structural model of the Pichler type it is assumed that the consumption of a production factor i in the field $j(x_{ij})$ depends, on the one hand, on the scope of production in this field (x_j) and, on the other hand, on a further number of factors m, so that the consumption function takes the form of:

$$x_{ij} = a_{ij}x_j + \sum_{k=1}^{m} g_{ijk}r_k,$$

where : g_{ijk} = correction coefficient expressing the degree of influence of factor k on the consumption of production factor i in the field j

r_k = factor k influencing the consumption (*e.g.* quality of raw materials, overtime work, production time, etc.).

LAYOUT OF TABLES OF THE STRUCTURAL MODEL

Organizational Classification	Field Classification
Consumption of semi-products and components of own production	Table I X
Consumption of purchased raw materials, semi-manufactures, and energy	Table II X_s
Wage costs	Table III X_m
Other production costs and profit	Table IV X_u
Labour inputs	Table V X_p
Production capacity requirements	Table VI X_k
Final production	Table VII y

The structural model following Leontief takes the following form :

$$\left[\begin{array}{c} A \\ \hline A_z \end{array} \right] x + \left[\begin{array}{c} y \\ \hline 0 \end{array} \right] = \left[\begin{array}{c} x \\ \hline z \end{array} \right] \tag{2}$$

where : $A = [a_{ij}]$ = the matrix of technological coefficients relating to consumption of own products

$A_z = [a_{ij}^{(z)}]$ = the divided matrix of coefficients for purchased materials, wages, profits, and capacity.

311

The structural model according to Pichler takes the following form :

$$
\begin{bmatrix} A & \vdots & Q \\ \hdashline A_z & \vdots & Q_z \end{bmatrix}
\begin{bmatrix} x \\ \hdashline r \end{bmatrix}
+
\begin{bmatrix} y \\ \hdashline 0 \end{bmatrix}
=
\begin{bmatrix} x \\ \hdashline z \end{bmatrix}
\tag{3}
$$

where : $Q = [q_{ik}]$ = matrix of correction coefficients for the consumption of own products

$Q_z = [q_{ik}^{(z)}]$ = matrix of correction coefficients for purchased materials, wages, profit, etc.

r = vector of correction factors,

and where $\qquad q_{ik} = \sum_{j=1}^{n} g_{ijk}$ and $q_{ik}^{(z)} = \sum_{j=1}^{n} g_{ijk}^{(z)}$.

As already mentioned, the structural models serve mainly for a rapid balancing of the production of individual fields of the system modelled, and for determining the demand for purchased materials, raw materials, energy, labour, etc. In doing this, we encounter three types of problem :

(*a*) For known production possibilities of the individual fields (known matrices A and A_z) it is necessary to determine the possible scope of final production (vector y) and the overall demand for purchased raw materials, materials, productive capacities, and labour (vector z). In this case, the model following Leontief takes the form :

$$
\begin{bmatrix} y \\ \hdashline z \end{bmatrix}
=
\begin{bmatrix} E - A \\ \hdashline A_z \end{bmatrix}
x
\tag{4}
$$

and the model following Pichler,

$$
\begin{bmatrix} y \\ \hdashline z \end{bmatrix}
=
\begin{bmatrix} E - A & \vdots & Q \\ \hdashline A_z & \vdots & Q_z \end{bmatrix}
\begin{bmatrix} x \\ \hdashline r \end{bmatrix}
\tag{5}
$$

(*b*) For known demands on final production, *i.e.* known demands for deliveries outside the modelled system (known vector y) and known consumption standards (matrices A and A_z) it is necessary to determine the required scope of production of the individual fields (vector x), in order to determine the productive consumption of individual fields of the system, as well as required deliveries, and to assure the materials, labour, etc., needed for this production.

In this case, the models take the following form:

Leontief model:

$$
\begin{bmatrix} x \\ \hline z \end{bmatrix} = \begin{bmatrix} (E-A)^{-1} \\ \hline A_z(E-A)^{-1} \end{bmatrix} x \tag{6}
$$

Pichler model:

$$
\begin{bmatrix} x \\ \hline z \end{bmatrix} = \begin{bmatrix} (E-A)^{-1} & (E-A)^{-1}Q \\ \hline A_z(E-A)^{-1} & A_z(E-A)^{-1}Q + Q_z \end{bmatrix} \begin{bmatrix} y \\ \hline r \end{bmatrix} \tag{7}
$$

(c) For known production possibilities of one group of fields x_1 and known demands on deliveries outside the production system for a second group of fields y_2, and for known direct consumption standards, it is necessary to determine possible deliveries outside the system for the first group of fields (*i.e.* y_1), the scope of possible production for the second group (*i.e.* x_2), and the total consumption of energy, labour, productive capacities, etc.

Leontief's model will now take the form of:

$$
\begin{bmatrix} y_1 \\ \hline x_2 \\ \hline z \end{bmatrix} = \begin{bmatrix} (E-A_{11}) - A_{12}(E-A_{22})^{-1}A_{21} & -A_{12}(E-A_{22})^{-1} \\ \hline -(E-A_{22})^{-1}A_{21} & (E-A_{22})^{-1} \\ \hline A_{z1} - A_{z2}(E-A_{22})^{-1}A_{z1} & -A_{z2}(E-A_{22})^{-1} \end{bmatrix} \begin{bmatrix} x_1 \\ \hline y_2 \end{bmatrix} \tag{8}
$$

A_{11}, A_{12}, etc., are sub-matrices which are obtained by dividing matrix

$$
\begin{bmatrix} A \\ \hline A_z \end{bmatrix}
$$

according to group of fields, for which production possibilities are known (first field group denoted by subscript 1) and for which demands on final production are known (the second group of fields, denoted by subscript 2), so that the following holds

$$
\begin{bmatrix} A \\ \hline A_z \end{bmatrix} = \begin{bmatrix} A_{11} & A_{12} \\ \hline A_{21} & A_{22} \\ \hline A_{z1} & A_{z2} \end{bmatrix} \tag{9}
$$

All three forms of the models form a whole, and are applied at various phases of balancing plans. Form (*b*) finds the broadest application. Form (*c*) is used mainly for re-balancing, and in those cases where production in some fields is relatively low.

SOME PROBLEMS OF THE CONSTRUCTION OF STRUCTURAL MODELS

One of the most important phases in the construction of structural models is the classification of production — that is, exhaustive classification into the 'fields' of the entire production activity of the system embraced by the model. The main requirements are : that each product must be produced by a single field ; that products included in different fields must not be substitutes ; and that a single technology must be used in each field, characterized with sufficient precision by a system of technological parameters.

Relations between individual groups in production are, however, such that these requirements cannot be respected fully in forming the concrete classification. A very detailed classification, in which each field would be formed by a single product, would seem to be the most advantageous. It is found, however, that even leaving aside the practical difficulties connected with obtaining the data, and with the exceptionally large size of the structural model, such a detailed classification is still inappropriate, since it conflicts with the demand of non-interchangeability of the products of different fields.

When setting up a definitive classification, it is desirable that products included in one field should have a similar raw material basis ; that the production technology of products belonging to the same field should be similar ; that the technological continuity of production should be respected ; and that the same treatment should be accorded products for productive and for non-productive use.

Present experience with classification for the use of structural models shows that in a given case a combination of different points of view must be selected. For those fields where output is mainly of producers' goods, the first three criteria should be fulfilled; for fields where production is aimed chiefly at final consumption it is more suitable to stress the fourth criterion. The classification needed for the model is also substantially influenced by the character of the branch of industry (engineering, chemicals, food processing, etc.).

A particular problem in constructing the model is the determination of parameters of the model, *i.e.* of direct input relationships or of corrective coefficients. These parameters may be determined largely by two methods, statistical analysis or technological synthesis.

The first method consists of determining the consumption of materials and labour within individual fields for some period in the past, and calculating from these data the required technological coefficients. An advantage of this method is its simplicity, for the required data may mostly be obtained from statistical and accounting material. The technological coefficients calculated will reflect the actual product-mix. A disadvantage of this method is the fact that it is based on past data, and therefore a model based on technological coefficients obtained in this way may be relied upon only for short periods of time. This method has been applied for all models constructed for levels superior to the enterprise.

The second method of constructing field technological coefficients consists in calculating standards on the basis of technological data. This is a difficult method, but its advantage resides in allowance for the projection of new techniques. This method of constructing field standards is suitable mainly for models which are to be used for long-term planning. It has been applied especially for models constructed on the level of enterprises or plants.

APPLICATION OF STRUCTURAL MODELS

In Czechoslovakia, structural models are being constructed for three levels of control and management, viz. the entire economy (inter-branch balances); branches of the economy (models for the production facilities administered by a single ministry); and enterprises (enterprise and intra-enterprise models).

Conditions for the application of structural models in planning have been experimentally studied: preliminary results are satisfactory, and show that the systematic application of structural models will permit an improvement in the quality of planning.

315

The first experimental structural models for enterprises were constructed in 1960 by a group of specialists of the Institute for Technical and Economic Research of the Chemical Industry. The methodology was worked out in that institute, and models were constructed for a number of chemical enterprises and plants with the collaboration of the technical staff. In 1963 a model was also prepared for the Ministry of the Chemicals Industry.

The first enterprise models were not formulated as complete : they included only the flow of materials and energy in the system, *i.e.* the first and second quadrants of the model, the parameters being mainly by technological synthesis. Structural models of the Leontief, as well as of the Pichler, types were used. Models were prepared for a variety of plants, including oil-refining, and the manufacture of cellulose and paper, inorganic chemicals, chemical semi-manufactures, and plastics.

Similar experimental models were later constructed for a number of engineering enterprises (*e.g.* a motorcycle factory), some metallurgical works (smelting and rolling), and factories for consumers' goods (textiles, wood-working, and food-processing).

These calculations have shown that the models all represent sufficiently precisely intra-factory material and energy relationships, and that they lend themselves successfully to use in planning calculations, and in determining demands for raw materials, other materials, and energy. Experience with these models has further shown that the construction of such simplified structural models is not difficult when done on the enterprise level. The data needed are more readily available in those production enterprises where there is no feed-back (*e.g.* producing cellulose and paper, plastics, etc.). There were great difficulties in constructing the structural models for enterprises where the production process did include feed-back (*e.g.* oil refineries). The particular advantage of structural models, as compared with the previous planning methods, lies in the considerable saving in labour involved in calculations, and in the greater precision.

Parallel to these enterprise models, work was pursued on the construction of models for individual branches of industry. Following the branch model for the chemical industry, a preliminary one for heavy engineering was completed in 1963. The model of the chemical industry included 106 fields of purchased raw and other materials, energy, and semi-manufactures, and 114 fields of production ; it was set up on the basis of calculations for 5,000 products for 1961. The first model for the Ministry of Heavy Engineering included only the mutual relations of 75 production fields in the first quadrant of the model, and was based on deliveries between individual enterprises of this ministry in 1961. The main object of this first attempt was the investigation of the amount of work involved, and the gathering of methodological experience.

In 1964, work was finished on two branch models, for the Ministry of Heavy Engineering and the Ministry of General Engineering. These models included the first, second, and third quadrants of the structural model, and covered 118 machine-production fields, and 70 fields of raw materials and energy. The basis for their construction was a statistical investigation of the year 1962, which was part of a special state-wide investigation carried out for the preparation of an input-output table. Evaluating and verifying work on these two models is still in progress.

Work on constructing the first comprehensive input-output table in Czechoslovakia started in 1962, and was completed in 1964. Most data were obtained by a single statistical investigation of inter-branch relations in industry and building, carried out for 1962 by the Central Commission for Control and Statistics. The investigation yielded input data in two breakdowns : first, the structure of material costs, expressed in money, for 122 fields (the basis for the branch input-output table), as well as wages and other costs ; second, the structure of material consumption in physical units for 216 selected products or groups of products (the basis for the product input-output table). An input-output table with 93 production branches was also set up according to so-called 'pure branches', formed on the principle of products (viz. not necessarily classifying an enterprise in any single branch by virtue of its predominant production).

Positive experience with the application of structural models has stimulated the gradual evolution of a hierarchical system of vertically-connected structural models for the use of planning and economic analysis. The main element of this system would be enterprise models, which in turn would form the basis of models of ministries (branches). On these a model of the entire economy could then be based.

Building up such a hierarchical system of models is, of course, very exacting. It has been particularly difficult to co-ordinate the classification based on industrial branches (*i.e.* on products) with the inferred stability and reliability of parameters, and the classification by organizations, arising from the actual management structure.

A necessary condition for setting up such a system of mutually-connected structural models is the formation of a standardized and generally-used classification of production, together with some modifications in book-keeping to ensure the systematic determination of the requisite data. The first steps towards this have already been taken. The Central Commission for Control and Statistics, together with economic organizations, has worked out a standard classification of industrial and agricultural production, with respect to the needs of the construction of such models. The classification is fourfold :

(1) field — about 400 fields ;
(2) group — a field has an average of 5 groups ;
(3) sub-group — a group has an average of 4 sub-groups ;
(4) product — a sub-group has an average of 6 products.

This classification, effective from 1965, will be obligatory for all economic organizations, and the changes involved in statistics and accounts will then be implemented.

By building up such a hierarchical system of models, conditions will be obtained for the systematic application of computers in planning calculations, and (through linear programming) also for the construction of optimum plans.

Chapter 28

SUMMARY RECORD OF THE DISCUSSION
— SESSION IX

THE APPLICATION OF MATHEMATICS
(In the Chair : PROFESSOR KAMENOV)

Dr. *Ophir* observed, in opening the discussion, that Mr. Bouska's structural model, being used in Czechoslovakia, could be traced back to Quesnay. Such models had also been adopted by Marx, but their modern employment began with Leontief in 1951. In Israel, an 85-sector model had been constructed to project import propensity : such an open Leontief model showed the bill of goods to be made available outside the inter-industry structure ; income and other elasticities of consumers' goods were calculated, and the imports were thence derived which were required to sustain that bill of goods.

Mr. Bouska's model had three main features. First, the calculation was done in stages — for the enterprise, for the branch, and for the economy as a whole. This sub-model procedure permitted a finer division of products, because the capacity limits of available computers constrained the number of sectors. Mr. Bouska did not, however, make clear how successful had been the final integration. Secondly, the model combined in tabular form the physical and financial relations of the economy, that is, both the flow of products and financial flows. Finally, the model refined Leontief's techniques on the lines of Pichler. In this manner, a constant was introduced to make the consumption of imports not solely proportional to output of the given sector, but to output plus a constant term.

It was unnecessary to reiterate the importance for a plan based on a balanced growth of the various sectors to be verified for consistency and for its bill of goods to be comprehensively translated into requirements. Another use, as described by Mr. Bouska, was to take gross outputs by sector as given, and to calculate the final bill of goods therefrom. Such a calculation could show the unfeasibility of the gross outputs (*e.g.* by negative entries in final demand). Mr. Kaser had pointed out that such a model did not optimize anything [1] : indeed, there was no function to be optimized. Mr. Bouska's view seemed to be that a process of optimization took place at the lower stages (when maximum outputs were determined

[1] M. Kaser, 'The Nature of Soviet Planning', *Soviet Studies*, October 1962, pp. 109–131.

The Application of Mathematics

with given inputs) and in the choice of techniques. As a simplification at
the final stage, each product could only be produced by one technique.
Dr. Ophir wondered whether the prices used in optimizing — *ex post*
after the final balancing — were correct. An iterating procedure might
be better, with the prices shown by the first round put into a new iteration
from the enterprise level.

He followed this exposition of the paper under discussion with some
general questions on the use of mathematical models. Dr. Hegedus's
paper had mentioned the problem of the reliability of mathematical
solutions, and he agreed that care must be taken with the premises
and assumptions used. In applying the Leontief model, the formal
statement of the relations showed the basic similarity of the two systems,
and did not introduce undesirable connotations, *e.g.* of interest and
profits. Such terms could be dispensed with by considering them as
mathematical functions, permitting, for example, the use of a rate of
discount.

The merits of centralization against those of decentralization were
as much at issue in the capitalist corporation as in the socialist economy. Dr. Ophir favoured decentralization in both. The computer
facilities now available not only permitted the planning board of a corporation to obtain more information, but also enabled it to exercise better
control over its lower agencies, by virtue of the same high-speed data
processing.

Professor Robinson was anxious to know how accurately socialist economists were able to construct their models and how far they were able to
trust them. He saw two particular problems. First, how accurately
could one predict future technical progress and the likely changes of the
technical co-efficients, which were an essential characteristic of any
advancing economy ? He offered an illustration from his experience in
India. He had been engaged in helping to plan the developments of
energy supplies — coal, oil, and electricity — to meet the needs for the
long-term plans for Indian development down to 1980. The groups with
which he had been working made their own first estimates of the future
technical co-efficients. When they had sought to obtain the agreement of
the various departments concerned to these co-efficients, they had almost
always found that the departments concerned were much more conserva-
tive in their estimates of future co-efficients, differing sometimes by 10
to 15 per cent. The responsible departments were perhaps naturally
concerned that they should not be accused of having over-estimated their
future needs for fuel. Did similar problems of projecting future technical
co-efficients arise in the socialist countries ? Did they really trust their
estimates when they had made them ?

The second problem was concerned with the achievement of targets.
In his own experience, targets were rarely achieved to the extent of 100
per cent ; some targets were apt to be bold and optimistic. If one were

320

planning a basic input such as electricity or steel, did one assume that all targets were simultaneously achieved, or did one make some small discount to allow for the improbability that all targets would be simultaneously achieved ? It was necessary to exercise judgement, and not merely to discover and apply existing facts and co-efficients.

Sir Roy Harrod had some similar thoughts. Even a growth rate of, say, five per cent over ten years resulted in a large cumulative increase : since this would not have been due solely to population growth, some technological change must have occurred. Thus, an expansion of this order of magnitude — which was below that recorded in socialist countries — implied tremendous technological change over a plan period, underscoring the difficulty of the projection. In the last eighteen fiscal years, the British Treasury had, on the average, under-estimated revenue or expenditure by £100 million a year.

With computers, the estimates would become less time-consuming and more accurate, but one should not have too great a veneration for the computer. The value of the computer for economic projections was chiefly to give the planners a lead to the sort of action or research needed (*e.g.* the direction of development outlays to achieve the required targets).

Professor Stefanov noted that the Soviet 'chessboard balance' for 1923–24 was the first use of mathematical techniques in planning. The idea that the utilization of the 'chessboard' could supply technical co-efficients, like those later developed by Leontief, had been put forward in a Soviet periodical as early as 1928 : Feldman, whose study had been mentioned by Professor Domar (p. 108), had worked along the same lines. Further progress in this direction had then stopped for extraneous reasons. Soviet scholarship also had priority in linear programming — Kantorovich's publication in 1939 preceded that of Dantzig in the United States, and Novozhilov had independently developed the application of linear programming to the determination of investment efficiency. He wanted also to draw attention to Bulgarian experience in these fields. In 1960 the Central Statistical Administration had produced a 'chessboard' table with 68 sectors, of which 59 were industrial. The Institute of Economics had elaborated such tables for 1957–62 on the basis of sampling data from 100 enterprises. Some elementary transport problems had also been solved by linear programming, and enterprises were presenting further programmes to the Institute for solution. The optimal mix of fodder production in the Rusé Region had been programmed.

Professor Stefanov felt that opportunities for the use of mathematical models were particularly broad in a socialist context, for information could be obtained from all enterprises, and not solely for the products, or from the corporations, on which data were available. This advantage was being notably exploited by the U.S.S.R. in its proposed Central Information System, which would feed data from individual plants into a national matrix. The big capitalist corporations could, of course,

The Application of Mathematics

employ such techniques, and it was possible for small enterprises to contract such work with special computing firms. The potential for standardization and large-scale data processing made such services cheaper and more accessible, however, under socialism. The same economies of scale could be derived in the application of cybernetics. Since the advantages of electronics and cybernetics were heavily weighted in favour of the large user — a socialist state or a big capitalist corporation — he was led to wonder whether a future conference of this sort would no longer be concerned with centralization or decentralization, but only with the forms of centralization.

Professor Grossman believed that Professor Stefanov had unnecessarily limited the notion of economic cybernetics to highly-centralized management systems utilizing electronic communications and computers. The late Academician Nemchinov had used the term to describe a partly-decentralized system, under which enterprise 'self-regulation' was responsive to parameters and signals generated either by central agencies or by the economic environment.[1] While the first system tended, as Professor Stefanov had stated, to centralization, the second supported decentralization. He did not wish to belittle Soviet contributions to mathematical economics, but he believed that Professor Stefanov (and, earlier, Professor Fauvel) had oversimplified history. Dmitriev's work had not been followed up in the U.S.S.R., for his aim, as the sub-title to his *Economic Essays* stated, was 'an attempt to synthesize the Marxist theory of value with the theory of marginal utility'. Leontief had, of course, nothing to do with the 1923–24 table (he was scarcely over 20 at the time), but his review of it stimulated his later work. It was fair to point out that it was not an input-output, but only a flow, table : it contained no co-efficients at all, let alone full co-efficients. Professor Stefanov had probably referred to Barengolts's paper,[2] in which he suggested the concept of technical co-efficients, but only direct, and not full, ones ; moreover, he did not see the way to develop a table of co-efficients. Leontief's contribution in this area was, of course, to invert such a matrix.

Mr. Nikiforov agreed with Professor Robinson and Sir Roy Harrod on the importance of accurate forecasts of technical co-efficients if input-output techniques were to be used in planning, and wanted to add to Professor Stefanov's remarks a contrast between economic cybernetics and the market system. The chief shortcoming of the market was its *ex post* operation, precluding its use under socialism, which planned activity on an *ex ante* consideration of allocations and signals. Cybernetics could assist the rapid adaptation of the plan, *e.g.* in avoiding overproduction by

---

[1] V. Nemchinov, *Ekonomicheskie metody i modeli* (Economic Methods and Models), Moscow, 1962.

[2] M. Barengolts, *Planovoe khozyaistvo*, no. 7, 1928, pp. 325–348 ; English translation in N. Spulber (ed.), *Foundations of Soviet Strategy for Economic Growth: Selected Soviet Essays 1924–1930*, Bloomington (Ind.), 1964, pp. 99–123.

prompt amendment of the plan. This did not mean that a market was excluded from a socialist system, but that its operation was counterbalanced by planning.

He found many reasons to favour the structural models described by Mr. Bouska. First, the speed of elaboration of plans was greatly accelerated. Secondly, the ideas of planners could be tested and compared more quickly. Thirdly, planning could be made continuous and not separated into periods. Finally, such models would be more accurate than those at present used. The solutions offered were nevertheless still unsatisfactory. The models required prior assumptions to be made on final demand, viz. exports, accumulation, and personal consumption, and such assumptions involved social and political, as well as economic, considerations. The process of correcting technical co-efficients by linear extrapolation was subject to a wide margin of error, and could not account for the discrete changes in technology which characterized rapid growth.

Professor Domar commented on Professor Robinson's remarks on the use of the input-output method in Indian planning. There had been much debate, since the appearance of Leontief's work, on the quality of forecasts or of plans based on such methods : the issue was not whether the technique was good or bad, but whether better methods were available. The Indian planners could choose between not planning at all — which they would scarcely welcome ; using some form of the input-output method ; or using some better method, which, as things now stood, was likely to involve non-linear relationships and thus be even more expensive in time and effort than ordinary input-output.

One of the outstanding virtues of using mathematics in economics was that it required assumptions to be stated explicitly and the reasoning to be rigorous. Most economic problems of today were too complex, and involved too many variables with intricate inter-relationships, to be solved without mathematics. Samuelson was reported to have said to a graduate student seeking his advice that economists without mathematics had to be twice as intelligent as mathematical economists. Professor Domar admired Keynes but had to concede that the *General Theory* abounded in vague and even inaccurate statements : only after Lange's comments had everyone understood what Keynes really had in mind.[1]

Mathematics, nevertheless, could be carried too far in economics : common sense had to be used at some point. Lenin once remarked that it was not the rifle that fired, but the man who pulled the trigger : thus it was the men who ran the computers who made the programmes.

Mr. Bouska concluded the discussions with the observation that, of the many mathematical models, most were unusable because they required unobtainable parameters : no way, for example, had been found to use curvilinear co-efficients. Models were, in fact, no better than existing

[1] O. Lange, 'The Rate of Interest and the Optimum Propensity to Consume', *Economica*, February 1938, pp. 12–32.

practice, and experience had shown that the improvement of data was slow. From the mathematical side, the models he had used in his paper were the simplest possible, but even they were only imperfectly applied because of inadequate information on supply-demand relations. Where information was lacking, recourse was to be had to probability factors — technical change, as many participants had pointed out, was the least quantifiable. For these reasons, the most that could be attempted was to illuminate ambiguity by short-run models, not exceeding five years ; for such a period, the projection of technical co-efficients had some realistic basis. Even so, such extrapolation had to be set out as average co-efficients for each branch, implying that the disaggregated constituents could be determined so as to derive a mean. For this purpose, his models applied probability techniques. There remained, finally, the problem of opening the model, *i.e.* to take accurate account of external factors. Work in Czechoslovakia was still simple and experimental, and it was hoped that the demand for more complex techniques could be met not only by intensive work at home, but by profiting from conclusions reached elsewhere.

He was less optimistic on the application of cybernetics to planning in the near future. Theory and practice were still far apart, and no satisfactory, medium-term cybernetic approach was yet available. Not only had no utilizable group of models appeared, but the way to study such models had only recently been discovered.

INDEX

Entries in the index **in bold type** under the names of participants in the Conference indicate their papers or discussions of their papers. Entries *in italics* indicate contributions by participants to the discussions.

Index

Index

327

Index

Index

5